Humanitarian Aid Work

Humanitarian Aid Work

A Critical Approach

CARLOS MARTÍN BERISTAIN

PENN

University of Pennsylvania Press

Philadelphia

Originally published as *Reconstruir el tejido social: Un enfoque crítico de la ayuda humanitaria*
by Icaria editorial, s.a.
Copyright © 1999
English translation copyright © 2006 University of Pennsylvania Press
Printed in the United States of America on acid-free paper

10 9 8 7 6 5 4 3 2 1

Published by
University of Pennsylvania Press
Philadelphia, Pennsylvania 19104-4112

Library of Congress Cataloging-in-Publication Data

Martín Beristain, Carlos.
[Reconstruir el tejido social. eng]
Humanitarian aid work : a critical approach : Carlos Martín Beristain.
    p. cm.
Includes bibliographical references.
ISBN-13: 978-0-8122-3943-0
ISBN-10: 0-8122-3943-1 (alk. paper)
1. Humanitarian assistance.   2. Humanitarian assistance—Psychological aspects.
3. Disaster relief.   4. Disaster relief—Psychological aspects.   5. Community mental health
services.   I. Title.
HV553.R36513   2006
363.34′8—dc22

                                                            2006042158

For Eugenio, Leo, and Francesc

With gratitude to the Solomon Asch Center for Study of Ethnopolitical Conflict at the University of Pennsylvania for its support

Contents

Foreword

Globalization has brought those from the Northern Hemisphere's economically more advantaged communities into ever more immediate contact with extreme poverty, natural disasters, pandemics, wars, and catastrophes. Recent catastrophes, most notably the multiple earthquakes and hurricanes that have devastated communities around the world in the first decade of this new millennium, evidence the vulnerabilities of all the world's people as well as the catastrophic consequences of political decision-making that fails to protect those most vulnerable to the effects of humanitarian disasters.

One policy-level response to these structural disparities and their consequences for the poorest and most vulnerable members of disaster-affected populations has been a series of international treaties, conventions, and agreements. For example, the eight United Nations Millennium Development Goals—which range from halving extreme poverty to halting the spread of HIV/AIDS and providing universal primary education by 2015—were agreed to by all the world's countries and its leading development institutions in one effort to redress these dramatic social inequities. Yet, despite these ideals, two-thirds of the world's population today live in extreme poverty and experience the threats and the realities of violence and catastrophe as daily routine. UNICEF's 2005 *State of the World's Children* reports that one of every two children in the world suffers some form of severe deprivation, with most living in poverty. Fifteen million children under the age of eighteen had been orphaned by HIV/AIDS by 2003. Moreover, international monitors have identified thirty-two armed conflicts in twenty-six different states in 2004. Recent comparative research links poverty and war, confirming that the more undernourished the population of a region of the world is, the more likely there is to be a war. For example, during the past decade 61 percent of states with more than 35 percent of the population malnourished experienced armed conflict, whereas only 15 percent of those states with 4 percent or less of the population living in extreme poverty had an armed conflict within their borders.

Individuals are increasingly challenged to respond to these global inequalities. Medical personnel have long-standing experience accompanying soldiers into war and responding to humanitarian crises. In recent years, growing numbers of psychologists, social workers, and other human service workers have joined their ranks in contexts as disparate as the aftermaths of the genocide in Rwanda, Hurricane Katrina in the United States, and the earthquake in Kashmir. As they enter these emergency situations, these workers frequently confront not only immediate disasters but also the long-standing structural and institutional inequities described above as well as patriarchal power structures, bureaucratic inefficiencies sometimes marked by corruption, and more needs than could possibly be addressed by the resources at hand. In the best of cases, internationalists and local professionals, para-professionals, and indigenous leaders and healers work collaboratively to render care to the most marginalized and least powerful in situations that are frequently chaotic and often perilous. In less ideal circumstances they compete for resources, undermine each other's confidence, and risk doing more harm than good.

Carlos Martín Beristain has devoted his life to working in these situations—contexts that the Salvadoran Jesuit and social psychologist Ignacio Martín-Baró called "limit situations." Trained as a medical doctor, he journeyed to El Salvador and Guatemala early in his professional life and responded to the voices of victims triply oppressed by extreme poverty, an ongoing civil war, and patriarchal cultural and political systems and structures of marginalization.

Drawing on over a decade of field experience in Latin America as well as a burgeoning literature about the psychological and social effects of war and disasters, Martín Beristain developed this volume at the interface of theory and practice as one response to these complex social and political realities. Writing in a language accessible to the wide range of helping professionals and volunteers who work in disasters, he describes the psychosocial effects of catastrophes and the community's capacities to integrate resources and creatively respond toward the goal of reweaving the social fabric of their lives.

Humanitarian Aid Work: A Critical Approach offers an excellent introduction to those seeking to address the complex social, political, cultural, and linguistic diversities to be found in any humanitarian crisis. These workers, often professionals from a variety of social scientific, legal, human service, and health fields, frequently are challenged by worldviews, meaning systems, and customary practices different from their own. They seek to respond to the immediate demands and complex realities within crisis situations while balancing theoretically sound approaches, sensitivities to cultural and linguistic differences, and a quest for comparability between these and other diversities. Rigorously trained social scientists wanting to help but also seeking to control, predict, or prevent greater distress and damage in the context of humanitarian crises face immense challenges. They also encounter moral, political, and economic ambiguities in situations that demand immediate action, challenging workers to respond to individual, family, community, and society.

Martín Beristain confronts these complexities theoretically and practically—and in a deeply humane voice. Reframing existing individualistic psychological theories about the individual, familial, and societal effects of war and humanitarian crises, he develops a mosaic, crafted from deep observations, a bond of commitment to those who have suffered, and solidarity with them as they seek to reconstruct their worlds and rethread the social fabric of their lives. As significantly, he demonstrates how this profoundly interpersonal bond is situated within, nurtured by a commitment to international human rights, and extended to seeking truth with justice. His collaboration in various Latin American truth commissions, as well as his expert testimonies at the Inter-American Court and within various agencies of the United Nations, further informs the work presented here.

Martín Beristain educates without being didactic. He transforms the ambiguous language of "psychosocial humanitarian care" into concrete practice informed by theory. He persuades through example, complementing thick descriptions of fieldwork with theoretical arguments supported by empirical evidence. "Psychosocial work" has multiple referents, and the phrase or its corollary, "psychosocial trauma," is frequently thought to be ambiguous, signifying everything and therefore nothing. Perhaps because this interdisciplinary work is at the interface of economic, anthropological, environmental, physical, cultural, and biosocial processes and outcomes, practitioners and theoreticians writing about it are blamed for not being clear or for using circular thinking to characterize endeavors that either are not well conceptualized or lack a clear objective. Martín Beristain embraces this challenge, discussing the complex situations, mixed emotions, ethical dilemmas, and concern for their own personal well-being that challenge psychosocial workers each day. He describes the common challenges they face when working within and across educational, economic, and cultural differences in local communities where they are seeking to insert themselves in the midst of often complex and contradictory relations among donors, local and foreign NGOs, and the survivors.

The victims are always visible in Martín Beristain's work, and their voices puncture an all-too-frequent official silence wherein impunity and a lack of justice exacerbate the painful consequences of disasters. He analyzes the diverse responses to horror and extreme deprivation. He does not minimize the intense pain of mothers and fathers whose children have been tortured or disappeared nor the sorrow and rage of women repeatedly raped by paramilitary forces in Colombia or death squads in Guatemala. Nor does he underestimate the resilience of Mayan children whose schools and communities have been destroyed by genocidal acts yet who rethread their social networks in refugee camps along the Mexico-Guatemala border. These stories inform and deeply humanize the theoretical and empirical work within these pages.

Euro-American or Northern Hemisphere humanitarian intervention work has often been criticized as being individualistic and prioritizing a medical or psychological focus on personal trauma and suffering as the primary consequences of catastrophe and war. In contrast, Martín Beristain and others living and working within the Southern Hemisphere affirm a set of common perspectives delineated in this volume. They include a more culturally sensitive, community-based, human-rights approach that emphasizes the "we" in contrast to the "I." This perspective is informed by a critical analysis of the structural violence and inequality at the root of the profound disruption of social and community ties pursuant to disasters and wars. Specific interventions are participatory processes through which humanitarian workers accompany local communities whose leaders, healers, and residents become, over time, co-participants in the reconstruction of the community. Emergency humanitarian aid is ever aware of the wider development agenda, and humanitarian workers strive to avoid paternalism through prioritizing the skills and resources of local communities.

Eschewing intra- and inter-professional debates wherein these differing humanitarian perspectives are frequently posited as oppositional, Martín Beristain discusses the distinctiveness of each approach. He identifies best practices, arguing that all humanitarian aid workers share a minimal commitment to accompany individuals and communities as they seek to rebuild and to promote the well-being of all affected by disasters. This volume thus defies facile characterization, demonstrating through rich description coupled with theory and supported by empirical research that psychosocial humanitarian aid is a developing field at the interface of indigenous and Euro-American knowledge systems. Moreover it is not a static discipline but rather a set of iterative teaching, learning, and action processes.

Humanitarian Aid Work: A Critical Approach is the book that many of us wish we could have read before responding to a catastrophe or war emergency. It discusses the consequences of both political violence and natural catastrophes. Although human-generated violence and catastrophes such as war have frequently been distinguished from environmental disasters such as hurricanes, recent experiences, most notably those in New Orleans, suggest that human errors and failures to allocate resources to preventively contain potential environmental disaster all too easily transformed what may have been the natural disaster of a hurricane to an unnatural catastrophe that inundated a city, took thousands of lives, and destroyed the social fabric of millions of lives.

Humanitarian Aid Work explores the dynamic interface of natural disasters and political violence, of individual trauma and structural violence, of personal loss and the rupture of social ties. Psychological theory is engaged dialogically with concrete examples from different geographical and cultural contexts, creating a discourse of applied knowledge that speaks for itself.

This English translation from the original Spanish was developed for use as a text in a master's program and in NGO settings. It thus contributed to the education and preparation of a cadre of psychosocial humanitarian workers for work alongside individuals and communities experiencing violence and catastrophes. Moreover, the volume contributed to improving communication among Spanish-speaking frontline workers and between them and policy-makers and political leaders who set budgets that support the work discussed herein. The English translation is a long-overdue and welcome resource for an increasingly large group of English-speaking psychosocial humanitarian aid workers to whom Martín Beristain's work has been previously inaccessible.

Humanitarian Aid Work: A Critical Approach is, first and foremost, a book of voices. It reminds us that only though genuinely listening to the victims and survivors, to their vulnerabilities and their strengths as revealed through their own words, do we learn how to accompany them in their journey from catastrophe to reconstruction. Through facing the other's suffering, we confront ourselves and together construct a world within which we want to live together.

M. Brinton Lykes and Arancha García del Soto

In these dark ages that we live in, under the new world order, to share pain is one of the essential preconditions for restoring dignity and hope. A large part of the pain cannot be shared, but the desire to share this pain can be shared. From this inevitably inadequate effort, a resistance emerges.

—*John Berger*

Introduction
The Premises of Humanitarian Aid

"Your head is full of little compartments," they told me, "where you put things. You put ideas in one, the struggle for justice in another, and your job in another."
"So how should it be?" I asked.
"Round instead of squared, things can't be separated like that."[1]

This book presents a psychosocial approach to the problems of groups affected by violence or catastrophe and to the challenges of humanitarian aid work and cooperation in situations of social emergency.[2]

In recent years, interest in humanitarian aid has been growing. Many more resources have been devoted to it, more organizations are carrying out cooperative projects, and emergency actions have grown without precedent. However, such growth has not meant that relief is always provided adequately to victims, that it has positive effects in reconstruction of the social fabric, or that it raises awareness of the unjust relationship between North and South.

A Psychosocial Approach

The approach presented in this book intends to help the reader understand the behavior, emotions, and thoughts of individuals and groups who survive a disaster, without isolating them from the social and cultural context in which they occur. Any project or specific action should be based on local needs and the events taking place in that area, and should be an exchange rather than a one-way effort. The role of cooperation in bringing relief to affected populations is not to transport ideas or to export models. The use of psychology provides a different understanding for those providing in humanitarian aid and a method of working with the people affected.

Many people believe that in emergency situations or crises material aid comes first and psychosocial matters are to be considered in the aftermath, if at all. However, if psychosocial issues are addressed from the beginning, aid workers can better understand the behavior and reactions of the population, develop plans for action and prevention, understand the mutual support of people in emergency situations, and gain a comprehensive understanding of humanitarian aid that encompasses the physical, psychological, and social requirements of the population.

Underestimating the psychosocial aspects of humanitarian aid can lead to the inability to understand people's experience and even to the failure of aid efforts. Too frequently, nongovernmental organizations (NGOs), agencies, and governments show their disregard—perhaps out of fear—for understanding humanitarian aid in a more complete way. To understand and to care about the psychosocial does not mean that the agencies and governments need always provide psychological support, just that they adopt a model of understanding and acting that is more complete. Providing aid for building a house, for instance, has psychological effects because it provides physical and emotional security. Alternatively, deciding to have an expatriate[3] distribute food could create feelings of distrust or dependency in a refugee population.

Objectives of This Book

This book is intended as a critical manual of humanitarian aid. The academic literature and debates have been summarized as much as possible to make clear, action-oriented statements based on current research in psychology and the social sciences as well as our direct experience[4] in Central and South America. This book also incorporates research conducted in Europe, Africa, and Asia.

The purposes of this book are

1. To describe how people react and respond to traumatic experiences in extraordinary circumstances (such as natural disasters or wars).
2. To formulate an understanding of the social and cultural context in which these reactions and responses occur so that they are recognized and they are able to reinforce the measures that already exist.
3. To offer a psychosocial approach and advocate a cultural sensitivity for humanitarian action and the work of collaboration, assistance, or accompaniment.
4. To suggest alternative ideas for the rebuilding of the social fabric in such areas as prevention, care of victims, collective memory, and respect for human rights.

Chapters 1 through 3 analyze the collective impact of human disasters and describe the phases of collective catastrophes and the various ways of confronting the danger. Chapters 4 and 5 describe the short- and long-term problems faced by victims and how survivors handle the consequences of violence and disasters. Chapters 6 and 7 describe the challenges faced by people, teams, and organizations involved in collaborative work as well as the cross-cultural interaction within humanitarian work. Chapter 8 describes and evaluates, from a psychosocial perspective, the meaning and effect of work undertaken to rebuild the social fabric of a community. The book ends by placing humanitarian aid within the framework of human rights and of prevention. Now we examine the concepts on which we base our analysis.

The Affected Population

In many countries where humanitarian aid projects occur, large parts of the population, especially the poorer ones, suffered frequent trauma of a sociopolitical nature such as violence or displacement. Also, in serious social crises or natural, environmental, or technological disasters, the poor are more exposed and have fewer resources for protecting themselves. In the case of political violence, ethnic or political opposition groups suffer persecution and serious violent acts. In many countries, anyone opposed to the established regime is considered an internal enemy and is subject to torture, murder, disappearances, or scorched-earth policies and religious and cultural harassment. As a result of displacement and violence, many have lost family members and have had to endure poor living conditions, misery, and poverty.

This victimization of a population poses a challenge to humanitarian aid because it cannot extract itself from the context and causes that have led to these situations. Working alongside these people prompts as well a questioning of the work models, the therapeutic approaches, and the role of cooperation in the prevention of these catastrophes—not just in dealing with their aftermath.

The Strength of the People

To politically condemn victimization helps to make suffering—and therefore the need for change—more visible, but victims should not be seen as passive. Even in the most critical moments, people develop mechanisms to confront their situation, as Bruno Bettelheim, a survivor of the Dachau and Buchenwald concentration camps, points out: "To observe and try to comprehend what I saw was a resource that appeared suddenly, to convince myself that my life still had some value, that I hadn't lost all interest in what had once given me self-respect" (Bettelheim 1973, 105).

These words of Bettelheim, reflecting on his own experience, present better than any other idea the approach of this book. Beyond the tremendous impact of many of these experiences, when confronted with extreme situations, individuals and groups sometimes react by increasing their cohesion, as a means of defense against suffering and social disintegration. Very often people draw on untapped resources or reconsider their existence given a new horizon, where human vulnerabilities and the complexities of the context can be taken more account of.

Focusing on the Situation, Not on the Condition

To understand these experiences, the aid worker's approach must focus on the external situation rather than assume that the problems relate to some personal characteristics of the individuals or to a condition of the particular group. James Appe, a refugee writer from Uganda, makes clear the importance of context. He argues that refugees are often confused with the situation in which they find themselves. In such cases, the crisis becomes an individual problem, despite its social causes, and the individual, rather than society, bears the responsibility for change. This tendency "ignores the fact that refugees are normal people in abnormal circumstances. Their problem stems from circumstance—the society in which they live, people's reaction to their presence, laws, the inhumane treatment they are subject to," and so forth (Appe 1993, 33).

Understanding the Experience of the People and Their Culture

Any humanitarian aid or accompaniment process must begin by understanding how people experience, interpret, and react to disasters. The people have previous experience, a past, an identity—all of which have to be understood. Both the victims and those who try to help them interpret what happens and respond to the emergency situation based on the influence of their own culture and history. How victims of disasters or political repression make sense of what is happening depends as well on the interpretations of close family members, learned through acculturation and socialization, which also apply in normal times.

In her work with women who had been widowed in the war in Guatemala, Judith Zur describes how the people from a mountain village in rural Guatemala try to interpret the violence through categories of causality that are familiar to them. Their interpretations are based in custom (Mayan traditionalism) and explain that luck (malignant faith), ancestral punishment, and malicious envy have caused the current sociopolitical crisis. Their interpretations also have a basis in Catholicism, as when they find similarities between their own suffering and that of Jesus: "They were killed in the same way that Jesus was killed, for speaking the truth" (1994, 11). Finally, they explain the violence in terms of political organization. They see the violence as a result of them having organized themselves to fight for better living conditions. For this, they were turned into criminals and accused of collaborating with the so-called subversives.

The First Need: Dignity

Frequently, organized violence not only causes harm but also tries to take away one's dignity. It can be done individually (as in the case of torture, which is a direct attack on a person's identity), collectively (as in the case of genocide or "ethnic cleansing"), or through scorched-earth policies. Attacks on the identity and dignity of the people are part of many repressive strategies. In other cases, contempt for the victims can legitimate violence against poorer people, as in the case of "social cleansing." In many other situations of disaster or social crisis, the perspective of human rights must be kept in mind because victims often suffer from injustice and social marginalization. As Aengus Finucane, the director of an Irish NGO, writes: "Health services, food, housing, and education could be described as basic material needs. For refugees, the basic human need is the restoration of dignity. Dignity is the vital missing ingredient when all the basic physical needs are covered in a mechanical and impersonal way. Often, however, respect for human dignity is the first casualty in emergency response efforts to help refugees" (Needham 1994, 17).

Many aid programs for refugees in asylum countries develop in an authoritarian way, with refugees confined and kept in a state of dependency, a situation that only magnifies the effects of prior events. In addition, Northern countries often treat undocumented immigrants as a security problem. Respect for human rights has a direct effect on people's well-being, and it is therefore a basic requirement for any type of action.

Who Defines the Needs?

Humanitarian aid happens not in a vacuum but in situations where history and society affect the relationship between those who give and those who receive. Humanitarian aid and development or accompaniment projects aim to alleviate people's suffering, but, whichever the task, the work of cooperation has deep psychosocial implications with regard to the definition of needs. Maslow (1970) presents a hierarchy of individual needs that go from physical (for example, water), to social (education), to communal (relationships), to spiritual needs.[5] "The agency-NGO relationship has to be rethought. Evaluation criteria and resource management have to be based on a temporary war situation, not on the criteria established in development projects under 'normal' conditions. The only way to improve relations between all sides is for there to be more dialogue, which in turn will lead to more efficient action" (CADDHHC 1997).

Although the actual situation determines what defines the importance of covering certain basic needs, "our" priorities are often different from "theirs." Two examples are deciding whether it is more important to provide economic resources or qualified workers, or whether informing the families of fatalities is more urgent than restoring ration cards.[6]

Patterns of Mutual Aid

Humanitarian aid occurs in a context where certain patterns of giving and receiving help already exist. In disaster situations, families, friends, and neighbors are the key agents in giving and receiving help, while organizations and people from outside play a much smaller role. Those who are being helped at one moment might also find themselves, in turn, helping others trying to cope with their problems. "Contrary to common belief, most of the help is found locally. What is missing from the aid model? To presuppose that all needs are uniform, not taking into account the connections and resources of the society, does not mobilize the people but weakens them all the more" (Benoist, Piquard and Voitura, 1997).

However, in many social crises or human disasters, social networks break down and people lose this social support. To what extent this occurs will depend on the situation, but any humanitarian aid should take these support systems into account so that the outside aid does not become an alien resource that calls into question or substitutes for the resources that already exist within the community. Humanitarian aid should support and stimulate what is already there.

Concepts on Which Humanitarian Aid Is Based

Humanitarian action is often based in the culture that happens to have the necessary resources or technology. However, that does not mean that Western models of aid are transferable. For example, in the case of mental-health programs, Western assumptions of humankind and the world are not shared by other cultures. Clifford Geertz provides the example of this difference in the concept of individuality: "The Western concept of a person as a unique, limited universe, more or less integrated with a social and natural foundation . . . is, however irrefutable it may seem to us, a rather peculiar idea among world cultures" (1988, cited in Bracken, Gilles, and Summerfield 1995, 1074).

Western thought and the concept of individualism shape political, cultural, and medical trends, which is why psychology emphasizes individual psychological problems and individual therapy. However, in cultures not centered on the individual, such as indigenous cultures, the psychological dimension is not isolated but linked to the spiritual and social worlds. Mental-health problems are considered to be caused by supernatural forces or social agents, and the treatment is carried out by religious authorities or traditional healers.

Chapter 1

The Social Impact of Disasters and Political Violence

War, Catastrophes, and Complex Emergencies

A catastrophe implies a negative event, often unforeseen and brutal, that causes material destruction and grave human losses, giving rise to a large number of victims and widespread societal disorganization. This destruction has long-lasting effects. Catastrophes are the result of violence or war, technological accidents (as in Bhopal[1]), or natural and environmental disasters (for example, earthquakes, floods, and droughts). An emergency is a situation that affects people's capacities and resources to such an extent that their lives are at risk.

The most common classification of disasters is natural versus human-created. In some cases, this distinction may be useful, but in others it may obscure the truth. For example, famine is caused by drought but also by distribution problems, the ravages of war, the lack of prevention policies, or the destructive economic effects of structural adjustment programs (as in the case of Somalia; Choussudovsky 1993). Sociopolitical disasters differ from natural disasters or accidents, even though they have some similarities such as large-scale material and personal losses, social disorganization, and some group behaviors in dangerous situations. Even in natural or environmental disasters, human factors can play a major role. Some disasters have their roots in lack of foresight and inadequate or misguided development planning. The impoverishment of a large part of the population is a key factor as well. Natural disasters are not as "natural" as they appear.

Although various definitions of disasters have been proposed, the International Red Cross offers the following definitions (International Federation of Red Cross and Red Crescent Societies [IFRC] 1993):

- Sudden or unexpected natural disasters: Avalanches, earthquakes, floods, hurricanes, storms, tornados, tsunamis, volcanic eruptions, and so on

- Long-lasting natural disasters: Desertification, epidemics, famine
- Sudden or unexpected human-created disasters: Structural, transportation, technological, or industrial accidents; chemical or nuclear explosions; acid rain, chemical, or atmospheric pollution; fires
- Long-lasting human-created disasters: Civil or international wars, riots, displacement

Even though the various types of disasters appear in this list separately, many occur simultaneously or form part of the same social disaster. The common term for these is "complex emergencies."

According to the IFRC, over seven million people died as a result of disasters between 1967 and 1991. Wars or civil disturbances have had the highest impact, causing 41 percent of the deaths. Famine, often brought about by the combination of droughts and wars, in Africa above all, caused 18 percent of the deaths.[2] It is likely that the number of dead has been underestimated because of the difficulty of determining who has been affected and of following up on them. According to these estimates, civil disturbances affected more than 135 million people. Most of these disturbances have been internal conflicts, taking place within one country. For example, between 1989 and 1992 there were eight-two wars in the world, of which seventy-nine took place within the borders of a country.

In natural disasters, the poor living conditions of very large numbers of people add to the dimensions of a disaster. Three million people, 80 percent of them in Asia, were affected by natural disasters between 1967 and 1991. In Africa, where only 15 percent of the natural disasters occurred, over 60 percent of the deaths occurred. In addition to the risk presented by poor living conditions, the risks of technological disasters with environmental consequences are growing (such as the nuclear accident at Chernobyl in 1986) as is the destruction of nature (such as deforestation, which has caused flooding and droughts).

AIDS is becoming not only a serious health problem but also a serious collective disaster in sub-Saharan Africa. The total number of people living with HIV/AIDS in the world was 36.1 million by the end of 2000, of whom 5.3 million were infected with HIV in 2000. There are 1.4 million children below the age of fifteen years living with HIV/AIDS in the world. The total number of AIDS deaths from the beginning of the epidemic to the end of 2000 was 21.8 million, 3 million of which occurred in just 2000. AIDS deaths have left thousands of orphans and other enormous burdens on the lives of the affected individuals and societies. Even though the number of disasters varies from one year to the next, the possibility of disasters is increasing because of the environmental

The North/South Divide

The geographic distribution of disasters is uneven. The highest number of disasters has occurred in Asia with 42 percent, followed by North and South America with 22 percent, Africa and Europe with 15 percent each, and Oceania with 6 percent. Disasters take place mainly in countries of the South.[3] From 1967 to 1991, an annual average of 117 million people were affected by disasters in developing countries, compared to 700,000 people living in developed countries. The rate of people affected in countries of the South over countries of the North is 166 to 1 (De Girolamo and McFarlane 1997).

An example of the disasters that occur in developing countries is the eruption of the Nevado del Ruiz volcano in Armero, Colombia. This volcanic eruption destroyed the village and killed 22,000 people, 80 percent of the inhabitants of the village. Disasters of this magnitude are hard to imagine in developed countries where better living conditions, warning systems, prevention efforts, and many types of support systems work together to decrease vulnerability.

changes caused by development, war, and poverty. Despite high levels of food production in the world, the death rate within populations affected by disasters has increased significantly in the last three decades, especially in disasters related to famine and drought. These conditions produce serious social and psychological problems for the affected populations. They also pose new challenges for humanitarian aid and call for a change in the concept of a disaster as a discrete event.

Governments and organizations increasingly believe that humanitarian aid may help to alleviate some problems and to offer support to the most affected people, without addressing the underlying causes. Humanitarian aid offers the opportunity to help people overcome the consequences of a disaster, but if the aid operates in isolation from the defense of human rights or political action, it will have little influence on the mechanisms that cause suffering.

The Nature of Disasters and Political Violence

In situations where people are faced with unforeseen, brutal circumstances over which they have little control, survivors experience high levels of loss, material and otherwise, and uncertainty as to whether similar events may happen again to threaten their lives.

The impact of disasters goes beyond the direct effects of the disaster itself. Disasters often cause greater degrees of social exclusion. Poverty causes disasters and disasters worsen poverty, giving rise to feelings of vulnerability and fatalism.

In 2000, Hurricane Mitch interrupted the lives of the people of Honduras just when the country was beginning to see positive economic growth at an annual rate of 4.5 percent. This economic growth, however, was not reaching the poorer populations. Between 1990 and 1997, poverty increased from 60 to 78 percent, a fact even recognized by a variety of research studies from official organizations (Meza 1998).

Psychological problems tend to be more serious and last longer when the event has been caused by humans and has not been merely accidental. The potential impact of a technological disaster is greater because those types of disasters create feelings of powerlessness and uncertainty with regard to the nature and duration of the effects.

The toxic oil poisoning disaster in Spain in 1981 affected 20,000 people; it caused 349 deaths and left thousands disabled.[4] The patients who survived the acute phase of the illness subsequently suffered from paralysis, atrophy, and infections, as well as household breakdown from the deaths of family members. A third of the affected people were referred to psychiatric care, more than 71 percent of whom were women suffering from anxiety, sadness, and depression. Half of them showed irritability and insomnia, and another 20 percent suffered from emotional instability and loss of short-term memory and vitality (López-Ibor et al. 1985).

Sociopolitical disasters such as wars or states of terror imposed by political regimes are more complex. They are usually part of a larger strategy that serves to dismantle public institutions. The state often becomes the enemy, which causes a greater sense of threat and social polarization that makes people feel more vulnerable. These experiences may cause worsened living conditions, family breakups, social chaos, and cultural changes. The phenomena of displacement and refuge often entail the rupture of familiar networks and social relations.

The variability of events implies not only different psychological effects but also different interpretations and responses. Nature may harm unintentionally, but humans are capable of harming intentionally. This difference brings about different interpretations. After natural disasters, people may begin to doubt the nature of things, whereas victims of human-created disasters tend to see the world and themselves in a more negative light (Janoff-Bulman 1992). Natural disasters kill, but they do not threaten people's self-respect as intentional human harm or violence may. Those in armed power harm those in opposition in order to dominate and destroy the social structure of the "enemy" and to capture, damage, or destroy their material resources; the other side defends itself; and local and international responsibilities are often involved in the conflict as well. "The truth is that many dreams have died in Bosnia in the last two and a half years: the dream that the world had a conscience; the dream that Europe is a civilized place; the dream that there is justice for the strong and for the weak. It would be no surprise if the millennial dream that the truth will set us free also died there" (Rieff 1996).

Given that most humanitarian aid takes place during wars, it is important to understand the psychology and social mechanisms of repression and civil conflict that appear in these situations. In the World War I, 5 percent of the deaths were suffered by civilians; in World War II, around 50 percent were civilians; today, more than 90 percent of these victims are civilians. The involvement of the civilian population is no longer a secondary effect. In fact, one of the objectives of recent wars has been to rend the social fabric of a country as a way of gaining control (Summerfield 1996). This is reflected in the lack of distinction made between soldiers and civilians. In very different armed conflicts such as those in Sudan, East Timor, or Colombia, civilians are supposed to be current or future collaborators with different guerrilla groups. In other places, violence against women is used as the plunder of war or, in Bosnia, as a form of ethnic cleansing. In contemporary wars, the people's way of life has become a military objective, as in Guatemala in the 1980s where the army's scorched-earth policy destroyed more than four hundred villages to be followed by a militarized social-restructuring program.

Many regimes have used psychological methods to increase control over the population. Faúndez (1994) analyzed the psychological war mechanisms most frequently used in Latin America to create terror in the population. They are torture, systematic propaganda, movement of the population, disappearances, political executions and murders, blackmail, dismissals, and raids. More recent wars in which the United States or the North Atlantic Treaty Organization (NATO), have been involved, supposedly to end violence toward civilians, such as the first and second Gulf Wars against Iraq (plus the embargo in between) and the war against Serbia for the repression in Kosovo, have clearly had violent consequences among the civilian populations in those countries. Despite an open declaration that the war was not against the Serbian population, the following statement of Lieutenant General Michael Short, then head of the NATO air force command in Kosovo, shows how the suffering of the civilian population was a goal of the NATO bombings: "I think that if there is no electricity for the refrigerator, or gas for the cooker, you can't go to work because the bridge has been blown up and you spend all your time wondering what the next target will be, you end up hoping that it will end" (*El País*, May 14, 1999).

The Impact of Traumatic Events

The impact of a disaster can be seen in the increased health problems and symptoms in the population.[5] Most victims of violence show some kind of symptomatic response. Epidemiological research shows that victims of disasters or violence present with severe symptoms in around 25 to 40 percent of cases. Those who were involved in combat and massacres have a similar rate. For rape victims, the rate increases to 60 percent. The measurement of the impact in the affected population is usually done by assessing symptoms; however, it is also possible to look at other social indicators (see Chapter 8).

As mentioned, psychological effects, as well as people's interpretations and responses, vary according to the event. One way of assessing the psychosocial impact of a disaster is to analyze the characteristics of the event. Generally, the more intense the event the greater the number of psychological symptoms that appear.[6] It has been confirmed that physical harm; the death of a partner; the involvement in atrocities; and witnessing deaths, rapes, or torture cause the greatest psychological impact. If the event is intense, is severe, involves darkness or noise, is unexpected, is uncontrollable, or involves personal losses, the impact will be greater.

Collective traumatic events also have a major psychological and social impact. During wars and periods of political repression, collective violent acts such as massacres and the destruction of communities often take place, which have a major impact on the survivors. For Mato, a nine-year-old boy from Dubrovnik, the destruction of the city is a symbol of the destruction of life: "They bombed my city. . . . The terrible war in 1991 destroyed everything. The city was attacked from the air, sea, and land. My city died" (Bonnet 1994). Open interviews with Guatemalans who had experienced different forms of repression confirm that massacres cause the greatest psychological damage (ODHAG 1998). The survivors of massacres showed more sadness, intense grief, despair, and feelings of injustice, as well as group effects such as displacement and the disintegration of the community. The larger community is also affected. The ODHAG study showed that massacres produced greater exodus, more panic, and a greater climate of distrust and social chaos. Apart from the damage done to individuals, the social losses can have a large impact in the medium term. Social and cultural changes also occur, as shown in the following testimony from Chiapas:

The Morelia community was always very united. Today the community is divided and that was a task well planned. [The government] planned army intrusions in key moments during the productive cycle, and people's economic life is very fragile. Intervention during the planting season or the harvest meant there would be a shortage of food. Then the government programs begin to appear, offering sheets of zinc or trucks full of gravel, and so forth, and people are in need so some families accept. Then they say that for the programs to work every-body has to agree. This is when the conflicts start. (Pérez et al. 1999)

These effects should not be considered in isolation from one another. The loss of land in rural communities, for example, not only causes the fear of losing the main form of subsistence and social status but also affects people's identity by uprooting them from their cultural environment.

These losses worsen living conditions, which already reflected of extreme poverty. Together with family losses, economic difficulties were the most frequent effects mentioned by the survivors of Guatemala's scorched-earth policies (ODHAG 1998). In this study, people emphasize both material losses, such as houses, crops, and animals, as well as social effects, which the survivors say continue to affect them many years on.

This rupture of the social fabric because of war, disasters, and neoliberal policies that often follow them or form part of their causes should be considered as a key element in the process of reconstruction. The loss of social organizations impedes the rebuilding of villages, so aid programs should consider the rebuilding of organizations and local capacities among their primary objectives.

The Impact of Violence

Intentional Effects and Dehumanization

In many countries, those in power use the violation of human rights as a strategy for social control. In an open war, or in the case of authoritarian regimes that use widespread repression as an instrument for political control, the entire society is affected. The following appalling story told by a boy-soldier from Mozambique shows the degree to which war promotes dehumanization, using deliberate mechanisms, such as training, to cause people to conform: "Renamo caught an elderly woman who was trying to escape. She was brought before our group while we were training. The leader of Renamo pointed to Manuel and ordered him to kill her. He took the bayonet and stabbed her in the stomach. The leader then ordered him to cut her head off. He did it and they said he was brave and they named him the leader of our group" (Boothby et al. 1991, 21).

War is not a sudden emergence of violence. It is a process that requires preparation and training. In Rwanda, one group's beliefs of superiority over another were reinforced, leading to violent clashes between groups whose prior relationship had not been based on ethnicity. In precolonial times, the three groups in the country (Hutus, Tutsis, and Pigmeos) were not tribes or ethnic groups; they were strata of the same group differentiated by political or occupational status and with reciprocal relations. For centuries, they peacefully shared a language, religion, and territory. The Belgian colonial administration destroyed this cohabitation and reinforced the differences among the groups and gave preferences to the Tutsis. The introduction of an identity card in 1926 specified to which group each person belonged. The criteria for being defined as a Tutsi (traditionally cattle farmers) consisted of owning ten cows or more (De Waal 1994, 1–2).

Military organizations demand discipline and loyalty based on a rigid ideology and moral absolutes. In a context where violence has become normal, changes of attitudes—such as insensitivity toward suffering, opportunism, disregard for human life, and changing mores arising from skepticism and despair—are frequent. "Here we no longer have freedom of speech or mobility. We can't say what we think because we could be killed, you never know who could be listening. Anyway, life is worth nothing. Most people don't care about anything. You learn not to trust anyone. There is no community. We have lost the right to think differently and that is demoralizing" (author's personal notes from Workshop in Sabana de Torres, Colombia, 1997).

THE DEGRADATION OF DIGNITY: THE IMPACT ON IDENTITY

Identity is a key concept in understanding many of the effects of violence and loss in social disasters. Identity helps to maintain emotional security and the ability to take action through the awareness of the situation in which one lives, the experience of being oneself, and the feeling of belonging to a group or community. We differentiate between an individual identity (based on the attributes and individual characteristics of the person) and a social identity (based on inclusion in one or more groups, social convictions, and so on).

Torture and rape are two extreme examples of the attack on dignity. Torture not only tries to extract information from a captured person, it also forces him or her to collaborate and degrades the person's self-image, destroying him or her as a person and as a member of a group. Finally, it makes him or her take on the identity of the oppressor. In the last twenty years, we have witnessed situations such as those in Rwanda, Bosnia, and Guatemala where torture had a social character, took a public form, and was exercised against a large part of the population with the strategy of destroying communities.

Rape is also a part of the machinery of war. Sexual attacks on women

TORTURE TECHNIQUES AND THE EFFECTS ON POLITICAL PRISONERS IN LATIN
AMERICA

Torture Techniques	Impact on the Prisoner
Arrest and initial torture	Initial weakening of the person and psychological upset in response to the torture
Isolation	Feeling of erasure and loss of habitual reference points
Physical and moral contamination (overcrowded conditions, sleeping with dirty clothes, humiliation, etc.)	Violation of the physical and moral self
Degrading ceremonies (obeying submissively, searches, etc.)	Profound weakening of the self-image
Admission ceremonies and dispossession (taking away personal belongings, assigning a number to the person, etc.)	Tendency to lose personal identity and degradation of the social identity
Regulations (submission to arbitrary and authoritarian rules)	Decreasing ability to react and submission to the rules of the prison

Source: COLAT 1982.

are common in wars as a way of demoralizing the enemy as a whole. A team of researchers from the European Union who visited the former Yugoslavia in December 1992 found that many Bosnian women and adolescent girls had been raped in Bosnia and Herzegovina as part of a systematic terror campaign. Thai pirates intentionally raped Vietnamese women in front of their families to ensure the humiliation of everybody—as in this example from Guatemala: "We were in a workshop with the interviewers who had collected the testimonies. I asked the [Guatemalan interviewers] (all of them men) about the raping of women, but they didn't answer. They looked at the floor and remained silent. I also stayed silent. That had been their answer: The women had been raped, which meant that the community had also been raped" (Claudia, personal testimony, REMHI project, Guatemala, 1997).

Victims of rape lose their confidence in others, their self-confidence, and social acceptance. They suffer from personal humiliation and often their families ostracize them. Spouses, brothers, or fathers may also feel helpless and responsible. Whereas the men and women who have been injured or murdered are considered "heroes" or "martyrs," the pain of rape is kept in silence or turned into stigma. As in the case of the disappeared, the suffering of the person and the family finds no validation.

AGGRESSION AND TERROR

The very dynamic of war brings with it aggression in many forms. Physical violence in personal and social relationships occurs that is not part of the actual war. The trauma of persecution, torture, or death can give rise to feelings of hate, with an element of revenge and a desire for justice, which, in many cases, is perfectly legitimate. The closing off of political spaces or the systematic persecution of peace campaigns often forces people to participate in a war. It can also be a way of saving their own lives or of trying to change the situation. However, the demands of military organizations for discipline and a vision of the world reduced to believing that armed clashes are the key to solving problems limit, in most cases, any prospects for social change. "I wrote that the war made me more human. That we learned to give it all, the measure of life. . . . More human? Rubbish! The war dehumanized us. I learned that those on the other side were 'the enemy.' I learned to obey without asking questions, without agreeing" (Arminda, El Salvador, 1995, in Martín Beristain 1997).

Hate is also used as a political weapon that often hides behind so-called security concerns. In recent decades, in many countries of Latin America, the system for training military bodies, which was later responsible for a great number of atrocities, was based on a division between "us" and "them." Such training centered on obedience, strong group control, and complicity. This system explains to a large extent the destructive nature of political repression and some of the violence that is taking place in postwar Central America.

In situations of political repression, the aim of violence is to create fear. While the violence itself physically eliminates those people who are its direct targets, its terrorizing nature tends to paralyze all who identify with any aspects of the victim. This apparent irrationality hides a very clear rationality: to make visible the threat to all those in opposition. Consequently, people often adopt an attitude of silence and passivity so as not to put themselves in danger, even when they witness disagreeable things. This increases conformism and may lead to a questioning of their identity, which affects all aspects of their daily life.

To not fear the turning corner, or the car that stops in front of you when you are on your way to work, to know that you'll return home every night, to be able to hear footsteps on the street at night without your heart missing a beat, to say yes, or no, whenever you want or when you go to the office. . . . To pass a policeman without being afraid, to look at yourself in the mirror, to be able to read the newspapers without feeling humiliated by the lies, to know where your loved ones are or that they haven't been thrown to the dogs and that they'll return in the evening, to speak simply of the time that we need in order to eat bread without tears. (Raymond Jacq, quoted in ACAT 1987, 14)

The characteristics of violence are changing in many countries. There is a shift from the political terror of the war years or the open military dictatorships to so-called social violence or criminality. Despite apparent normality, serious violence is taking place in many countries because of deterioration of political regimes and unstable economic structures made worse by neoliberal policies, poverty, and the existence of organized networks protected by impunity or by the actions of the state itself.

When faced with insecurity, fear, or the emergence of new internal enemies (the marginalized or socially excluded), the assumptions of social stability take their meaning from the paradigms of war, which justify the repression of civil liberties (death penalty or degrading prison conditions, for example). In many countries in Latin America, the new "war against crime" risks reproducing the effects of the previous violent situations. In Argentina in the mid-1990s, for example, some of the support teams for families of the disappeared were also working with victims of the so-called "easy trigger"—the impunity under which the police acted and the legitimization of "social cleansing."

Forced Displacement

It is estimated that around fifty million people have taken refuge in other countries or have undergone forced displacement within the borders of their own country. When a population is displaced, families separate and social ties fall away. Changes in the social structure range from the loss of basic services and support to the creation of new forms of social organization in response to the new situation. In the case of refugee populations, life in the camps may bring about a new way of life, being subjected to new forms of authority and forced to live with other groups. Cultural changes may also take place, such as the loss of symbols, traditions, and rites or even a hiding of one's own identity. "The central event—from the violence to the exodus—meant that every person's life was disrupted, each family, each community, each village was affected. The identities—still being formed—suffer a new transition marked by the effects of displacement. Before: peasant, tenant farmer, Black, native Chocoan. Now: 'displaced person from Chocó'" (Giraldo et al. 1997).

All of these facts frame the lives of the displaced and refugees, and they present many problems and tensions for families and individuals. It is important that those accompanying or supporting displaced populations take these social issues into account because the routine needs and activities will in large measure revolve around such situations. It also helps to consider the rhythm and dynamics of the communities involved.

In some countries, the displaced populations have organized themselves to negotiate with the government over the conditions of return (such as security, health, and autonomy). In many cases, the displaced face, in addition to pressures to return, problems of violence and security. People often try to figure out how to return, despite insecure conditions, in order to avoid permanent losses and to rebuild their lives.

From June 1997, the Colombian government proposed to the displaced Urabá Chocoan population a return to their places of origin. Since then, the government has pressured the farmers in different ways to return. The displaced communities wrote up a series of petitions (things they wanted guaranteed for their return), and they were willing to negotiate on these points. . . . But the truth is, forced returns violate the regulations set out in international instruments, which oblige states to respect the voluntary returns of refugees or displaced people with guarantees for their resettlement, ensuring the necessary resources from the state for the economic, moral, social, and political reconstruction of their uprooted families and communities. (CADDHHC 1977, 14)

In the 1997 return to Rwanda, military sieges and fear instigated the movement of the population. In this case, the difficulty the humanitarian aid agencies faced in simply finding the refugees and understanding what was going on within these communities showed how far these agencies were from understanding their problems, and this led to a poor response to the return process. More recently, a similar situation occurred in the massive deportations in Kosovo in 1999, where military priorities were placed over the needs of the people. While NATO forces were carrying out air raids and searches using satellites and high-technology airplanes that could take detailed photographs, the UNHCR reported that somehow ten thousand Kosovars "got lost" in the Prizen Mountains after eviction from a border camp in Blace (*El País*, February 15, 1999).

The following table shows some of the problems that displaced people or refugees have to face at different times.

Research on refugees indicates different phases in the experience of taking refuge or being forcibly displaced. Before departure, economic problems, social or family disruption, physical violence, or political repression are likely. Many families suffer the difficulty of economic loss or lack of food. Even though in most cases violence is the main reason for leaving, other factors such as the closing of schools or the absence of basic necessities can make life untenable, as in testimony from Guatemala describing the situation before scorched-earth policies were implemented: "The market closed in 1981 and 1982. You couldn't buy anything in the shops, not even medicine or food. Our work, our crops, nobody was buying. It was only for ourselves and our children" (ODHAG 1998, 101).

THE EXPERIENCE OF REFUGEES AND DISPLACED PEOPLE

Before departure	Economic problems Social and family disruption Physical violence Political repression
Departure	Separation Dangers of the journey
Reception	Reception and initial settling Fear of repatriation or threats Obtaining some form of recognition Resolving needs such as food, clothing, shelter, etc. Daily hardships of the new regimen
Settling in	Language barriers Cultural conflicts Finding work Conflicts between generations

Repatriation	Family conflicts
	Separations
	Threats to life
	Integration back into a country that has changed
	Expectations collide with reality, the attitude of the
	    population of the country or origin; identity problems
	    (refugee-repatriate).

Source: Ager 1995.

In the departure phase, the main experiences will be the separation from family, friends, and home and the danger of the journey. The precarious conditions of escape often cause extreme suffering, even deaths from starvation or sickness, especially in young children and the elderly.

My daughter and I got on the bus. My wife and I looked at each other. After fourteen years together, this was the moment of separation. My hope was that one day we would be reunited, but I knew that wouldn't happen for a long time. . . . We were the first to get on board [the boat] and were very nervous when other illegal passengers got on board. If someone discovered our secret we would have been imprisoned. . . . By the next morning we had drunk all the water, and some people had died. We threw their bodies into the sea. One night nearly twenty people died. It was terrible. We could hear screams and people crying. One mother lost her two sons and then threw herself into the sea. (K. Doung on his escape from Vietnam, Refugee Program Network 1994)

In the reception phase, refugees and the displaced face various problems: fear of repatriation and threats of persecution; obtaining some form of recognition—or, conversely, concealing their situation—and taking care of basic needs such as food, clothing, shelter, and so on. Most refugees are taken in by neighboring countries and do not stay in camps but disperse into various locations. The main problems in such cases are isolation and economic hardship. Refugees are often taken in by families, especially when there are family or ethnic ties between the populations. For example, in Chiapas, 60 percent of the population internally displaced by political violence has been taken in by families from other communities. More than 50 percent of the Kosovar refugees who sought refuge in Albania were taken in by families. People forget about these receiving populations even though they can be an important factor, especially later if problems in the camps arise, such as overcrowding and lack of supplies.

Other problems—such as dependence on the organization and daily hardship—emerge in the refugee camps where humanitarian aid is distributed, as described in this testimony from a refugee in Mozambique: "I'm not happy in the camp. Lots of things worry me. I cannot dress my family adequately. I have no say in this situation. I miss home. I want to ask the government and the rebels to stop so that I can go home in peace. I can't go until there is peace." (Ager 1995). Refugees and displaced people are often treated as a public problem instead of as a population that has suffered terrible violence and injustice. Humanitarian aid workers and agencies should recognize this and not become another aspect of the policies that control those they are trying to help.

During the settling-in phase, problems with a new language, cultural conflicts, work difficulties, or conflicts between generations may arise. These are major problems for refugees in Europe, the United States, or Australia, which are home to only 15 percent of the total number of refugees in the world. Even when fewer cultural differences exist, the experience of spending a long time in another country can pose similar problems, such as the case of the Guatemalan refugees in Mexico. Even when most serious threats have been overcome, problems still result from the separation of families, social exclusion, or financial difficulty.

Repatriation is difficult, even when the situation leaves no other option or when humanitarian aid agencies enforce it. The repatriation process entails many family conflicts, over who returns and who does not, causing even more separation. Forced return sometimes happens during a conflict, which can make the journey life threatening. Many of the problems the refugees had to confront on their departure appear once more as they try to reintegrate into a country that has changed during their absence. Their expectations do not match the reality of what they find at home and in the attitude of the population of their country. This movement between refugee and repatriate status can cause difficult identity struggles. The following table summarizes the elements influenced positively and negatively by the social reinsertion of those refugees who returned to El Salvador and Guatemala at the beginning of the 1990s.

THE CONDITIONS OF SOCIAL REINSERTION (EL SALVADOR AND GUATEMALA, 1989–97)

	Negative Aspects of Social Reinsertion	Positive Aspects of Social Reinsertion
Sociopolitical situation	Financial problems Political instability and continued danger Scarce infrastructure in the area of the return	Public discussion and information on repatriation Negotiations International accompaniment for the return
"Receiving" communities	Financial competitiveness with other populations Political image of the refugees Ethnic or historical conflicts	Achieving balance of common interests Conditions for living with other families
Refugee population	Traumatic memories and experiences Habits acquired on humanitarian aid Organizational dependency	Experiences and abilities acquired during life as a refugee Own organizational structures

Chapter 2

From Emergency to Reconstruction: Stages of Collective Disasters

> *Any disaster is a live phenomenon, but the Páez disaster had a distinguishing element: it is uncommon for an earthquake to cause ecological destruction of this magnitude. An enormous area was destroyed. Sixteen hundred families were forced to leave. Another element was the diversity of the population—indigenous people from the Páez region who speak only their native language; indigenous people from Guambia, who are completely different; black communities; mixed race communities; Catholic communities; evangelical communities. The variety of people involved brought about conflicts, and the resolution of these conflicts has become an essential part of the reconstruction process.*
>
> —G. Wilches, 1995

This chapter presents the different stages of the response to emergency situations, and the main problems that must be managed during the period after a disaster. Based on information taken from longitudinal studies and historical studies on epidemics and disasters, the following stages can normally be identified: preliminary stage, stage of alert, stage of shock and reaction, first responses after a disaster, and adaptation and reconstruction stage. Most research is based on natural disasters, but we also refer to "human-created" violent experiences such as massacres or the destruction of communities. In the case of complex emergencies, these stages may overlap.

Preliminary Stages

Descriptive research has demonstrated the existence of a preliminary stage and a stage of alert. The *preliminary stage* is that of the preparation of the authorities and the population for a disaster. However, before a disaster, and also in the first stages of a disaster, it is common for the authorities and the public to deny or minimize the threat. When the threat of the plague appeared in the fourteenth century, doctors and authorities tried to calm people down by denying the possibility that the plague would occur or by minimizing the severity of the situation. People were told that it was not the bubonic plague but some other, more benign illness and that the increasing rate of death was from other, less threatening problems such as food contamination. It was rumored that the authorities had invented the disease. Similar attitudes emerged around cholera outbreaks in the nineteenth century, and we can see something similar with the AIDS epidemic in the late twentieth and early twenty-first centuries—in France, authorities minimized the risk of contracting AIDS through a blood transfusion, which resulted in the infection of many hemophiliacs and others (Delumeau 1993). Similar risk minimization was present in the U.S. government's response to Hurricane Katrina in New Orleans in 2005.

People tend to believe that others expose themselves to danger because of a lack of knowledge. However, being aware of danger or the possible exposure to disasters is not enough for people to avoid those situations. Generally, people live in places where they can survive even if they know they are at risk, especially if they do not have the means to change their circumstances. It is also common for people who live under threat to avoid talking about the possible danger. For example, people who live in areas where the risk of contracting a disease is great or people who live near nuclear power plants avoid talking about the issue or think that the problem is not particularly threatening. Surveys have shown that the nearer people live to a nuclear plant, the safer they think they are. In the same way, industry workers in high-risk jobs deny that their jobs are particularly dangerous, to such an extent that it is difficult to make them enforce the necessary security measures (Zonabend 1993).

THE STAGE OF ALERT

The *stage of alert* is defined as that time between the moment danger is announced and the appearance of the disaster itself. It begins with various alert signals that provoke a general state of useful anxiety, with vigilance regarding preparation and installation of security measures. If this stage is managed without instruction or precise information, however, it can give rise to rumors and panic.

Early warnings and late warnings differ. Early warnings are the first alarm signals that warn of approaching danger and the importance of prevention actions and preparations to leave. Late warnings, made in the face of imminent danger, include precise information on decisions that have to be made, how to flee, and what support is available. Those who are used to living with imminent danger—such as people who live

---

The Explosion of the Space Shuttle *Challenger*

The *Challenger* space shuttle disaster in January 1986 illustrates how group thought processes minimize the threat of disaster. The engineers opposed the launch because they were aware that cold temperatures could cause the rocket to explode. NASA officials wanted to launch the rocket as soon as possible, and they asked the engineers to prove that the rocket would not work. Because the engineers could not prove this, the launch went forward. The officials' insistence reveals their illusion of invulnerability—in their minds, the worst-case scenarios were the least likely to happen.

The NASA administrators pressured the engineers to conform, asking them to "give their opinion as administrators, not engineers." The engineers were told that they should not put obstacles in the way of launching the space shuttle. An illusion of unanimity was created by relying only on the administrators and not the engineers as to whether the rocket should be launched. Finally, because the criticisms of the engineers had been censored, the executive who made the final decision was unaware of the concerns of those who had designed and manufactured *Challenger*. The result was that the shuttle [exploded just over a minute into the flight, killing all on board].

Source: Páez and Marqués 1999.

close to rivers that overflow or people who experience typhoons or tornados—have many resources available to cope with these events. Sometimes they have even adapted their daily lives around the possibility of such an emergency.

The displaced population of Yondó had lived near the Magdalena River for twenty-five years. The river had occasionally flooded their village but not their homes. They had learned to read the signs and communicate with it. When the river warned that it would flood, the people raised their houses with sticks onto the small hill. They waited until the water disappeared, and then they would take their houses down again. They lived by the river for twenty-five years, but then the violence began and they couldn't cope with the guerillas. The guerrillas harassed their fleet that left to patrol the river; eventually they were evacuated. Later, some of them returned. (Author's notes from a workshop in Barrancabermeja, Colombia, 1997)

Nevertheless, daily contact with danger can also create apparent indifference that corresponds to resignation or denial and a focus on normal daily activities. In addition to this attitude of denial, some will accuse others in the group of being fearful or of exaggerating the threat. Recent research confirms that in the moment of disaster, or when a threat persists, even when rumors about the event circulate, people prefer not to talk or think about it. This avoidance mechanism is a way to adapt to the imminent confrontation with great tension.

**Elements Associated with the Lack of Response
When Faced with an Imminent Danger**

- Difficulty in abandoning belongings, land, and so on.
- Denial about what is happening ("This can't happen here").
- The belief that a supernatural being will protect those in danger.
- Lack of clear and precise information.
- Excessive length of time in period of alert.
- Lack of previous experience in similar situations.
- Poor organization of the immediate alert when danger is imminent.
- Lack of credibility in the source that informs about the threat.
- Spreading of contradictory rumors that play down the need to escape or take refuge.

Source: ODHAG 1998.

Pennebaker (1990) compared two communities that experienced the eruption of a volcano and found that in the community that had been affected very little by the volcano but which could still have been affected more, people refused to be interviewed more than once about the event, insisting that they were not emotionally affected by the event. In contrast, in the community where the disaster was felt to be over, people were willing to be interviewed more than once. This shows that those who find themselves in the middle of an unfinished task, such as coping with a disaster, may try to deal with it by inhibiting their thoughts and feelings. Pennebaker confirmed this theory with laboratory studies that compared people who had accomplished equivalent tasks but with different expectations. The group that was made to think it had more work ahead of it was less tired than the group who thought it was finished.

This adaptive mechanism of inhibiting thoughts, feelings, and communication may, however, be costly. A group of survivors of the Chernobyl disaster described that the people from the nearby city of Belaris had found denial mechanisms to decrease their anxiety ("We don't want any information," they said) (Teter 1996). They maintained an attitude of passivity and impotence, and they resorted to drinking alcohol. Epidemiological studies suggest that over time this mechanism of denial or inhibition is linked to higher rates of illness and death (Pennebaker 1995).

Such denial is also common when faced with serious sociopolitical threats such as massacres during an armed conflict. Despite imminent danger, many people function with a proportional logic ("I haven't done anything, so they won't do anything to me"), as was the case in the massacres of Ixcán, Guatemala, in 1981 and 1982. When there is maximum threat of danger, the credibility of the source that sounds the alert is a key for the effectiveness of prevention efforts. In the massacre carried out by the army of El Salvador in El Mozote in 1981, the people had given total credibility to the local leader who said that El Mozote would be the only village not affected. Similarly, during the Armero volcanic eruption, local leaders gave reassuring messages and the government's communications were unclear. The people's lack of previous experience with volcanic eruption was another key element in their denial of danger.

Within institutions and among elites, critical voices tend to be silenced and optimistic hypotheses affirmed, which leads to an illusion of group invulnerability. Such institutional behavior may occur for economic reasons, from insensitivity toward the most vulnerable populations, or because of a need to appear to be in control of the situation. However, such behavior has caused many deaths that could have been avoided.

STAGE OF SHOCK AND REACTION

According to estimates from the British Crisis Centre for Disasters, 15 percent of people facing a disaster show a pathological reaction, another 15 percent maintain a stable attitude, and the remaining 70 percent appear calm but are covering up a kind of emotional numbness. A key factor in achieving an adequate reaction is to have those able to maintain stable attitudes help those who are emotionally numb become aware of what is happening. Conflicts with the minority who exhibit a less adaptive reaction should be avoided.

There are different types of victims and different types of movement. A study of the effects of an earthquake in Peru describes the following types of victims or affected people, which can be applied to all kinds of disasters: (a) direct physical victims, (b) contextual victims—those traumatized by the material and sociocultural conditions after the impact, (c) peripheral victims—nonresidents who have suffered losses, and (d) "imported" victims—volunteers and aid workers who suffer from stress and the miserable conditions created by the disaster (Oliver-Smith 1996).

Although many variations can occur depending on the disaster and its characteristics, different zones are commonly identified based on how affected people are by the disaster and on the distance of the people from the location of the disaster.

The stage of shock—brief and brutal—is a state of collective stress in

---

Zones of Impact in Disasters

Central impact zone: A massive number of victims and a great amount of chaos. At first, people are in shock, but flight takes over.

Destruction zone: Primarily material destruction, with fewer injured or dead people but still many who have been affected by the disaster and by the social devastation. People are uneasy over what to do and they attempt to flee; at times, widespread panic results.

Marginal zone: Neither victims nor destruction but disturbances in the systems of communication. There may be uncertainty, rumors, or escape from the central areas toward the surrounding areas.

Exterior zone: Surrounding areas that remain intact in every way except from a "moral" perspective. Often family members and others will go from this zone to the disaster zones to help out.

---

which people are emotionally shaken and experience a sense of disbelief ("This cannot be happening; this is a nightmare"), inactivity, and inability to concentrate. It is a stage of shock, inhibition, and a sort of stupor. The person cannot think clearly, cannot believe what is happening, and wanders about or is unable to respond in a deliberate manner. There are many other examples of people who are unable to react in the face of danger and remain paralyzed—such as not jumping from a train even though it is clearly going to crash. The stage of reaction—the stage immediately after the stage of shock—is a continuation of the shock-inhibition-stupor process, but in this stage agitation, panic, and escape appear as well. The reaction stage is very brief and does not usually last more than a few hours.

At the moment disasters occur, victims mainly experience fear, impotence, or anger, but supportive behaviors are also common. According to a study on disasters, which included fires, accidents, and terrorist attacks carried out in the Basque Country, 40 percent of people felt intense fear, a third of whom expressed their anxiety through anger, screaming, or crying. The majority, about 75 percent, said they were not prepared for the event they experienced. Two-thirds of the sample requested help and received it (Páez, Arroyo, and Fernández 1995).[1]

The First Responses

THE EMERGENCY STAGE AND MOMENTARY RESOLUTION

The resolution stage, which follows the shock and reaction stage, is a period of clarity and social rebuilding characterized by a decrease in turmoil, panic, and flight and a development of new behaviors adapted to help, support, and rescue. Research on responses to natural disasters shows that, immediately after the event, an emergency period occurs that lasts two or three weeks. People may experience high levels of anxiety, intense social activity, and repetitive thoughts about the event. Then a stage of inhibition tends to follow, which lasts between three and eight weeks. In this stage, people repress their feelings and tend not to share

---

Acting in the Midst of Danger

1. A large group of people crowded into a small area can provoke a stressful situation. Maintain a calm attitude from the beginning and communicate instructions clearly.

2. Take a few minutes to think ahead and try and imagine what the general reaction to a collective disaster will be. Try and obtain a complete picture of what is happening. What will people do? Will they come together? Will they escape? Where will they escape to? Will we get help? Where will the aid arrive? What will make the work easier? From these concerns, develop a survival strategy.

3. Locate the people who are reacting to the situation with clarity and awareness to design a plan. The aim should be to integrate those in shock—most people will be in a state of shock and will feel numb—by giving them simple tasks to do, tasks that do not require thought or decision-making. For example, have them try and look for their family, clothes, or something to extinguish the fire; or instruct them to stay in one place so that their family can find them, and so on. It is important to reunite families, especially lost children or the elderly, for example, by establishing meeting points or a key person who is clearly visible.

4. Know both how to be a leader in a moment of confusion and how to back off when better prepared people with more authority take over.

---

their experiences with others. This is often an attempt to overcome what has happened, but it also shows the difficulty of finding other people to talk with because others are usually "burnt out" from talking about the event. "In the case of the [1989] earthquake in San Francisco, after talking about the event intensely for weeks, some T-shirts were printed that illustrated the saturation point. They said, 'Thanks for not sharing your experience of the earthquake'" (Pennebaker 1990). Similarly, in the 1995 massacre of Xamán in Guatemala, after expressing their grief intensely for the first few weeks, the families of the victims resorted to silence, isolation, and attempts to forget about what had happened. In this stage, there may be an increase in anxiety, psychosomatic symptoms, minor health problems, nightmares, arguments, and disruptive collective behaviors.

Very often, the media appear during the emergency stage and

become added participants in wars and disasters. Journalists' main concern is the news story above and beyond any other issue, but they each have their own attitude. Their work has multiple effects: On the one hand, journalists help to spread the news and obtain aid; on the other, they may complicate the recovery by reporting contradictory information or exaggerating or ignoring certain problems.

The Media in the Stage Following the Disaster

Positive Aspects
- Make known what is happening.
- Provide information on how to handle the disaster.
- Provide information about where to look for help.
- Collect testimonies and help to identify those responsible.

Negative Aspects
- Tend to trivialize and simplify complex emotional problems (e.g., showing people completely out of control).
- Tend to personalize events, causing problems for those people involved (e.g., using confidential information; disclosing names in dangerous situations).
- Are often invasive and interrupt the work of the rescue teams or survivors who are helping people.
- Tend to create "model" heroes and victims ("frozen" images) among the people affected by the disaster or involved in the rescue so that the person singled out becomes a "star," stands out from the rest of the victims, and attracts jealousy or criticism.
- Change focus rapidly, abruptly abandoning the victims and rescue teams who, after being in the spotlight, may feel once again isolated or ignored.

Source: Stewart and Hodgkinson 1991.

Support teams are also present during this stage. Although a large part of their activity will be aimed at security, looking for survivors, and taking care of basic needs, they also need to pay attention to the psychosocial needs of the community. The support teams should intervene early, without waiting for victims to come and ask for help. This active victim support should take the following action:

1. Offer aid to all victims to help aid workers to understand the people's reactions better and to communicate the following message: "The feelings you have are understandable, and your reaction is normal given the circumstances." This kind of intervention reduces anxiety and feelings of isolation. If survivors blame themselves for the deaths of close relatives, it is important to calm them

down and reassure them from the beginning: "You did the right thing, you did all you could. It was impossible to do anything otherwise." These assurances given during or immediately after the crisis will help people to stop blaming themselves more than those given after a few days.

2. Remain calm. Some people may lose control—for example, as a result of the stress, a survivor might insult or attack a member of the rescue team. This is an understandable reaction, and aid workers should be careful to not react aggressively.

3. Active intervention allows people at risk to come into contact with people who can help them. Make contact with the victims as early as possible, but do not interfere with other forms of aid that are normally given right away.

4. Offer assistance in adapting to the disaster conditions, which encompasses performing a wide range of specific tasks. Provide practical help in the initial stages to build a foundation for trust between aid workers and the victims.

5. Provide short, simple, and concise instructions to the affected people who help. Some of the affected people may not be thinking clearly even if they are very active—for example, they may be removing rubble without assessing the risk of collapse or the risk of harm to those who are buried underneath. These people need to be active, but they should not be allowed to make their own decisions when there is a need for coordination.

6. Adapt the specific forms of aid to the culture and motivation of the people. Offering assistance should not include forcing people to undergo psychotherapy, counseling, and so forth. Preferably, self-help groups should form after two weeks and especially for people who, after two months, are still suffering from anxiety, traumatic memories, and health problems.

ADAPTATION AND RECONSTRUCTION STAGE

The final stage of postdisaster adaptation is characterized by social-organization activities and the rebuilding of daily life. In this stage, people have to learn to go back to a certain normalcy and rebuild their lives despite the impact of the disaster they have experienced. The four key aspects to the impact are the grieving process, the fear of an uncertain future, the heavy burden of rebuilding, and the need to overcome the "condition" of being a victim. A leader of the Xamán community in Guatemala described this phase a few months after the massacre, when many development activities were being carried out together with a follow-up of the judicial proceedings and the reconstruction of the cooperative production project: "More hunger, more sleepiness, more work, more exhaustion, more complaints and demands, more worry about the future and that the achievement and success of our work will be slow" (Cabrera et al. 1998).

The long-term effect of this collective stress may manifest itself in overwork and a fear of the future—fear of epidemics or problems with resources, loans, or the law—or in secondary manifestations such as psychosomatic or traumatic symptoms. These aftereffects diminish substantially over time, but they may affect some groups or individuals differently. Within this process of adaptation and reconstruction, it is necessary to emphasize the structuring of collective grief. During this reconstruction phase, survivors try to reestablish autonomy and social activity. However, in the long term, the postdisaster mentality may reappear, including an acceptance of what has happened ("Fate!"), blame, and an attitude of dependency on public powers.

In either human-created or natural disasters, the convergence of different rescue teams and the presence of national and international organizations can produce other effects such as raising the cost of living or placing the community in a dependent situation. Therefore, not only the positive effects but also the negative effects of humanitarian aid should be considered. In Xamán, offers of financial aid and NGO projects that were intended to help the community generated an atmosphere of rapid responses and a greedy attitude toward resources. This dynamic activated the expectations and demands of a population that had been refugees in Mexico and helped by NGOs, becoming dependent on the NGOs for support. For example, the dependency of people on external aid was increased, the organizational process was conditioned, and the humanitarian aid generated a social differentiation that did not exist before the massacre (Cabrera et al. 1998). Similar problems were found in the survivors of Armero, causing the newly founded community organization for victims to fall apart. However, not all the effects are negative (see, for example, the section Disasters and Social Movements in Chapter 5). In the disaster in Páez, Colombia, the strong indigenous organization played an important role in the reconstruction process.

Chapter 3
Emotion and Behavior in Emergency Situations

> *All day long I am terrified that they will come back. I'm injured and I'm scared that the soldiers are on their way. My stomach is burning. Our hearts are always sad. We don't want to do our daily chores. We're scared. When people died—oh God—how our hearts ached.*
>
> —Midwife, survivor of the Xamán massacre, Guatemala; Cabrera et al. 1998, 15

This chapter reviews the emotions and collective behaviors that appear during threatening and destructive situations like those frequently brought about by wars or social disasters. This chapter focuses especially on the effects of shock, fear, and rumors.

Collective Behavior and Collective Emotions

In emergency situations, human behavior is usually described as a fight-or-flight response: people escape from danger, face it, or remain in a state of shock from the impact of events. In the case of war, population displacement has been on the increase in recent years, but natural disasters too have led to uncontrolled flight. Collective behavior depends on the following factors:

1. *Scale of impact:* If the entire population is seriously affected, general defenselessness is more likely; if only part of the population is affected, the remaining people will come to their aid.
2. *Speed at which events occur:* If the event occurs very quickly, there is no time to evaluate the situation or to consider alternatives.
3. *Preparedness of the population:* Some populations are more accustomed to disaster situations, and they will be better prepared.
4. *Length of threatening situation:* The event might be an isolated occur-

rence (an explosion) or a repetitive one (continuous massacre from military forces).

5. *Nature of the event:* Natural disasters (flooding from heavy rains) cause different effects than those provoked by human actions (genocide in Rwanda).

Researchers have rejected some of the concepts that are often used to describe behavior during disaster situations (Fernández et al. 1999). Widespread panic, asocial and illegal behavior, emotional devastation, and mass exodus is not common. This illusion of panic results from diverse and uncoordinated activities being carried out by numerous rescue teams at one time. The misperception arises from the convergence of people and groups from the outside offering help; people looking for family members and or trying to obtain information; or the inefficiency of aid organizations (as in the aftermath of the 1999 earthquake in Armenia, Colombia). In most cases, only 5 to 15 percent of people (depending on the situation) react in an uncontrolled way, with inappropriate behavior. Most of the population remains in shock and wanders around in a state of delusion; 10 to 20 percent remain calm and act in a controlled and rational way.

In many disasters or situations of risk, one finds appropriate group behavior (as in the orderly evacuation of a population or solidarity with the victims), which in turn allows for the prevention of the rapid spread of danger or rumors and for the rational organization and distribution of resources. Cooperative and coordinated behavior is more common than inappropriate behavior.

In other circumstances, however, one finds inappropriate behavior brought about by a disorganized exodus of a group or community or when people think that the situation is not real. Inappropriate behavior increases the sense of chaos and the exposure to danger. In these emergency situations, a psychosocial need to face the danger and to maintain emotional stability exists. The psychosocial needs in emergency situations include the following:

1. *Security and instrumental support* are needed to improve security measures during the escape, to maintain social cohesion, and to encourage mutual aid.
2. *Information* is needed to explain what has happened, to describe the effects of the disaster, and to report the status of family members in order to stop the spread of rumors.
3. *Management of fear* is needed to identify the risks, control impulsive reactions, and analyze the situation in order to prevent upsetting people's sense of reality.

Fear and grief influence how people react to the events and how they face the reality in front of them. Social emergency situations can trigger a chain of episodic group emotions that may last days or weeks after the traumatic event. However, prolonged violence as a result of a war or a dictatorial regime can provoke prolonged emotional states that create a climate of persistent fear (such as the fear instilled in the Mayan indigenous communities by decades of military dictatorships). Such an emotional climate might be more stable than an episodic emotional state (for example, as seen in the chain of emotional reactions of the communities affected by Hurricane Mitch in 1998) but less stable than other emotional states that characterize a society over long periods of time (De Rivera 1992).

SHOCK-INHIBITION-STUPOR

> *About four hundred soldiers arrived at the San Francisco ranch that morning. They arrived by helicopter. People helped them unpack boxes but only one of the people survived. The only one to survive such horror said that the soldiers had had death on their faces. He managed to escape. He walked in silence, but he wasn't sad. That dark night he walked until dawn. They killed his wife, his children, grandchildren, nieces, and nephews, but he wasn't sad. "I can't feel anything," he said.*
>
> —*Ricardo Falla, Guatemala, 1996, from the author's notes*

The most common group behavior immediately after a disaster is the shock-inhibition-stupor reaction, in which survivors, suffering from emotional shock, leave the scene of the disaster in a slow exodus. Examples of this are the destruction of Pompeii, the earthquakes in Lisbon and Mexico, and the bombings of Hamburg, Tokyo, Hiroshima, and Nagasaki during World War II. Witnesses to these events describe slow, silent lines of survivors following each other out of the ruins. Such a reaction can last a few hours. Many may also feel vulnerable and dependent on aid workers.

FEAR AS A REACTION

Intense fear is a common reaction in disasters, war, and other threatening situations, but it is not sufficient to provoke panicked behavior. Most people are frightened in those situations, and, despite feeling an intense fear, some people carry out heroic and coordinated actions. This ability is apparent not only among victims of war but also among people who work in dangerous occupations (firefighters, for example). Research on fear during disasters suggests that panic usually lasts a short time and that even the most frightened people are capable of following rules laid down by the authorities or local leaders. Fear has an adaptive value in many different dangerous situations, and many groups' experiences of organizing and of resistance have demonstrated the importance of the proper management of fear.

As humans we have fears. We experience it as fear but we say we are being cautious. . . . We know that people have disappeared, and we don't want to disappear as well. Some people say, "That one is a coward," but those who were not cowards are no longer alive. . . . The important thing is how can we use our fear? Fear makes a person think and tells him when to withdraw, when to advance, when to do something or not. . . . If there was no fear, the fight would have been lost a long time ago. The fight is not lost because of fear, it is won because of it. It gives the individual the ability to devise a strategy, the ability to say: "This is where it ends." (Testimony of a trade unionist from El Salvador, Rivas, 1986; (Martín-Baró 1989)

Indigenous refugees in Guatemala, who had been subject to massive repressions, said that those who considered themselves fearless were no longer with them; those who remained either to face or to elude the military repression had died.

In addition to the defensive function of fear—the perception of risk— fear causes other effects, including illness or other physical manifestations, an intensification of fear, impulsive emotional reactions, and mental reactions such as the distortion of reality. Many of these are individual reactions, but they can influence group behavior. A climate of fear isolates people, keeps them from communicating, encourages them to hide their thoughts and feelings, and breeds apathy.

PANICKED BEHAVIOR

Panic is one of the least frequent but most feared group behaviors. It could be defined as intense group fear, sensed by the individuals of a population and capable of triggering primitive reactions such as sudden flight or mindless violence. Group behavior that leads to panic occurs as follows: First, people start feeling trapped. Second, they start feeling uneasy because they are not able to escape the situation (for example, because of blocked roads). Third, people are unable to call for help or to communicate with others. Fourth, repeated attempts to escape prove fruitless. Finally, the feeling grows that death is imminent.

MASS EXODUS

The exodus is the largest type of collective behavior. Examples include the exodus of populations from the north and east of France during the German advance in 1914 and again in 1940, the exodus of the German

Physical and Emotional Effects of Fear

- *Physical reactions:* Diarrhea, stomach pain, palpitations, rapid breathing, and trembling are ways of showing tension. People must learn to control some of these reactions—by relaxing the body, for example—and not to be carried away by the negative feelings the physical reactions can produce.
- *Intensification of fear:* If it is not confronted in a positive way, fear can grow. Repressing fear has a negative effect because it can bring about insensitivity or obsession, as does transmitting fear to others. Fear must be shared and analyzed to figure out how to manage it.
- *Impulsive reactions and disorganized behavior:* Impulsive reactions can be a defense mechanism, but they can also provoke even more danger. People must be prepared to face dangerous situations and to avoid negative responses caused by fear.
- *Distortion of reality:* Fear distorts one's sense of reality so that a person is confused about what is real and what is not. The person has to make an effort to objectify the fear and not to be carried away by it. The group must analyze the problems it is facing and clearly identify the threats.
- Fear as a defense mechanism: In the face of danger, *fear can help a person to perceive risk,* and so it should be seen as sometimes positive. When fear is considered only negative, people will often hide it so that no one notices, or they do not ask for help, which makes the situation worse.

Source: Martín Beristain and Riera 1993.

Social Effects of Fear

- *Inhibits communication.* "It was very dangerous during the day, very dangerous, nobody was allowed to speak. Every so often an order was given to keep quiet. That's what I heard, it was dangerous for everybody."
- *Causes separation from organizational processes.* "When they began to see the dead bodies, people were very frightened and they began to withdraw."
- *Creates social isolation.* "Sometimes I thought I was going to die. Who could I talk to? My mother was dead, and my father was scared to be with me, because they told me that they would come and kill me and my children."
- *Prompts questioning of values.* "They put fear in us and that is humiliating. We weren't able to say anything."
- *Results in community distrust.* "People changed their mind about the army. They couldn't believe in them anymore."

Source: ODHAG 1998.

> **Anticipating Panic**
>
> Keep in mind that panic depends on the following:
>
> 1. The degree of perceived coordination.
> 2. The amount of information provided.
> 3. Previous experience.
> 4. The degree of calm in dealing with the situation.
>
> To prevent panic among survivors,
>
> 1. Provide information or training beforehand on how to deal with the situation.
> 2. Have considered the different ways to get out of the situation (escape routes, etc.).
> 3. Present an appropriate plan of action.
> 4. Give clear instructions, calmly and reassuringly.

population fleeing Soviet attack in 1945, and the exodus of the inhabitants of Somalia and Rwanda in the 1990s because of war. The unstable or threatening conditions associated with an exodus often creates new threats to people's lives. For example, in the Bhopal chemical accident, the exodus of people was the cause of many deaths: of the thousands of bodies found, a large proportion had not only been poisoned but also had been crushed by the vehicles driven by people trying to escape (Fernández et al. 1999).

In other sociopolitical crises, even facing imminent danger, people manage to plan strategic escapes after evaluating the risks of leaving versus those of staying, but, nonetheless, on many occasions, these escapes escalate into mass exodus, as in Guatemala (1980 and 1982) and Rwanda (1993–96) as the consequence of widespread massacre. During epidemics, escape can be an adaptive behavior.

The Influence of Rumors

Rumors abound after any disaster or collective tragedy, and they can undermine a group's ability to function. As mentioned earlier, rumors can provoke panic, especially when no alternative, unbiased channels of information are available. However, in disasters that disrupt channels of communication (as in the floods in Holland in the 1950s), a panicked response is much less likely because of the difficulty of spreading a sense of danger.

A preexisting climate of anxiety prompts both rumors and the possibility of panicked behavior. An incident (such as a signal or a rumor)

The Case of Epidemics

Even though there are clear differences between Europe in the fourteenth century and Europe in the nineteenth, the reactions to the plague and to cholera epidemics were similar. The plague and cholera epidemics caused

a. Scenes of panic, intense fear, and massive flight.
b. Isolation and abandonment of the sick, even by family members.
c. Attacks on the sick or on groups of people who were considered to be responsible for the epidemic (foreigners, Jews, and doctors, among others).

Some of these behaviors have continued to appear in recent outbreaks of cholera and in the spread of AIDS.

Not all fatal epidemics have the same impact, however. For example, in the influenza epidemic that killed half a million people in the United States in 1918 and 1919, no outbreaks of panic or violence were reported because the causes of the epidemic were known, a vaccine existed, and preventive measures were taken such as the use of masks, street cleaning, and so on. Although these measures were not effective in stopping the virus, the semblance of control decreased the fear of being infected. The plague and cholera epidemics caused fear and panic because the social beliefs of the time could not explain what was happening.

These group behaviors occur when: (a) the illness is fatal, (b) the illness appears suddenly, (c) the death rate increases rapidly, (d) people believe the illness is contagious and that many people are at risk of being infected, and (e) the cause of the illness is unknown. These characteristics appeared at the beginning of the AIDS epidemic, causing stigmatization, prejudice, and the isolation of people who were HIV positive. Some of this behavior continues today.

Source: Fernández et al. 1999.

can easily turn this anxiety into a specific fear (for example, that the dam has burst) and provoke out-of-control behavior.

The risk of rumors spreading is proportional to the level of anxiety, the number of people who have spread the rumor; the level of general uncertainty, and the credibility of the rumor. If the motive behind the rumor (risk of flooding, arrival of the army, and so on). provokes a lot of anxiety, then it is much more likely to spread. Rumors are spread out of ignorance or out of the ambiguity of the situation. They express emotions. The repetition of a rumor depends on the number of people who have influenced the person telling the story: The more people the subject has heard telling it, the more likely he or she is to repeat it, regardless of its believability or importance. Mere repetition reinforces the belief in the rumor and strengthens it. Rumors arise from a general

Rumors and Escape Behaviors

On August 17, 1955, floods overtook a town in the United States that had experienced floods three times in that century. The water rose on August 18 and continued until 6 A.M. the next day. Firefighters evacuated 700 people out of a population of 9,000. On the night of August 18, rumors started spreading about polluted drinking water, a typhoid epidemic, and the bursting of a nearby dam. The public denial of the rumors helped to avoid panic.

The rumor about the dam rupture started again on August 19 at 10:30 P.M. (when the flood was already under control). Rescue workers and authorities denied the rumor at 11:30 P.M. During this time, 2,500 people evacuated the town. Sixty-two percent of the population believed the rumor after hearing it only once, and 45 percent believed the public denial of the rumor. Only 23 percent of the people who evacuated the town returned after hearing the first denial, 11 percent after hearing two denials, and 50 percent returned after hearing three or more denials.

The escape was neither irrational nor arbitrary: The people who escaped were those who had experienced the previous floods (this is true for 90 percent of those who escaped) or lived in the lower part of town, which was most under threat by a rupture of the dam. Of those people who thought the rumor of the rupture was true, 50 percent tried to help others, versus 33 percent from the general population. Rather than provoke individual escape, a rumor can actually reinforce helping behavior.

Source: Marc 1987.

atmosphere of uncertainty—for example, if contradictory information appears in the press about the extent of a disaster or if official information cannot be confirmed by personal experience. In those situations, rumors arise as a way of dealing with that ambiguity.

The believability of a rumor also influences its spread. The repetition of a rumor might be a way of confirming certain emotions or attitudes, either positive or negative. To confirm them, the person may think that the rumor is true. However, if the rumor implicates a person—if it pertains to a person's group or has consequences for the individual—that person is much more likely to process the information carefully and is less likely to repeat it to avoid damaging his or her image, judgment, and so forth (Páez and Marqués 1999).

A good way to combat rumors is by providing adequate and reliable information as soon as possible not only about what has occurred but also about what could occur and how to handle it. To avoid the spread of rumors, the members of a rescue and support team need to know what to say as well as what is expected from them.

Rumors are also common after serious violent acts. Following the Xamán massacre (carried out by an army patrol in Guatemala in 1995),

Preventing Rumors

1. Transmit the idea that a story, even if told carefully, tends to change its shape.
2. Analyze the credibility of the source.
3. Clarify the facts about the situation and other matters that are provoking anxiety.
4. Anticipate rumors through information, coordination, and so on.

rumors originated both from external sources (accusations made against them) as well as internal ones (accusations from the community itself). People spread rumors because they were trying to make sense of their experience, looking for explanations; they feared more violence; and they wanted to know how to get help. These accusations and rumors contributed to the problems faced by the community for months after the massacre.

Negative rumors have much more of an impact and spread much more rapidly than denials of them, so it is necessary to concentrate on sharing positive information. A common strategy to avoid rumors is to strictly control information that is given out. However, attempts by authorities to control the information will provoke trouble and increase the rumors and criticisms.

Critical rumors produce negative effects such as creating insecurity in the group. Many rumors can give rise to atypical group behavior, causing divisions, loss of support for victims, conflicts, and panicked behavior. In the aftermath of natural disasters such as the eruption of the Armero volcano in Colombia, many rumors revolved around the humanitarian aid (such as "members of the rescue teams want to rob the victims"); what actually happened (many people were said to have been trampled during the escape); or the significance of particular events (such as "the prostitutes were saved because God had mercy on them").

Behavior and Cultural Differences

Finally, cultural differences are another influencing factor in determining group behavior in human disasters. For example, despite being as deadly in North Africa as in Europe, the plague did not cause panic or violent behavior there as it had in Europe. The illness was not perceived as being contagious; rather, it was seen as an illness that punished nonbelievers or, in the case of the Muslims, was a punishment sent from God. The assumption is that these cultural or ideological differences prevented group fear and therefore the panic and violent behavior associated with it (Rushing 1995). In many cases, religious people who believe that there is an external cause to the disaster react in a more adaptive way than people who think that they control the situation themselves. In some way, this "fatalism" can act as a shock absorber during disaster.

People in some collectivist cultures, such as in Japan, exhibit a lesser degree of illusory optimism than those in individualist cultures, as in the United States, who exhibit an illusion of invulnerability. Therefore, people in the United States see themselves as less likely to experience negative events (illnesses, disasters, accidents) than the average person. They exhibit illusory optimism. Japanese people, however, think that they are just as likely to suffer negative circumstances as anyone else (Markus, Kitayama, and Heiman 1996). It is possible that collectivist cultures might respond with greater acceptance of disasters and negative events. However, studies of the survivors of Hiroshima and Nagasaki (people from an Eastern, collectivist culture) do not show marked behavioral differences from those in Western, individualistic cultures. Passivity in the face of death can be found throughout Western cultures whether the threat is from epidemics, lethal illness, or extreme circumstances such as concentration camps. The cause of such passivity is usually physical exhaustion and daily contact with misery and death.

Community values or cultural differences in coping with grief also influence the response to dangerous situations. Despite the preeminence of danger and other political factors that can explain group behavior, the internal workings of a community, such as people's attachment to the past and to their families, can explain such group behaviors as escape or resistance: "I lost my father here, like many of us did. Some people went to Mexico because it was too dangerous here, and others stayed here refuged in the mountains. Our land is here, and here is where our dead loved ones rest. If my father is here, I cannot leave him. That is why I stayed with the resistance" (Francisco, CPR, Guatemala, 1995, from author's field notes).

Chapter 4
From Victims to Survivors

> *We've lost more than our closest relatives. We've also lost the friends and memories that it took our whole lives to create. Everything has been destroyed. Nearly all our friends have been murdered. We have to start again. Everything, even our friends. This is the hardest thing to bear.*
>
> —*African Rights 1995, 1184*

Humanitarian aid often takes place in situations where collective experiences such as this moving account, from a Rwandan woman, are common. We have discussed the emotions, behavior, and social effects of emergency situations. This chapter describes the medium- and long-term psychological effects people who have been affected by violence and social disasters experience.

Concepts Used to Evaluate Experience

A person's mental health is normally assessed using clinical tools and concepts. Understanding these concepts is useful because they are used not only by professional clinicians but also by the media, NGOs, and so on. Identifying the frequency of symptoms is a way to prove there is a problem, to make the suffering of affected people visible, to evaluate the necessity of putting in place psychosocial programs, and to identify the people who need special attention.

It is important to note the limitations to the use and application of these concepts. First, the origin and definition of our concepts are based on Western medicine and psychology. As we will see, great cultural variation exists in how people respond to disasters and in what form support is given and expected to be given. Second, our basic concepts reflect an individualistic approach, but in some cases, because of the nature of the circumstances, it may be best to apply a group or community approach. Some of our concepts are not applicable in disaster situations because of the collective and political nature of disaster experiences. Third, the nature of the catastrophe is not only a circumstantial element, it has considerable bearing on the social and individual meaning given to the event as well as on the resources used to deal with the consequences. For example, the experience of a tortured person who has been held for political reasons in a detention camp cannot be understood psychologically only from the perspective of the interpersonal relationship between the torturer and the tortured. Last, clinical approaches continue to be based on a definition of good health as the absence of symptoms more than the presence of well-being. They also tend to pathologize people's experience, running the risk of stigmatizing people and isolating them from the group. Keeping these difficulties in mind, we now define some of these terms and their characteristics.

Traumatic Experiences

Trauma is the emotional shock caused by a violent experience that leaves a lasting impression. The affected person has been subject to one or more events of great impact, which are extremely stressful, and this gives rise to a sense of vulnerability, helplessness, and dependency on others until the person reaches a breaking point or a loss of control over his or her life. The concept of trauma, however, can also vary from culture to culture: "In some indigenous communities in North America, trauma damages the person's capacity to relate to himself, with the community, or with the universe" (Mental Health Handbook 1993).

Martín-Baró (1989) identifies three types of trauma: psychic, social, and psychosocial. Psychic trauma is specific damage inflicted on a person through difficult or exceptional circumstances. *Social trauma* is the mark left on entire populations by certain historical events. Martín-Buró places psychosocial trauma between individuals and historical events, to represent the dialectical nature of the phenomenon: "Psychosocial trauma refers to trauma produced socially but nourished and maintained in the relationship between an individual and his society. But this doesn't mean that the trauma produces a uniform effect in the population. The extent to which each person is affected will depend on his experience, which is conditioned by his social origin, his degree of participation in the conflict, and other aspects of his personality" (Martín-Baró 1990).

Arcel (1994) describes the social experiences and characteristics of the war in the former Yugoslavia in terms of "potential" trauma. Among the factors that contributed to the trauma, he cites the large proportion of the population involved in the war, the perception of unpredictability, the geographic concentration, the internal source of the violence, and the level of terror transmitted through mock executions and rape.

These circumstances make the impact of trauma even worse because that impact takes on a social dimension for which the people could not prepare themselves and which turns neighbors and even family members into enemies. These circumstances have presented themselves in other countries with wars or mass political repression such as Cambodia, Rwanda, and Guatemala, as described in this moving testimony: "Then they said that we had to kill so that Guatemala would be in peace. First they made us dig graves, and then they took Diego Nap and grabbed a knife that each patrolman had to pass along and stab him with. Then they did it to Tomás Luxtillo, and lastly my cousin, who said: "Swear that one day you'll get revenge" [crying]. I'm very sorry. . . . This is very painful for me" (Chiché, Guatemala, 1983, in ODHAG 1998).

Value and Impact of Symptoms

Despite their traumatic impact, serious human disasters do not always cause long-term negative effects in individuals. Most victims of violence show some type of negative effects,[1] but others do not. The impact depends on the person and the intensity of the situation. The fact that a person shows psychological or emotional effects (that is, symptoms) does not always imply that the person is suffering from a disorder or an illness, and even if that were the case, there is not always a need for treatment. Many people show symptoms of some disorder, and yet only a minority of them requires specific psychiatric treatment. Also, affected populations exhibit many reactions and effects that are often described as symptoms or psychological problems when it is possible that they are simply normal reactions to abnormal situations (Perren-Klinger 1996). This is not to deny that problems exist; rather, it is to show that a person's experience cannot be reduced to a collection of symptoms.

Symptoms are visible signs of a difficult or traumatic experience. For example, insomnia, fatigue or lack of energy, and concentration difficulties are symptoms of depression; however, but nearly everybody experiences these symptoms at some time. In emergency situations or traumatic events, both victims and aid workers can suffer from these and other symptoms. As Dr. Anica Mikus Kos, a child psychiatrist in Slovenia points out, though, "Being sad is not the same as being ill" (Arcel 1994, 11).

In other cases, the symptoms are examples of the difficulties in adapting to a loss or stressful context:

I haven't slept properly since I left Africa about a year ago. I go to bed and I start thinking about Africa, the family, work . . . papers. . . . As soon as I'm left alone in the room I start thinking. My eyes are wide open and I can't sleep. I don't fall asleep until five or six in the morning. Then I get up late. At night of course I'm not tired, I can't sleep, and I start thinking again . . ." (Abdulresak, Ivory Coast; Díaz 1998, 50).

The meaning given to symptoms varies according to culture. In many rural cultures, symptoms of suffering are expressed through the body. People show their suffering through headaches or stomach pains; or, in other cases, they give bodily symptoms a broader significance—for example, to speak of heartache as a way of expressing sadness. "In Nicaragua, the rural people who had suffered violence expressed themselves with a mixture of psychosomatic language: for example, 'There is sadness in my body,' and 'My blood is frightened'" (Summerfield 1996).

Apart from this cultural variable, the intensity of symptoms varies from person to person according to the seriousness of the violent experience, the individual's personality, or the support they receive. The seriousness of the situation can be assessed by taking into consideration (1) the frequency of symptoms, (2) the duration of symptoms, (3) the amount of suffering or difficulties the symptoms cause, and (4) the danger the symptoms pose for the life or well-being of the person.

Nonetheless, regardless of the psychological symptoms, the disappearance of organizations and community routines, the social and symbolic losses, and other losses are generally just as important or more important than the physical problems or psychological symptoms.

Stress: Sources and Consequences of the Impact

Stress is another concept frequently used to understand the experience of people affected by violence or serious social crises. Normally we refer to stress when describing the effects of disasters as well as the causes (stressors). Stress consists of a psychological and physical state of tension before a threat, challenge, or change in the environment that exceeds the resources of the person or the group.

Models based on the concept of stress have their limits, such as in comparing different experiences or in limiting the impact of an experience to the psychological effect that it produces. However, those models do have some advantages, such as evaluating the strategies that people use to cope with situations and recognizing the importance of social support and responses as a way of diminishing aftereffects. Therefore, the impact of a disaster is the result of the relationship between the causes (for example, losses), the protective factors (support), and what is done to deal with the situation (coping mechanisms).[2] This way, survivors can be helped to manage their response better by trying to diminish the causes of the tension, identifying negative effects, adjusting their coping strategies, or improving the support they are counting on.

Also, survivors can identify experiences that are life threatening or that generate tensions, which may not be exclusively linked to a traumatic experience. To consider these factors together helps us not to decontextualize people's experience and not to focus the aid through our own predefined criteria. In Chile, after the dictatorship, a program was set up to help victims of torture and political violence (PRAIS).[3] Most of the people who asked for help wanted also to solve other social or health problems, not only those related to the consequences of torture.

Hauff and Vaglum (1995) interviewed Vietnamese refugees living in Norway when they first arrived and then again three years later. The researchers did not find a decrease in psychological distress. The main factors that contributed to the distress of the refugees were related to experiences in their country of origin (the war, imprisonment, the danger before the escape, or separation of the family), negative experiences in Norway (unemployment, moving from city to city), lack of friends, and chronic estrangement from relatives.

The Challenge of Extreme Situations: The Impact of Guilt

During traumatic events, people confront difficult situations and tough challenges. People have to cope with feelings of anger, confusion, and guilt over what has happened. Refugees that have left their country may feel guilty because they were able to escape whereas their family members or friends died.

Guilt is often induced socially—that is, the victims themselves or their families are blamed or accused of having provoked their misfortune. "This government has also tried to enforce collective guilt, telling us we are all responsible, we are all guilty. But it is not true. The people are not guilty or responsible. People were scared because of the dictatorship. There are other people responsible, those who passed the Due Obedience and Full Stop bills" (Madres de la Plaza de Mayo 1988 in Martín Beristain and Riera 1993). Guilt, therefore, becomes an instrument for social control, a justification for the atrocities, and a way of not punishing those responsible. Recent history of countries that have suffered wars or military dictatorships, such as those in Latin America, is full of examples of these processes of making the people in a society feel guilty for what happened.

Guilt is a common reaction among victims. When experiences exceed our normal frame of reference or they shatter the concepts that we normally use to understand them, guilt can be an attempt to make sense of something that does not make sense. Even though it may have a destructive effect on the person, feeling responsible for what happened can be a way of finding a sense of control over an experience that might have

---

Guilt

Guilt is psychological suffering associated with thoughts and emotions of a self-accusatory nature.

1. The person believes that he or she has violated a personal or social rule. The feeling of guilt from not having helped someone else may spring from the breaking of internal standards (one's self-image as a supportive person) or external standards (the social value of solidarity).
2. There is a difference between being responsible for something (determined by evidence and proof) and feeling guilty about something (determined by feelings).
3. What has happened violates the image that person has of him- or herself and what he or she portrays to others (e.g., that he or she has disappointed his or her friends).[4]
4. There is the element of reparation. Depending on the person's beliefs or culture, the situation can be amended in different ways (through action, symbolic redress, punishment, etc.).

Source: Pérez Sales et al. 1998.

been avoided. Guilt is often retrospective. By looking back and seeing the succession of events in a clearer way, the person feels guilty for not having read the "signs" that indicated something would happen. The following testimony summarizes some of the problems involved in handling guilt that took place after a massacre in a community in Guatemala.

After the massacre of Xamán there were a lot of rumors about who was guilty. Some said the leaders were to blame for allowing the army into the village. Others said that it would have been better to take a less direct attitude with the patrol, to give them something to eat so that they leave us in peace. We had to work hard to see how the community was being accused from outside and how this increased the rumors within. It was also important that each group showed its different forms of resistance and understood the others: returnees defending their rights, residents adapting to the militarization and finding indirect ways to resist. (Cabrera et al. 1998)

The impact can be felt for a long time. The survivors of Hiroshima and Nagasaki, the *hibakusha*, have been described as "immersed" in death for many years after the event. None of them understood what had happened. The cause of such complete destruction and the horror of seeing family members and friends lying dead in horrifying conditions, crying for help that would never come, were incomprehensible. This experience is too appalling to be healed with time. Some explain this reaction by saying that the survival instinct of these people broke down, and so many *hibakusha* have spent the rest of their lives tormented by feelings of guilt for having abandoned their loved ones to save their own lives. Because of the social destruction and long-lasting psychological effects, many have come to accept that they have "a permanent encounter with death" that will be with them for the rest of their lives. The *hibakusha* have not received any type of official recognition for their suffering and have become a stigmatized and isolated group (Fernández et al. 1999).

Another long-term psychological effect is the "survivor guilt." Many survivors of large-scale disasters ask themselves why they survived when others did not. Other types of guilt include existential guilt, when people ask themselves: "Why me?" or "Why did God choose me?" and guilt more focused on specific actions: "Why couldn't I have saved more people?" or "Why didn't I do something so that my son would not have died?" As well as being an individual reaction, this guilt can also be caused by social rejection. "I survived the massacre. I was tortured like the rest, but in the end they set me free. I was the only one and I don't know why. Since then, my life has been hell. All the families suspect me, and the situation has been unbearable. I can't stand it" (Survivor of a massacre, Colombia, 1998). Again, the effect of survivor guilt will vary from culture to culture; in some collectivist cultures in Asia, as seen for example among Cambodian refugees, the guilt of the survivor seems to be less common (Friedman and Jaranson 1994).

Survivor guilt has also been observed in relation to the AIDS epidemic, especially in the homosexual communities. Behaviors include complex grief reactions; increased fear of death, discrimination, and one's own sexuality; social isolation; and a reluctance to share with others what has happened. A study of German homosexuals who had lost a close friend or partner from AIDS confirmed that the denial that AIDS has had an effect on their lives and their feelings of demoralization were reactions closely linked to symptoms of trauma (Baer 1989). "He is the only survivor of his group of friends. The rest have all died. Each time Fabio meets a family member of one of his friends, they look at him with contempt. Some have even asked him what he has done to deserve to live when their sons have died. He is very depressed; he wants to move to another city to escape the contempt as well as the impact of having lost all his friends. He is beginning to feel guilty for being alive" (Support group, Madrid 1998).

In other cases, demoralization can occur in highly stressful environments, as in the aftermath of disasters or violence, when people do not know how to deal with the situation. People are often demoralized when the results of the struggle for social change do not correspond to their expectations. After the war in El Salvador in 1994, the NGOs working in the health sector pointed out that despair was the main mental-health problem.

Mental-Health Problems

Mental-health problems or disorders occur when a person cannot function in his or her daily life because of the frequency or intensity of a series of symptoms. Even if people had previous mental-health problems, wars or disasters can aggravate them or indeed cause others. Anxiety and depression are the most common mental-health problems. *Depression* is a mood state characterized by pessimism, sadness, or irritability with symptoms such as lack of sleep, listlessness, fatigue, loss of interest in daily activities, poor memory, and difficulties concentrating, thoughts about death or suicide attempts, changes in appetite, or loss of self-esteem. *Anxiety* is a generalized state of psychological tension or psychosomatic upset. Its characteristics include rapid breathing, accelerated heartbeat, gastrointestinal discomfort, nervousness, or emotional stress.

Repression discourages us: it makes us feel sad; it inhibits communication with groups and communities. The chronic effects are tiredness, sadness, and mistrust, which can cause misunderstandings. We feel guilty. Sometimes we cry alone. We feel ashamed. We don't show our feelings, and we put on a brave face. We isolate ourselves from the group or community. We don't want to know. We think everything they say is rubbish. We are reluctant. Sometimes we provoke. Sometimes we are offered help and then feel even more hate, and we hurt people and the community. Sometimes we feel superior to the rest and sometimes we don't even know who we are. (Martín Beristain 1997)

Keep in mind, though, that it is important to avoid describing the affected population in negative terms or focusing only on the damage done: the vulnerability to depression, anxiety, antisocial behavior, violence against women, alcohol and drug abuse, or psychosis.

One of the most frequent terms used to describe the state of people after a traumatic event is post-traumatic stress disorder (PTSD). According to this psychiatric diagnosis, the impact of a traumatic event makes itself known through three types of problems: intrusive symptoms such as images or repetitive thoughts about the event, avoidance of the memories and the hurt, and a state of exaggerated alert. "The worst thing about the torture is the psychological problem. How they have scarred me! By which I mean, what they did to me, what I saw . . . it is always with me; it never leaves, and I can't distract myself from it. This is how they scarred me psychologically" (José, Chile 1981).

The first dimension of PTSD is a response of exaggerated alert (psychophysiological hyperactivity) that is manifested in hypervigilance,

Clinical Characteristics of PTSD

Experiencing an event or cause that produces significant symptoms of distress.

1. Staying in an alert state, with problems sleeping, difficulty concentrating, unexpected responses, and irritability.
2. Reliving the traumatic event through dreams, nightmares, or repetitive thoughts.
3. Exhibiting emotional numbness in one's responses or in relation to the outside world together with avoidance of stimuli associated with the trauma.

unexpected responses, irritability, and difficulties both concentrating and sleeping. This high reactivity increases when the person confronts a stimulus similar to the violent event or disaster. Second, the person tends to remember the traumatic event repetitively (through intrusive recollections, daytime flashbacks, and recurring dreams) and to easily relive it, especially when an external stimulus reminds him or her. These intrusive thoughts are the longest lasting symptoms—about 40 percent of people affected by a disaster continued having these types of responses sixteen months after the event (Horowitz 1986; Steinglass and Gerrity 1990). Many torture victims suffer from insomnia and disturbed sleep patterns long after the event.

Third, people who have experienced traumatic events avoid thinking or feeling in relation to the event. In addition to avoiding all types of stimuli linked to the event, a psychic numbing occurs that causes difficulty expressing emotions and being involved in intimate relationships.

Studies on PTSD have been carried out in various countries. After the volcanic eruption in Armero, Colombia, 54 percent of the affected population were found to have symptoms that matched those of PTSD. Also, a study carried out ten weeks after the 1985 earthquake in Mexico City showed that 32 percent of the victims had symptoms of PTSD. This evidence suggests that PTSD occurs across cultures, but it doesn't mean that there cannot be other responses or that support to the victims should be based only on the aspects of PTSD. Many people, especially professionals working within non-European cultures who take a more global, and less clinical, approach to victims' experiences, are critical of this approach.

Criticisms of PTSD

Even though many of the PTSD symptoms are common, other common reactions—such as feelings of guilt, changes in self esteem, and so on—

are not given as much importance. In addition, the importance of social support, the social meaning given to the trauma, and the political dimension of the harm are not considered. Often little differentiation is made between very different traumatic experiences such as rape, a car accident, or a massacre. The PTSD approach, like other approaches based on individualistic medical models, risks labeling instead of helping to understand people's experience and the circumstances in which they ask for or need help. "When I returned to my country, many doctor friends told me I had to stop worrying so much about what I had experienced in the war in El Salvador, that the problem was that I had low levels of serotonin and I was suffering from traumatic stress. I tried to explain to them what I had gone through, what it meant to me to see my patients die . . . but my colleagues didn't understand me" (Paula, United States, 1992, in author's field notes).

In the case of refugees, PTSD does not differentiate the nature of the stressor or the cultural experience. Eisenbruch (1990) introduced the concept of cultural grief. *Cultural grief* is the experience of a person or group that loses its roots as a result of losing social structures, cultural values, and identity. For example, in indigenous communities in Cambodia and Guatemala, which have experienced mass violence and displacement, people or groups continue to live in the past; to suffer feelings of guilt for having abandoned their culture, their country of origin, their dead; or to see constant images of the past in their daily lives (including traumatic images).

By understanding some of the problems refugees exhibit as part of their cultural grief, we can avoid mistakenly labeling them as having psychiatric disorders,[5] when their symptoms instead reflect a deep collective suffering the meaning and expression of which is culturally determined. From a cultural-grief perspective, the areas to explore would be memories of family members, communication with ancestors—including dreams—feelings of guilt, experience in the receiving country of separation and escape, experiences of death and grief, and the resources to deal with situations such as beliefs, religious traditions, and other cultural practices. "She couldn't sleep, she couldn't walk, she just stayed still, traumatized. I had stepped on the bones, that's when I felt even more fear. It feels like the dead are running after me and I can hear them talking in the clinic" (Survivor of the Chichupac massacre in Guatemala; ODHAG 1998).

One of the most common criticisms of PTSD is that it generalizes symptoms found in Western cultures to populations of Latin America, Africa, and Asia. Among Mayan refugees from Guatemala, intrusive memories, high reactivity, and to a lesser extent avoidance behavior were quite common, whereas cognitive avoidance and emotional numbness were not (Martín Beristain et al. 1996). Both hyperactivity and rec-ollections seem to have neurobiological bases and are much simpler responses, so they are naturally found across cultures. Cognitive avoid-ance and emotional numbness are more complex responses and depend on how a person from a certain culture evaluates and interprets the event. It is also true, however, that some of these responses are adap-tive. An alert state can help a person sense danger in a continuous or an uncertain threatening situation. Emotional numbness can help to pro-tect against pain while a loss is being assimilated.

It is important to take these differences into account because many psychosocial assessment or diagnostic tools are based on Western or clin-ical categories barely adapted to local forms of expression or to the meaning of the symptoms. After a flood in Puerto Rico, victims' emo-tional upset was categorized under "nervous attack" rather than under the clinical categories "signs of alert" or "hyperreactivity." The typical symptoms of "nervous attack" were periods or outbursts of crying or shouting. Thus 13.8 percent of the representative sample after the Puerto Rican disaster reported they had suffered a "nervous attack," and nine out of ten people who said they had suffered nervous attacks were given a different psychiatric diagnosis under Western criteria. This shows the importance of taking culture into account when trying to understand the response to the disaster and when organizing assistance (Oliver-Smith 1996).

Evolution and Changes in Effects

During an emergency, protecting lives, mobilizing people, and focusing attention on the situation at hand is most important. Therefore, an alert state and a reactive behavior such as escaping or fighting back is com-mon. Immediately after the traumatic event, people begin to suffer from psychosomatic problems—flashbacks, nightmares, or a possible sense of helplessness and emotional shock. In this phase, the person can alter-nate between flashbacks and a complete avoidance of the issue. Depend-ing on the duration of the situation, some people will overcome these symptoms within a few months. Others, however, will be more affected in the long term.

In some countries, people frequently have to confront traumatic experiences. For example, the trauma faced by the refugees in Cambo-dia was not only a result of the war but also lack of food, water, and shel-ter, as well as bombings in the camps (Mollica et al. 1993). In many countries where humanitarian aid is carried out, people have been born into and lived through sociopolitical crises that have marked their lives, from the macrosocial down to the most private aspects of their lives. In these situations, different traumatic events can run together and reinforce their effects. People can also become accustomed to continuous or sequential experiences as an adaptation mechanism (Becker 1989).

According to studies on human or natural disasters, 45 percent of directly affected people in the first year show psychological problems (PTSD, anxiety, or depression), whereas this figure goes down to 20 to 40 percent in the second year. This tendency of psychological problems to decrease over time can be altered by unfavorable conditions. For example, in a study carried out by a team of psychiatrists in Santacruz, Colombia, in 1993, seven months after the Armero disaster, 50 percent of the survivors found in shelters and camps showed signs of PTSD (cited in Saavedra 1996). In subsequent studies, one conducted after a year and a half and the other after two years, this percentage increased to 67 and 70 percent, respectively, instead of decreasing. According to Saavedra, the explanation lies in the situation of the survivors who stayed in the camps and shelters for two years after the event without privacy, without incentives, and with paternalistic treatment. Although 60 percent of victims do not show any serious effects after a period of two years, these figures clearly show the need for support, as in many cases the level of stress does not decrease over time (Hodgkinson and Stewart 1991).

The level of PTSD, anxiety, and depression varies from one study to another. People affected by disasters provoked by humans show more symptoms of stress and their symptoms tend to last longer (Raphael 1986).[6] This greater duration may be explained by people feeling a greater loss of control than people who are affected by natural disasters. Traumatic events caused by human action compromise victims' sense of themselves and of others because they have been degraded or their dignity has been violated. Horowitz (1986) has pointed out that after a disaster, people go through a series of stages: experiencing shock and numbness; alternating between denial and avoidance (trying not to think), accompanied by flashbacks of the episode; making sense of what has happened, allowing the person to overcome the impact of the disaster; and finally assimilating.

Studies that review ways of confronting extreme events suggest the following stages. In the first stage, up to the first six months after the disaster, people mobilize their psychological resources in relation to the event. A high level of physiological stimulation, many obsessive thoughts, and frequent outbursts of anxiety and anger occur. The period from six months to a year and a half is more stable, with a decrease in physiological activity and thinking about the event. In this stage, the grieving process takes place and depression may appear. Finally, after a year and a half to two years, the acceptance process ends and the emotional impact goes away. These periods may be shorter when the person has had a previous experience or if the person has received social support (Pennebaker 1990).

Some theories state that recollections and repetitive thoughts about the event can help to assimilate the disaster. However, one study has shown that people who dwell on their state of mind after an earthquake are more likely to suffer from depression than those who do not, even after having the initial effect under control. Similar results have been found in relation to human loss: people who most dwell on the grieving process take longer to recover. It must be noted that those who tend to repress their feelings and to avoid thinking also suffer from periods of repetitive thoughts, which shows that avoidance and rumination are part of the same dysfunctional process (Nolen-Hoeksema et al. 1997). Nonetheless, despite all of the difficulties, most survivors of traumatic events, including sociopolitical crises such as concentration camps, are able to fully adapt years after the event (Janoff-Bulman 1992; Silver and Wortman 1990).

Changes in the Image of the Self or the World

From a more sociocognitive perspective, Janoff-Bulman (1992) defines a disaster as a traumatic event that deeply alters the essential beliefs that people have about themselves, the world, and others.[7] These beliefs can be shared among social groups or communities and they vary according to the culture. For example, not all cultures show a positive bias toward themselves or their group. Markus et al. (1996) found that North Americans who live in cities that are susceptible to earthquakes believe that their neighborhood is more prepared than the average. However, Japanese people who live in areas affected by earthquakes believe the opposite—that surrounding neighborhoods are better prepared to face an earthquake than their own. In the same way, another study has shown that only among North Americans does there appear a relationship between a fatalistic view of the event and taking fewer security and prevention measures for disasters (Markus et al. 1996). Fatalism is normally associated with an attitude of helplessness or abandonment in the case of individualistic cultures, which differs for people from collectivist cultures as in Asia.

Many reports given by people about disasters show a positive bias about their sense of what happened. Those people who escape and are fearful tend to overestimate the collective fear and panic—they believe that more people were afraid and escaped. Their view is slanted toward a false consensus that their emotions and behavior were widely shared ("I did it, but everybody does it"). A study of a flood in the United States showed that people who had escaped and felt fear tended to think that others had had the same experience and behaved the same, in contrast to those people who had not fled (Marc 1987).

People tend to think, though, that they dealt with the disaster better than the rest. For example, 40 percent of people interviewed about their experience in a disaster stated that they had felt fear, whereas they perceived that 60 percent of the rest had felt the same—indicating that they had felt less fear than everyone else (Páez et al. 1995).

As mentioned earlier, it is common for people to have illusions of invulnerability. This feeling arises from having (1) no direct experience; (2) individualistic values that reinforce an independent self-image; (3) stereotyped images of the type of people who are victims of accidents; and (4) management of anxiety—as a way of reducing anxiety, people believe the event is less likely to occur to them (Van der Pligt 1995). These beliefs can change temporarily, but they can recur. For example, immediately after an earthquake in California, the victims lost their optimism and sense of being less vulnerable. The loss of the illusion of invulnerability did extend to other possible events—the victims still believed they were less vulnerable to other types of negative events than others. After three months, they had recovered their illusion of invulnerability (Burger and Palmer 1992).

Biases of Individualistic Cultures

- *Illusion of control:* Things do not happen by chance and they can be controlled.
- *Belief in a fair world:* People get what they deserve, what happens to them is fair.
- *Self-image:* People tend to have a positive image of themselves, their past, and their future; feel more positive emotions than negative; and remember more positive facts about themselves.
- *Phenomenon of false consensus:* People believe that their opinions and emotions are shared by the rest or by a large number of people.
- *Phenomenon of illusion of control and false sense of uniqueness:* With respect to ability and skills, they consider themselves among the most able.
- *Positive view of the future:* They feel relatively invulnerable, have a tendency to predict that the future is positive, and are less likely to suffer negative events and more likely to experience positive events.

This set of cognitive biases can vary according to economic status and other social conditions, but the biases are stronger characteristics of Western cultures than of collectivist cultures.

Source: Janoff-Bulman 1992; Markus et al. 1996.

Looking for Meaning: Attribution of Responsibility

People need to attribute a meaning to traumatic events. Much of the people's discussion after a disaster is about the causes, the possibility of prevention, and the attribution of responsibility. After a disaster, public opinion tends to attribute responsibility for the event to a specific group of authorities who can be criticized and punished. The press plays an important role in setting out a list of those possibly responsible. This attribution of responsibility often has a grain of truth but also tends to follow the prejudices and dominant stereotypes to accuse the usual scapegoats. For example, toward the end of 1998, a series of assassinations took place in Milan, a settling of scores between mafia organizations. Although the majority of the accused were Italian, the autonomist group Lega Lombarda organized a protest against "multi-ethnic Italy," blaming immigrants for the violence.

In cultures based on traditional beliefs, everything has a cause and problems are seen to be caused with intent (for example, envy) or tied to the behavior of the person (a transgression). "Then came the hurricane. It took away a lot of roofs and brought a lot of fear. The old people said that the wind had come to remind the people that they had not asked the land for permission to live there. Then they did the traditional prayers of sacrifice to establish the relationship with the land, the way it always had been" (Martín Beristain 1997).

In some cultures, psychological suffering can be considered normal or it can be considered shameful or even malignant. For example, because of the cultural significance of sexual purity, many women who have been raped are often marginalized or unable to fulfill their family or social expectations (Kane 1995). In poor rural societies, individual psychological suffering is seen as part of a difficult life and the daily fight for survival.

Even in serious political crises, people use traditional concepts as well as their direct experience and the political or ideological meanings to explain the events that are occurring around them. For example, a study on the impact of the forced disappearances of family members in Chile found that the Mapuche people explained events as the result of local causes like envy, or someone reporting another to the police over land disputes, or turning people in to save themselves. Other Chileans gave similar explanations, but when they did they had included a broader perception of the general context of state repression and dictatorship: "He was a friend of the military, he gave them food and shelter. They came to our house and took away my father and brother. He told them we were communists because we held meetings in the house. He did it to end up with our land" (Pérez Sales et al. 1998).

Guatemala Never Again report shows a similar tendency in the explanations of political violence, encompassing traditional culture but also the impact of violence on the social fabric. This report is the result of an investigation by the Catholic Church, based on information gathered during the historical memory project. It is also based on interviews with survivors, witnesses, and even perpetrators of the abuses, most of which were carried out by the Guatemalan military. In order of frequency, the explanations recorded in the testimonies in the report were (1) accusations about conduct ("they killed him because he was accused of collaborating with the guerillas"), (2) envy, (3) not knowing how to explain what happened, (4) more general explanations like power and military actions, or (5) the fight for land or conflicts between ethnic groups. "He was courageous, caring, well respected, and kind, but the people were envious of him and that's why it happened. He was accused by the people themselves, because when a person works for the people, they don't appreciate him, they feel envy" (Parraxtut; ODHAG 1998). In this case, explanations varied, based on the way the violence occurred in that area, the previous social conflicts, and the consequences of the events on the lives of the people. This set of factors, more than ideological or religious explanations, are present in most testimonies analyzed. Still, it is common for people who have lived through extreme situations to never arrive at a plausible explanation of the event (Janoff-Bulman 1992).

People who believe that events are subject to external control (luck, destiny, and so on) tend to respond differently from people who attribute them to internal causes (controlling events through action). In a series of studies on natural disasters, Ross and Nisbett (1991) found that the "northerners" in the United States had a more internal locus of control and "southerners" a more external locus. When the weather report warned that a tornado was approaching, northerners confirmed that they listened to the news more carefully; whereas the "southerners" said that they looked at the sky. (It appears to be assumed that looking at the sky is less reliable for appreciating the real danger than listening to the news on television.) When the subjects were given unfinished statements such as "The survivors of a flood . . . ," people from the culture with internal control (northerners) were likely to finish the sentence with "need help." The southerners, who believe more in luck or divine intervention, focused more on the negative emotions that survivors would have experienced.

Even though fatalism can lead to disorganization, the attribution of disasters to external causes does not always have a negative effect. Various studies have examined what happens when, for example, disaster strikes in a family. In some cases, people with a more external or religious orientation, or who believe that it is from bad luck or because it is God's will, are able to recover more quickly and go back to their normal lives. Earlier anthropological research suggested that traditional cultures confronted natural or human disasters in a fatalistic and inadequate way. However, current research on natural disasters has shown the adaptive capacity of these cultures when responding to such events (Oliver-Smith 1996).

Confronting the Losses: The Process of Grieving

> *I felt sad and I still cry for my son because he was my only child and now I am alone, I can't sleep, my life is sad without him. Losing a loved one is hard and painful, and nobody can fill that empty feeling, only God. We are traumatized, sometimes we try and hide it, we laugh, but our souls are wounded because we lost our loved ones and that's very difficult.*

—*ACAFADE 1990*

Collective disasters cause human, material, and cultural losses. How do people confront these losses, and how can aid workers understand and help during this process? In psychological terms, the form in which a person confronts a loss is called the *grieving process.*

PERSONAL AND CULTURAL DIFFERENCES

Various authors have described a process of stages when confronting grief: denial, anger, compromise, depression, and acceptance. First, the person denies the fact and has a sense of disbelief about the event. Then the persons feels anger for the loss of the loved one, or even toward the loved one for no longer being there. The next stage is one of ambivalence, and the person will begin to consider the tragic event from different points of view and with different feelings. This is followed by a period of depression in which the person feels the impact of the loss profoundly, realizing that it is irreversible. This stage leads to the acceptance of the loss and a reconstruction of life and social relations. These stages are part of a process more than of clearly delimited phases. However, research has shown that only one out of three people goes through the stages as described, half of the people confront the situation without passing through all the stages, and one out of five experience chronic or delayed grief.

No consensus exists on the duration of the grieving process. For some, it might be between a year and a half and two years; for others, it might be much longer. There is also debate on the various stages of the grieving process. According to some researchers, beyond the majority reaction, 20 percent of family members show slight grief from the beginning whereas 10 percent show very intense reactions that can last for over two years, which is considered prolonged grief (Middleton et al. 1996).

All of these differences are both personal and cultural. In Mozambique, for example, people remember and talk about the dead for some months, after which the dead are not mentioned again. In some indige-

---

Mayan Cosmovision

According to Mayan cosmovision, everything is linked. There are no divisions between parts and the whole, person and nature. Nature reflects the body, and the body reflects nature. In the *ixil* language, the elbow is the hill of the arm, and the upper part is the valley. A woman is fertile because she has valleys and mountains: "If you ask about the dead, then you must also ask about the living, unless you understand that the dead are alive. The earth is also alive, which is why when I drink, I also give some to the earth. The earth can feel, but not in the same way."

The priests in Nebaj hold the key to the church. The people from the village wanted the key because the church belongs to the people, not to the priests. The priests said no. The people were angry and they insisted, and they came and went until one day they broke down the door and rang the bells for about two hours.

When I arrived, they told me, "The dead people of the village are lost. If the bells don't ring, the dead would not be saved." So they kept the key and every Tuesday went and rang the bells to save the dead—"Otherwise they get lost, and if one of the dead gets lost and goes to Sacapulas . . . They don't speak *ixil* there and they have thin clothes, can't bear the cold, and don't like chilis like we do."

I asked them if the dead were not in heaven. "They have their type of heaven," they told me, "but not like the priests said." Where is heaven? "Our village is heaven. How can there be a heaven if there is no village? How can anyone who is not in the village be happy?"

Source: Martín Beristain 1997.

---

nous cultures of the American continent, however, death is not thought of as absence of life, and the relationship with ancestors becomes part of daily life. Humanitarian aid workers have to bear these differences in mind so as not to offend people or create conflict with the community.

Grief amid Disasters and Violent Experiences

The sudden and brutal nature of the deaths caused by disasters and the subsequent feelings of helplessness, fear, and isolation complicate grieving processes. The emergency situation itself—ongoing war or repressive social circumstances—can impede ceremonies, public recognition of what happened, and other activities that restore dignity to victims and survivors. "My mother died a year ago and I told myself that she would rest in peace. My father died when I was young and I told myself his death would make me mature and responsible. But this death, unjust and inexplicable, I can make no sense of" (Report of the National Commission for Truth and Reconciliation, Chile 1991, 767).

Violent deaths are senseless and unjust. The sudden nature of events robs people of the opportunity to do anything to stop it or to say good-bye, leaving people with strong feelings of helplessness and repressed anger. The brutal nature of the death also increases the agony of survivors, some of whom have nightmares about the suffering of their loved ones before dying. Not being able to have a proper burial and knowing of improper treatment of the body not only add to survivors' suffering, but it degrades them as well.

The following testimony from a survivor of genocide in Cambodia shows the suffering caused by not being able to hold a proper burial and by the mistreatment of the bodies.

Nobody in my family could find a piece of wood to put in the hole we had dug for a grave. Do you know what I mean? When you dig a hole, the part at the bottom is wet. But you have no choice. You have to put your parents in there. Luckily, I managed to wrap my mother in some beautiful outfits she had. Then, something horrible happened. Two or three days later after burying her, someone told me. . . . This is still a nightmare for me they told me—how can I say it? A wolf had gotten to her because they hadn't buried her deep enough. How would you feel if you were me? The most important person in your life dies and you think she is at peace. Not even the body can be at peace. (Mollica 1999)

Also, in situations of violence, family members cannot carry out ceremonies or name the victims, talk about what has happened, or point to the guilty. Sometimes, family members are even accused by the guilty as a way of justifying their actions. The family members of the victims of the Trujillo massacre in Colombia were only able to carry out ceremonies and name the victims in public five years after the event (1995) because of the climate of fear instilled by the military rule and drug traffickers.

In other cases, uncertainty about the whereabouts of family members, as in the case of forced disappearances, can leave a permanent open wound. Having to live with this loss and absence can be more difficult than knowing what happened. Family members of missing people are condemned to suffer in silence as the disappearance is never officially recognized and those responsible also seem to disappear into silence. In such cases, the reactions of grief and ambivalence can be much more intense and persistent. The family has to learn to tolerate the ambiguity of the situation and face the task of grieving as best they can. Part of this process is the fight for truth and social amends. The disappearance of victims during some natural disasters—floods, avalanches, and even airplane crashes—can also cause similar difficulties of ambiguity and disrupted grieving.

The AIDS epidemic in Africa, in addition to the toll it has taken in human lives and the consequences it has had for development, is also disrupting funeral traditions. In Zimbabwe, where AIDS claims 700 deaths a week, the growing number of deaths has meant that numerous burials have to be carried out very quickly. This practice clashes with traditional beliefs, which hold that the dead person may drift without a resting place or even seek revenge from the living (AFP 1998).

Tasks of the Grieving Process

Grieving involves complex tasks that derive their meaning from within a cultural context. From a psychological perspective, the key to confronting the grieving process is related to acceptance of the loss and regaining the will to live. The key to confronting the grieving process is shown in the following list:

1. Accept the loss with appropriate rituals and ceremonies.
2. Express feelings about the person and the traumatic situation.
3. Adapt to the new situation, to changing family roles, to one's sense of the world, and to one's own identity.
4. Relocate the dead and establish new ties to the dead and new relationships with the living.

Many of these tasks must be carried out in specific ways or within certain time limits according to cultural traditions and religious beliefs. For example, most traditional cultures have a period of time in which family members dress, pray, or participate in activities with other members of the community. The Mapuche believe that, after this period of time, dreams in which the dead person appears calling the family or with an erotic theme are negative signs. The dream could be a sign that the person is not following the new path or that the acceptance process has not yet happened. A vision of the deceased during the day—seeing that person on horseback or on a path—is called *Peyewün* and is considered normal if it lasts only a few months. If the deceased ancestor appears in dreams after a few months, he or she is understood to be accompanying or advising the living (Pérez Sales et al. 1998). In many indigenous cultures, the apparition of the deceased in dreams is seen as a common form of communication. The following statements are interpretations of dreams from Mapuche families of disappeared people (Pérez Sales et al. 1998, 265):

"When he appeared in dreams, he told me not to be sad, that he would soon come to look for me so that we could be together."
"In the dreams I felt that he was suffering a lot for me, worrying. He said that he wanted to take me far away from this place."
"I can still feel something like he is waking me up, he is calling me."

Common Grief Reactions in Survivors

It is common for survivors to show different reactions of grief, which may be normal and should not be considered pathological if they do not persist—for example, denying that there has been a death; trying to forget what has happened; experiencing deep pain and sadness, anxiety, anger, or rage; having constant thoughts about the deceased; having nightmares; feeling helpless; and not eating. People involved in humanitarian aid should be sensitive to these problems and understand these reactions and accept them. They should also learn to recognize those who need more support—for example, those who cannot talk about the person without feeling great sadness even a long time after the event, those who are constantly ill and see no meaning to life; those who are self-destructive or become alcoholic, and those who have not been able to rebuild their lives and are still living in the past.

Helping with the Grieving Process

Aid workers can best help a person or family who has suffered the loss of a loved one through the following procedure:

1. *Help the survivors to face the loss.* Talk to them about what has happened, what the person was like, what rituals they have performed, and so forth. They may need to talk, and it is important that they are listened to and understood by others.
2. *Help the survivors to express their emotions.* Accept their show of emotions, especially in cases where those emotions are hard to recognize, such as helping them to overcome guilt. When they say, "I didn't do enough," ask them, "What did you do?" and "What more could you have done?" Do not tell the person to stop crying or to not express his or her anger. It is no use telling the person how he or she should feel or that he or she should forget, which might give the impression that you do not understand at all and could block communication.
3. *Develop ways to remember the deceased.* Maintain the memory and the meaning of the person's life, through sharing positive memories and collective ceremonies with a group of trusted people.
4. *Give people time to grieve.* Allow time to pass; keep in mind the rhythms people have for rituals and group and family activities. Be attentive to delayed reactions, which may be greater on anniversaries.
5. *Help the survivors understand grief behaviors as normal.* Especially in cases where grief has been disrupted by violent circumstances,

reactions may persist. It is important for people to understand that they are becoming neither mentally nor physically ill.
6. *Symbolize the loss through forms of expression.* This can be done by using symbols that represent the family member; writing or drawing messages that family members would like to say; reconstructing the memory of that person, written or spoken about how he or she was, what he or she believed in, and what he or she taught.

THE IMPORTANCE OF RITUALS

Group commemorations and a funeral or grieving rituals help to assimilate the human loss caused by a disaster. As mentioned earlier, the absence of group farewell rituals can complicate the grieving process. In some cases, these rituals cannot take place because the location of the dead person is unknown and, in other cases, because of a climate of fear and violence. "Many years after the Vietnam War, the people finally visited their homes and held rituals. This was the first opportunity the community had to cry together over their loss" (Kane 1995).

Commemorations not only have a social function for the grieving process, but they also benefit people's physical health. Some research shows a link between group rituals and positive effects on physical health; the link between rituals and psychological well-being is not as strong (Levav et al. 1988; Weiss and Richards 1997). The explanations for this are varied. On the one hand, factors that correlate health and behavior may not correlate to emotional experience, such as in our work with the Communities of Population in Resistance in Guatemala (1992; see Cabanas 2000), where we found that most people were in good spirits despite the daily persecution they were subject to; yet, they complained of physical problems from the climate of tension. On the other hand, according to various authors, commemorations and rituals reinforce emotional reactions and social mobilization. The opportunity to hold rituals and ceremonies allows people to express their emotions, but that does not mean they will suffer less emotionally. Durkheim (1967) states that rituals intensify group emotions and create a feeling of solidarity. The effects are similar with positive rituals and the commemoration of losses, creating an emotional effervescence through collective emotion; a sense of unity with others; and, even in the face of death, a renewed interest in life and trust in the community.

Rituals help family members and members of the community (Bowlby 1980). For family members, rituals can

- Mitigate the separation and allow people to pay their respects to the dead.

- Emphasize death as part of life's changes, confirming that death is real.
- Allow the public expression of pain and define the phases of grief.
- Allow new social roles to be assigned and define the rhythm of their reintegration into social life.

For members of the community, rituals can

- Allow the public expression of pain and other emotions.
- Allow recognition of the loss.
- Provide the opportunity to pay respect to and honor the memory of the deceased.

Results from research into the effects of participation in funeral ceremonies in Guatemala confirm that people who participate in funerals show more sadness, fear, anger, and intense grief as well as feel a greater sense of injustice than those who do not participate. Only when a person has experienced an extreme trauma can participating in rituals relieve the intense grief. Following massacres, the cultural demand for rituals is great, partly confirming the function that ceremonies play in helping survivors of human disasters.

RESPONSES AMONG THE BEREFT

	Attended Funeral Ritual (percent)	
Response	No	Yes
Fear	24	36
Sadness	25	39
Intense grief	7	9
Family reconstruction	4	9
Help to others	10	22

Source: ODHAG 1998.

Participation in funeral rituals did not protect against negative emotions. However, participation in rituals correlated with solidarity and group mobilization. The people who participated said that the rituals had helped to reconstruct social and family support and had been a help to others. Participation in rituals is associated with more intense emotions and with greater social cohesion and social mobilization.

Rituals and social support seem to protect against social isolation but not against emotional isolation. In a review of funeral rituals in Africa, Pradelles (1996) concludes that funerals, in allowing for the separation of the deceased from the world of the living to become an ancestor, guarantee social order but do little to address the psychological effects of the loss. A ritual can help to alleviate the loss of a person because it reinforces cohesion and social order, but this does not have a direct psychological impact on one's experience of the loss. Pradelles attributes this overestimation of the psychological function of rituals to individualistic conceptions of grief, which come from psychoanalysis and other Western sources.

> Alejandra, Roberto, and Walter return from the exhumation. They had taken a camera with them. When the first remains appeared, a family member took them home, and they lit a candle and burned incense. Walter asked for permission to take photographs of the event, but "only two or three," he says, afraid that the light from the flash would outshine the candles.
> "Don't be sad," they tell him.
> Then it was they who asked for pictures to be taken of the family. They dressed, combed their hair, but they didn't smile because photographs have the air of a miracle. They couldn't keep still. As he was looking through the lens, they were moving to the left. Then he realized that they were standing next to the boxes of bones which had been lost for so many years.
> "Of all the family," they said to him.

Source: Exhumation in Alta Verapaz, 1998, author's field notes.

The following are some principles to support the relatives of victims during the processes of exhumation of clandestine cemeteries as they have occurred in countries like Guatemala, Rwanda, and Bosnia:

1. *Give support out of human and social commitments.* Solidarity should form the basis of trust and the reconstruction of relationships.
2. *Promote an active stance.* Do not victimize the family members. Promote mutually supportive processes and social recognition.
3. *Facilitate group identification.* Apart from mutual support and empathy, the group can help family members to give a social dimension to their loss and to contribute to the group process of looking for alternatives.
4. *Take into account explanations of circumstances and the emotional climate.* It can be difficult for people to understand why something happened and to confront that reality. The manipulation of the truth in the form of an "official version" can make people feel more frightened.
5. *Respond to family and group expectations.* The ceremonies and rituals following a massacre must have a sense of collective amends

(going from "my dead family" to "our dead") and a sense at the family level (reburial of remains).

6. *Consider practical issues* that may facilitate or interfere with the process: place, excavation, movement of remains, scientific analysis, and so on. These bring up cultural issues and may provoke reactions that must be respected.

7. *Respect religious and cultural expression.* Listen to what people say and pay attention to how they prepare ceremonies, rituals, and so on. Adapt the exhumation to the grieving process. Too much outside attention of a political or an instrumental nature may interfere with the process and disregard the sensitivities of the family or the community.

8. *Understand the impact and meaning of legal procedures.* Help the family members deal with the work of investigators, provide them with the initial basic information, and assess how well people understand and agree. These are basic conditions for the process to run smoothly. Respond to requests, but do not generate false expectations.

9. *Consider the impact of social amends.* Reparation may come in the form of compensation, which may create new problems of favoritism, discrimination, or comparison of grievances. Establish clear criteria for the management of aid and promote a shared feeling of benefit for all to diminish these risks.

10. *Develop a comprehensive vision.* Legal processes, the impact of impunity, previous conflicts or conflicts worsened by the event, experience with victimizers, the criminalization of the community—all these factors must be taken into account for the preparation, the development, and the eventual accompaniment (Martín Beristain 2005).

The study carried out in Guatemala (ODHAG 1998) clearly shows that, given the character of events and repression, rituals and ceremonies are needed, as are clear information about the location of family members, public recognition of events, institutional responsibility, and the recovery and restoration of the victims' dignity.

Chapter 5
The Strength of the People

Some organize, the rest sing to the people to alleviate their suffering.
—*Amelio, Colombia, 1998*

People are not passive. They confront disasters in different ways and use unsuspected resources to cope with difficult situations. This chapter reviews the experiences of different populations and the way they face tragedies.

Experiences of Affected Populations

The effects of a disaster on the people and the coping strategies people use differ according to age, gender, social situation, or the characteristics of the event.

Children go through their own traumatic experiences and are particularly sensitive to the separation of the family and the effects of war and political repression on their parents. Apathy, regression, withdrawal, and fear are common reactions in children who have been orphaned because of war. Children whose parents are missing or have been tortured also exhibit emotional problems, loss of appetite or sleep disorders, difficulties at school, or evasion of reality.

War may become a "normal" situation for many children because they have grown up amid an armed conflict. Boothby, Upton, and Sultan (1991) carried out a study in Mozambique among 277 boys and 227 girls between the ages of six and fifteen. They found that 77 percent had been witness to homicides and massacres, 88 percent had seen physical abuse or torture, 51 percent had suffered physical abuse or torture, and 64 percent had been separated from their families.

Among the children separated from their families, 28 percent, all of them boys, had been trained for combat. Because boy recruits are separated from their families, they do not have access to school or training for teachers. Part of their military training may be to mutilate or kill their victims; as a result, their social and moral development can be seriously damaged. Such brutal behavior by children arises from being forced to perform these acts and from the possession of arms and the power to threaten others.

Nevertheless, children who have an adequate family and social support present fewer problems and symptoms in the short term even when faced with highly stressful situations. Punamaki (1989) has underscored the fact that children are not only passive victims and that in some countries, such as Palestine, they have found active ways of confrontation and resistance. However, even in those cases, inhibition, emotional stress, and fear may appear (in the form of nightmares, loss of appetite, psychomotor retardation, or unwillingness to separate from their mother). Children who live in refugee camps outside the danger area still feel afraid a long time after the event or whenever there is talk about returning to their country, as was the case in the Mayan refugee communities in Mexico in the 1990s. Even though problems are often concealed from children as a form of protection, their need for security and information should be taken into account in dangerous situations. "Marcela is ten years old and very bright. She was present in a workshop for displaced women. At the end, when we were talking about fear in children, one of the women asked her: "What do you think about all this?" Marcela told us that the mother and father have to talk to their children. Children ask their mother to confirm things they already know, and it's not good for them to shout or to lie" (Workshop for displaced women, Colombia, 1997).

In populations that have been refugees for years, adolescents in particular have to develop their identities in a cross-cultural context. During a war, group-identification patterns or the rejection of violence or recruitment influence the identity of adolescents. "We are what we have suffered, but we don't know how to organize ourselves as young people. We don't have experience, we are afraid. Sometimes fear overcomes us and we are paralyzed. But now we have woken up and can organize our activities. We young people have exchanged ideas about our past, of how we escaped, how we have lived. This is how we manage to understand ourselves." (Group of young returnees, Guatemala, 1994).

Depending on the severity of the situation, problems such as aggression, alcohol abuse, and suicide may appear during adolescence. However, adolescents may also display attitudes that affirm their identity, such as initiative, being open to change, identifying with a group and with positive role models, and so forth.

The young people of the group see the big picture. Whereas the adults speak of fear of the army, they speak of fear of the future; whereas the women speak of fear of the shootings, they speak of fear that they will become insensitive or of fear of not ceasing to feel fear, which Fear is the mirror in which all fears are seen. Anyone might say it is a matter of experience, but no. When they speak of death, they speak the fears of Colombia: to die and not even know why. (Workshop with displaced people, Colombia, 1997)

The pattern of work distribution, the occurrence of specific events, and the ability to adapt create different effects in the adult population. Women may be more exposed to rape, overwork, and heavy emotional burdens, especially when they have to take charge of the family on their own and when they have fewer opportunities for social participation. In the camps in Hong Kong in the 1980s, women were more anxious and depressed, with poor expectations of the future. Women with children were especially concerned about how their children experienced the detention camps. In some situations, women may cope better by focusing on daily tasks. In many countries, it has been groups of women who have confronted political repression by looking for their missing relatives, opening an arena of debate that violence had shut down.

When we women begin to make demands for our disappeared relatives, for life, for freedom against the military dictators, women's participation begins to be more evident. Even the army is surprised. They can't believe that those weak little girls could confront an army that everyone is afraid of, you know? Nobody could believe that we could confront, pursue, run after the army, but that's what happened. It wasn't a question of whether we could do it, but that we dared to do it. (ODHAG 1998)

Men suffer differently, from militarization or from the crisis of their role in the family, but they receive more recognition and have greater social participation. According to a study in Sarajevo, the majority of psychiatric admissions before the war were women, whereas after the war 70 percent were men between the ages of 25 and 44, suffering mainly from stress disorders. Many women said that they would have felt better prepared if they could have done more to confront the situation in order to give some meaning to their experience instead of just dodging the bullets. According to Ceric, "If you are with the children, preparing food, looking for water, heating without gas or electricity, you have no time to be stressed" (Jones 1995, 1053).

The elderly are physically weaker, are less able to adapt to new or rapidly changing situations, and find it difficult to live far from their homes. The loss of friends or family may affect them more as they depend on their families or the community for support (UNHCR 1994). However, the social status of the elderly person varies within cultures or societies, from marginalization to protection as an authority. The experience of other disasters or wars may help the elderly to cope with situations better, as was the case in Sarajevo during the war in Bosnia. During that war, the experience the elderly had had during World War II helped them to cope with the harsh living conditions (Jones 1995). "Our grandparents have taught us many things about our culture that we didn't know. They have explained the dreams and the history of our ancestors. The young people invited two elderly people to the meeting so that they could explain to us how they had been captured by the army and forced to be soldiers" (Group of young returnees, Guatemala, 1994).

People who have serious physical or mental illnesses are extremely vulnerable to social ruptures, which include the loss of community support systems or health services. For example, during the war in Bosnia, the families with mentally ill relatives found it hard to continue looking after them, which led to them being admitted to institutions. Stressful situations or abrupt changes can provoke crises that may worsen their condition or expose them to danger. However, in some countries like El Salvador and Nicaragua, groups of disabled people have formed mutual support associations—such as one for those wounded in war—and these groups have played an important political role at various moments.

Ways of Confronting Situations

Ways of coping with losses or dangerous and challenging situations may be more or less positive, depending on the situation or the person, and can vary according to age and social status. The "instrumental response"—for example, precautions at home and organizing with friends or neighbors—is more common among younger victims or those in the middle or upper socioeconomic classes, who have more access to information and greater means than the poor in a community.

> A study carried out in the Basque region of Spain confirms some of the most common forms of coping mechanisms used by people in a natural disaster. "Active confrontation" deals with the problem by devising a plan of action. "Focused rational confrontation" focuses on the problem and waits for the appropriate moment to take action. "Expressive confrontation," or the search for social support, uses talking to others who have had the same problem and expressing anger over the situation. Last, "resignation" and "avoidance" are also ways of coping, but they are less common.

Source: Páez et al. 1995.

Coping strategies involve thoughts and feelings as well as problem-solving behaviors. People may try to cope with problems by devising plans to solve them, minimizing them, or searching for meaning. On an emotional scale, people may share their experiences, relax, repress feelings, and so on. The behavioral coping mechanism refers to what people do to handle the problem, such as search for information or support, react passively, and so forth. These three categories of coping—planning, feeling, doing—complement one another.

The Importance of the Context

The same coping mechanism may be positive or negative depending on the context, the perception of the person, and the individual characteristics. Distrust may be adaptive in a hostile situation such as an arrest, but in less violent situations it could be an obstacle for getting help. Repressing feelings or trying not to think about an event may help while doing something important to save oneself and help others. However, continuing to repress feelings long after the event is stressful in itself and may cause people to become numb or suffer from repetitive thoughts or nightmares. Teter (1996) describes how rejection of information and discussion about the disaster was among the coping mechanisms of a group of survivors of the Chernobyl nuclear disaster. This rejection offered protection against the uncertainty of short- and long-term effects of the disaster. Passivity, despair, and the use of alcohol were other negative coping mechanisms.

According to Pennebaker (1995), inhibition, which is frequently conscious and automatic, can become a habitual form of low functioning. An extreme case of this low functioning would be the use of drugs or alcohol to avoid thinking or feeling. High functioning, however, allows one to consider the complexity of the problem and to be more conscious of what's going on and one's own ability to do something about it. Even though the degree of control over the situation is low, the ability to see the different aspects of a situation and the possibilities of asking for help is a distinct advantage.

Other research has shown that those people who think about the positive side, such as the value of lessons learned, the sense of sacrifice or struggle, and so forth, may feel better than those people who isolate or blame themselves. Ideological or religious perspectives may be used either individually or collectively as a means of coping or of self-protection. These perspectives help to make sense of experiences, to look for comfort, or to promote solidarity.

There is the problem of fear. People have this idea that there are powerful forces out there and that there is nothing they can do to avoid the threat posed. Even though they aren't the majority, the problem of these fearful people is that it keeps them from getting over the situation and the effects are much worse. They can't find a way of coping. They have no initiative. Something that has helped the [Communities of Peoples in Resistance] is the idea that the [state's] repression has an explanation, and this helps people to understand and to deal with the deaths. If you understand it, it is less destructive. The repression has some kind of meaning. (Miguel, Guatemala, 1992)

Traditionally, a distinction has been made between passive and active coping mechanisms, the latter being the most efficient. However, when

---

Coping with Violence

A study in Guatemala (ODHAG 1998) on the coping mechanisms for mass violence revealed the following positive coping strategies, listed in order from the most common to the least common:

1. *Direct coping strategy and self-control.* Includes a set of adaptive strategies for living amid violence: not talking, mutually supportive behaviors, resignation, direct resistance, searching for information, self-control, and self-containment.
2. *Collective or community coping strategy.* Refers to the return and rebuilding of family ties following displacement.
3. *Collective instrumental coping strategy.* Brings together precaution, vigilance, and community organization; associated with collective displacement into exile (refugee camps) or in the mountains (communities in resistance).
4. *Adaptive emotional coping strategy.* Encourages resistance on an individual level to strictly bounded situations, like torture, through talking and seeking comfort or solace.
5. *Ideological and cognitive coping strategy.* Provides a sociopolitical commitment to a positive reinterpretation of what has occurred, by getting involved and trying to change the situation.

---

a direct confrontation is not possible because people are in a position of weakness or dependency, they develop other coping strategies. In research on mechanisms for adapting to the working conditions on the farms of landowners, Scott found that farmhands worked more slowly, talked among themselves about the problems without bringing notice, or ridiculed their overseers during their rituals and celebrations (Berry et al. 1992).

In many cases of political repression, imprisonment, or torture, the victims also develop their own active adaptation and defense mechanisms even though they may not appear to be doing so. Political or religious convictions; knowledge of the methods and strategies of power; as well as maintaining an active stance, preserving autonomy, and trying to resist the imposition of authoritarian rule are key aspects of the resistance of many surviving people, groups, and communities (Martín Beristain and Riera 1993). "'You are an animal not a person,' they said to me, 'and we are going to treat you like an animal, that's the only way you will understand.' But no, I'm not mad and I'm not an animal. I'm OK, I feel fine. As a defense mechanism, I try and keep my mind blank and I try not to think about anything at all except a dot suspended in mid air" (Testimony from H. Anaya, El Salvador, 1984).

Cultural Differences

> It's four o'clock in the morning in this truck and it's cold. That damn window is open. In front of me, Carlos and Pablo, my Mayan friends, put their hats on and huddle together for warmth. Meanwhile, I'm asking myself why they don't just shut the window instead of covering themselves up. My imagination is up much too early, turning over ideas about how to cope one way or another with our problems. When I stop going round and round about it all, I get up and close the window. If the cold stops, sleep may come. After a couple of minutes, the window falls down. I push it up and it falls down again, this time even further and more quickly: the window is broken. Finally, I look for my clothes and curl up, sending my imagination to sleep.
>
> —Martín Beristain 1997

Culture has a strong influence on adaptation and coping strategies. Although some coping strategies appear to be universal, others vary considerably according to the dominant beliefs, values, or ways of responding to life's uncertainties. This means that aid workers need to learn to recognize particular adaptation strategies instead of following Western models or stereotypes. Traditional cultures and populations affected by violence have their own enormous funds of knowledge on how to cope with problems. Efforts must be made to keep an open dialogue with the local reality—generally some sort of mixture of Western, popular, and traditional concepts and practices. Such a dialogue is only possible from a position of sincere respect and equality and not just from intellectual curiosity.

Support and Social Networks

> Little by little we separated ourselves from them, like when animals wean their young. At first they feed four times a day and then they go down to three. It's like that until they become independent altogether. They wanted us to accompany them every night but we didn't have much time nor was it good because they got used to it. But this is what we did until they recovered their moral strength.
>
> —Manuel, a member of the human-rights community group; Riera and Martín Beristain 1993, 173

Disasters are collective experiences that bring about the search for help, first among the people affected trying to help themselves and then look-

Common Elements	Individualist Cultures	Collective Cultures
• Family support • Social support • Increase in group cohesion • Working, to avoid thinking about what is happening • Self-discipline and responsibility • Support from religion or ideology	• Accept individual responsibility. • Search for the deep meaning of an experience. • Use psychology to undermine the aggressor. • Strengthen identity and personal values. • Develop compensatory fantasies.	• Passively accept events. • Deny and remain silent. Avoid. • Focus on the new problems to be solved. • Focus on the body and relationships with others. • Highlight responsibility and the collective solution to problems.

ing to other sources outside. This support may be informational, emotional, instrumental-material, or social. Aid consists of an objective network set up for the fulfillment of various needs; it is also a network of help that people perceive as supporting them and understanding them. The mere presence of humanitarian aid does not mean that the people perceive that their needs are being considered or that they fully trust in it.

The Importance of Sharing

Sharing experiences is a way of coping with traumatic events because it helps to validate, recognize, understand and make sense of what happened. Generally, people who do not share their memory of a negative event with others suffer from more physical and mental-health problems. Having a partner who had experienced the same event and being able to share and talk about one's experience were two factors associated with better psychological adjustment in survivors of concentration camps (Janoff-Bulman 1992).

In most cultures, people share their experiences. However, how often one talks about those experiences and for how long varies by culture. In general, people in individualist cultures talk more and longer than people in collectivist cultures, where the opportunity to share experiences is more linked to the cohesion of the group. The types of traumatic events differ by culture, as well. In many places, rape is considered to be a stigma for the victim, so victims may not want to talk about it because they may face rejection from the community, which would of course isolate them and affect them even more.

Sharing does not always reduce tension. When the problem that caused the person suffering is still ongoing, sharing experiences may inflame people's concerns and cause rumors to spread. In difficult situations, people need to share bad news, and sometimes this will lead to the exaggeration or distortion of reality.

IMPROVING HEALTH

Social support is associated with a lower death rate and improved mental health.[1] Help that validates and recognizes the traumatic experience of people and that helps them to understand and make sense of it is very important for the assimilation of disasters and traumatic events. Those people who receive support feel much better than those who are isolated and unable to confide in anyone.

The results of a study on the residents living near the Three Mile Island, Pennsylvania, nuclear reactor showed that, one and a half years after the 1979 accident, they suffered from more stress and more physical symptoms and anxiety when compared to people from other areas (Bromet et al. 1982). The residents also had high levels of catecholamines[2] in the blood, which is linked to stress. Those with lower levels of stress had received a moderate or high degree of social support. This help reduced the psychological and behavioral effects of stress. Sharing, however, does not always diminish the physiological effects, as mentioned earlier. For example, in this case, those who received social support did not necessarily have a lower level of catecholamines. From this, we see that support helps people cope with the psychological effects of a disaster and helps reduce the behavioral effects of stress, but it does not decrease the hormonal effect and thus does not guarantee the elimination of stress-linked physical effects.

DIFFICULTIES IN FINDING SUPPORT

In general, people who look for social support to cope with traumatic events have difficulty finding it. Some support may come from people who have been equally affected by the violence or the disaster—people who have had similar experiences and who may understand things better—but it may be difficult to find support even among these people if they have different ways of grieving. Difficulty finding the opportunity to get help combined with the feelings generated by the terrible experience may limit people's ability to find support. Moreover, losses often create personal or family crises. One study, for example, has shown that in the United States it is common for couples who have lost a child to divorce (Pennebaker 1995). It is also difficult for close friends and relatives to listen to someone's traumatic experiences because talking with depressed people can make other people feel depressed, too, and they in turn can be strongly, and negatively, affected by the person. The search for social support under these circumstances "burns out" their social network and increases problems for survivors who are left without the support of others or the social recognition of their suffering.

Moreover, disasters can be stigmatizing. In the words of Janoff-Bulman (1992), victims are a permanent testimony to the ill will that exists in our world and of our own eventual vulnerability. This is why people react to stigmatized people in a contradictory way: In a formal evaluation, for example, they may verbally react positively (for example, by making positive comments), but in nonverbal communication they may react negatively with signs of rejection and distance. In terms of social approval, those people who "put on a brave face" are thought better of and are reinforced as opposed to those who express how affected they are by the traumatic event. If we add to this that close friends or relatives do not know what to say, avoid talking about the issues, or wait for the victim to take the initiative, we realize how difficult a task social support and coping with these events is.

People do not usually express their negative experiences or negative states of mind for the following reasons: they want to protect other people, they feel their experience will not be understood, or they find it painful to recall the traumatic event and they prefer not to. These were the three reasons survivors of the Holocaust gave as to why they had not shared their traumatic experiences (Pennebaker 1995).

Sometimes people don't know how to cope with this. Some are amazed, as if the torture could not have been possible, and that stops you from wanting to speak; some are really scared of talking about it, and we are scared enough as it is; some don't want to talk about it at all, perhaps because they don't know what to say or they don't want to make it worse. Sometimes we don't want to talk about it anymore, we want to forget, stop going over it again and again. We all have the same difficulties and everyone has to know what to do. (Support group; Sarea 1994)

Coping with the Extreme: A Catalyst for Change

After a disaster, the difficulties of the social reconstruction or the disappointed expectations in a climate of increasing economic difficulties can often lead to more trauma and despair. Despite the fact that people are seriously affected and their capacity for personal and social reconstruction is damaged, not all the responses after a disaster or serious sociopolitical crisis are negative. People can also become very active when faced with extreme situations. They develop resistance mechanisms and begin to reorganize their lives in the hopes of a better future.

Under certain conditions, disasters may have a constructive effect on the social system. The interruption of the status quo and the clear need for cooperation and common efforts to repair the damage may combine to eliminate differences in status and to promote change and solidarity in the community. Similarly, it has been found that during political conflicts certain psychological problems decline because of the increase in group cohesion. This activation of support networks should be taken into account during the reconstruction process.

In a study on survivors of a tornado in the United States, 84 percent said that they coped with the experience better than they thought they would have, and 69 percent felt that they had overcome a great challenge and had grown as human beings as a result. About a third found that their relationships with friends and family had improved and their relationship with their partner had become more satisfactory (Hodgkinson and Stewart 1991).

This has also been found in Guatemala where the collective massacres not only had a greater impact on the individual and the community; but the people who faced these massacres also developed more strategies of social cohesion and mobilization. For example, the survivors of the massacres demanded recognition of the truth (as a sociopolitical demand) more than the survivors of other events did.[3] In short, those who had experienced a collective disaster exhibited greater community organization and stronger political demands for the truth and for human rights than did those who had survived other events.

Disasters and Social Movements

After the 1985 earthquake in Mexico City, a group of neighbors organized themselves and demanded social improvements. Evaluations on the impact of disasters have shown that disasters tend to accelerate the social changes that were taking place before the event and, by shedding light on social contradictions and encouraging solidarity, become contexts for social reorganization. As research on Guatemala shows, even though the humanitarian disaster caused by military repression was responsible for tremendous destruction, the number of social organizations remained stable because of victims' efforts (ODHAG 1998).

In many postdisaster or postwar situations, the victims and survivors have developed their own support or even social movements based on certain claims and demands. The movements and organizations that emerge in these situations combine various interests and social aims to manage the aid and demands of survivors, to foster mutual support among the survivors, and to organize public denunciation and political force.

The organizational movements of victims and support groups that take place during the reconstruction stage are focused on the management of the material aid, including demands on the state. Institutional reconstruction programs often state as one of their main priorities the participation of the affected population, but this is limited by a paternalistic orientation that is often a source of conflict.

The activities of the organizations set up by victims of disasters include laying out the criteria for the management of the aid and monitoring the agreements and claims to the governments. These normally last until the end of the aid management or reconstruction process. Sometimes new social organizations emerge during this period that have their sights set far ahead, as was the case of the 1976 earthquake in Guatemala. Many factors, including an increased awareness of social injustice, the presence of political organization, and the support of the Catholic church led to a fruitful organizational process in indigenous communities.

In addition to promoting material aid, some organizations of affected populations emerge from the need to rely on a trustworthy functional network that is perceived to be a source of support and understanding. Examples of mutual aid, such as the anti-AIDS organizations throughout the world, show the importance of self-help in collective disasters. In other cases, especially in sociopolitical disasters, victim movements worked toward the demand for justice, mutual support among the survivors, and the defense of human rights—all of which constitute collective coping mechanisms. They are not free from common organizational problems, however, such as leadership problems, the risk of stigma, fear of participation, and internal conflict. "We started because in other organizations we didn't feel comfortable; it was more bureaucratic. In the plaza we were all equal. We asked each other 'What happened?' 'How was it?' All of us had had our sons taken away from us, we were all going through the same thing. We had gone to the same places. There were no differences, there was no distance. For this reason, we felt good and our group came together and we were strengthened" (Mothers of the Plaza de Mayo, in Martín Beristain and Riera 1993).

Some associations combine aid management to the families with the reconstruction of the collective memory as done by the group AFAVIT (Association of Relatives of Victims) with respect to the massacre of Trujillo, Colombia. Others are aimed more at mutual support or political demands, such as is the case of the Mothers and Grandmothers of the Plaza de Mayo and other associations of relatives of the missing in many countries of Latin America and Asia. These groups keep the memory of the atrocities alive and continue the pursuit of demanding truth and justice. Some Vietnam War veteran associations, for example, contributed support to antiwar efforts and U.S. involvement in wars such as that in El Salvador. These are collective ways of coping with the consequences of traumatic events, rebuilding the social fabric of the community, and often fighting against the causes of suffering. Humanitarian aid faces the challenge of strengthening the social fabric and opening spaces for the population's own types of mutual support to be exercised.

Chapter 6

The Experience of Humanitarian Aid Workers and NGOs

> *Humanitarian action—quick, simple, and specific, at least when compared to the political treatment given to faraway problems—appears easily accessible and allows immediate assessment: the victim-helper partnership has become one of the emblems of the end of the [twentieth] century.*
>
> —Brauman 1993, 155

For people and groups involved in humanitarian aid, crisis situations can have psychosocial implications. This chapter discusses the motivation and role of humanitarian aid workers and NGOs, as well as the ethical dilemmas and the impact of stress on humanitarian aid.

Brauman (1993) critiques the role of the media in crisis situations and how overseas workers fulfill a symbolic function in their societies of origin that contributes to a particular representation of reality. The distortion and selective filtering of images affects both what is considered to be an emergency and the nature of the action taken. In recent years, the "humanitarian" has become news and aid workers have become personalities. The representation of the "humanitarian" in the media influences the motivations of the different actors and the impact of aid, and it enters the area of collective emotions, especially through television. That certain situations become news while others remain in obscurity means that situations such as the famine in southern Sudan went unnoticed at the end of the 1980s. Another example is the gassing of Iraqi Kurds, which also went unnoticed until Western opinion changed regarding Saddam Hussein. Humanitarian aid must keep these scenarios in mind and not risk losing its perspective or the purpose of its existence. It should also try to maintain its criteria of what is important and not let itself be swayed by public opinion, collective emotions, or short-lived and self-interested policies.

These challenges and many others have a political and organizational dimension as well as a personal one. Humanitarian aid often risks extinguishing the effects caused by failed economic development policies (for example, structural reform programs) as was the case of the famine in Somalia (Choussudovsky 1993) or of protecting the political inertia of states by reassuring the altruistic and pacifist sensitivities of the citizenry (Hermet 1993).

In recent years, many changes have taken place in the conditions under which humanitarian aid is provided. Unstable environments and difficulty reaching the population in need pose new problems for humanitarian action. Confusion between the humanitarian and the political, now emerging in various situations, runs the risk of changing the nature of action and the type of relationship aid workers will have with affected populations. Aid organizations and agencies now work in complex situations where their role can often be ambiguous. Overseas workers face these challenges in their everyday work in addition to the difficulties of humanitarian work itself. This complexity can both call into question and give more meaning to their work.

Psychosocial Implications of Humanitarian Aid Work

The work of agencies, NGOs, and overseas workers takes place in emergency, reconstruction, and "development" contexts. Although the meaning of humanitarian aid is often taken for granted, in reality we find different types of visions, priorities, and activities. These visions, priorities, and activities depend not only on the needs of the population or the problems caused by the crisis but also on how the aid is conceived. If humanitarian aid does not have a historical perspective or a view to the future, it risks imposing on the people something that is far removed from their lives.

Humanitarian aid is usually made up of a series of tasks such as providing basic care to the affected population, giving support, and improving living conditions. Even though these tasks are clear, the confusion arises because the individuals or institutions involved often have different interests or priorities (Fisas 1994). Jean (1993) describes how differences between the United Nations and NGOs were apparent in the humanitarian aid in Somalia. Justification for the protection of NGOs was used as a disguise for political objectives, and the confusion between the military personnel and humanitarian aid workers caused a feeling of insecurity for the humanitarian organizations and reduced the space in which they had to work. The war in Kosovo (April–May 1999) also involved disguised political aims. The justification for military intervention to protect Kosovar civilians, who were subject to repression and ethnic cleansing from the Serbian regime, led to the war being considered a "humanitarian war." However, the bombings accelerated Serbian plans for deportation and caused countless civilian casualties. Meanwhile, military plans took priority over the needs of refugees, giving rise to a lack of preventive measures to prepare for the mass of refugees (*El País* April 25, 1999). Even NATO soldiers were used to supplement the work of the NGOs.

Despite this, a naive view persists in the humanitarian orbit that leads to seeing its work as specific, neutral, and without consequences beyond a helping relationship. People with little capacity to assess the situation are at risk of not being aware of what they are doing and of the influence that humanitarian aid can have. To do their work properly, humanitarian aid workers need various abilities and skills: the ability to relate to the affected population; the technical knowledge adapted to the social situation and local culture; the sociopolitical knowledge of the situation and the purpose of aid; and the ability to relate to the authorities and other groups in a difficult context. Cooperative work has similarities to other helping professions. Relationships with people can be the most important stimulus and the main motivation for many. Unrealistic expectations about the nature of the work, however, often clash with monotonous tasks such as resource management, report writing, and everyday work routines.

Humanitarian work is carried out within NGOs, international agencies, or governmental agencies that contain different structures, interests, responsibilities, and requirements. International or governmental agencies are sometimes more concerned about public opinion or institutional politics. The central administration of NGOs might be more concerned than aid workers with maintaining good relations with overseeing institutions or being aware of their priorities when providing resources to secure financing. Aid workers, because of their contact with life on the ground, are often more aware of people's priorities and are more sensitive to their needs, especially those aid workers who have lived among the population for a long period of time. Agger (1995) points out that a committed and professional attitude on the part of those who work in humanitarian aid requires energy, and this requirement often conflicts with the number of "beneficiaries"[1] and the visibility of their actions. These challenges are faced by local NGO workers, too.

The policy of contracts is one example of how a certain organizational culture can have psychosocial implications on humanitarian aid. Structuring aid work around deadlines for the awarding of funds has implications on the mobility of workers and the continuity of their work in a given context. Such complicated issues as having to work in Rwanda, for example, for two months and then in Haiti for a few weeks, or working under the uncertainty of whether a project can continue because of lack of funding affect the health of the volunteers and their degree of commitment. These issues also affect the usefulness of the programs for the population in need. Assuming that immediate action is the most effective way to handle emergencies without the conditions necessary to make the aid truly work obscures the fact that it may be ill suited to the situation and the cause of the failure of many interventions.

Motivations and the Role of Help

The discussion so far shows how different agendas can affect the effectiveness of aid. Although there is currently a debate between agencies and NGOs on the motivations and concerns of humanitarian aid, hardly any research has been done on the relationship between motivations and the way in which the work is carried out by organizations and workers.

In general, there tends to be a lack of interest in the aid, and workers and agencies refuse to consider the possible negative effects of their actions (De Waal 1987). In reality, however, the lack of a critical perspective on their own work and the assumption of the role of "helper" can have negative consequences on the population (Harrell-Bond 1986). For instance, the organizational criteria of aid condition the attitudes and structure the relationships between the workers and the population. The spatial organization of refugee camps often suggests to the residents that they have no access to information and that the staff controls decision making. This organization is similar to what Goffman (1969) described in his research on "total institutions."[2] In such a context, the relationships have already been established, regardless of individual motivations or attitudes.

People participate in organizations for one or more of the following reasons:

- *Idealism.* Through identification with the values and convictions of the organization.
- *Adhesion to the group.* Belonging to the organization is a way of being accepted socially or having a group of reference; a way of meeting new people.
- *A new experience.* To understand the world better; to learn from the people one works with; to satisfy intellectual curiosity and to gain awareness, skills, knowledge, and practical experience (first-aid skills, project management, and so on).
- *Professional benefits.* Possibility of finding work or a promotion in the medium or long term.
- *Equilibrium.* Being in the group can satisfy psychological needs such

as overcoming a sense of helplessness, anxiety over a personal situation, or feelings of guilt.

- *Escape.* Resolution of emotional conflicts; flight from an unpleasant or a threatening situation (in one's family or country of origin, and even in oneself).
- *Political commitment.* Participation seen as a political struggle to change social living conditions of the people or to support opposition groups.
- *Improvement of self-image or purpose of living.* Some people leave stable jobs and their social and family lives, which they see as empty and purposeless, to emigrate somewhere else.

Most people are involved in organizations because they believe in what the organization is doing or what it stands for; other factors can come into play, however, especially in moments of crisis or when relationships worsen. Unclear motivation or the use of humanitarian work to satisfy other types of personal needs (something to put on a resumé, quest for adventure, or escape from personal problems) carry risks for the development and purpose of humanitarian action. A lack of conviction in what one is doing can make people less sensitive to the needs of the population, especially when the action is risky or involves discomfort. A motivation that seeks social recognition can be frustrated if that recognition is not achieved. An idealistic motivation not based on reality can cause disappointment. When political or economic problems appear—as is often the case—the reality of the situation does not correspond to the idealized image that the person had before becoming involved.

Personal attitudes can also affect the aid workers' relationship with the population. The implicit presumptions of those who have the knowledge (legal or technical) or the power (the management of aid)—while the population is in a state of dependency—suggest an attitude of superiority. In addition, the idealization of the people and the actual aid can give rise to a paternalistic attitude and a model of dependency based on management of the aid and an underestimation of the abilities of the population. Such attitudes are fairly common. The tendency to believe oneself to be omnipotent (a Jehovah complex) or an overidentification with the role of caregiver (a Magna Mater complex) can lead to confusion and a reinforcement of the victimization and passivity of the population (Stearns 1993).

We have to try and avoid extremes in the way we confront our experience with the people. Both overidentification and underidentification have negative effects on the work. An overidentification is a mistaken attempt to take on the experience of the other, which increases the emotional load and doesn't allow us to see problems objectively. At the other extreme, underidentification implies a lack of human sensitivity and makes our work lack quality. Given the difficulty of managing this individually, it is important to look for the support of others. (Volunteer workshop, Basque Country, 1998, in author's field notes)

Recognizing the abilities of the population implies an open attitude to training and reciprocity based on respect for the population and oriented toward social justice.

Cooperation and NGOs

> *Aid to the Third World is based on the premise that the West has the capital and training to help. Those who have the resources should "plan and carry out the transfer." Therefore, the donors, however far they may be from these cultures or from the aspirations of the intended beneficiaries, control the process through their experts. If the receiving country would like this aid, they have to respond positively and accept the terms and conditions, even when they are not clearly defined.*
>
> —F. M. Mburu

Government cooperation often depends on political and commercial concerns. Sometimes, development projects are already part of the platform for negotiations between countries. An example is the case of the relationship between the European Union and Morocco. Morocco negotiated fishing agreements and a policy of police control of illegal immigration in exchange for development projects and withdrawing support for the Saharan cause. Morocco is more and more the recipient of these official projects as well as NGO projects.

The process of formulating a project, getting approval from a financing agency, receiving the money, and starting the project normally takes from six months to a year. In a context of war or political violence, often what was thought at the outset to be urgent changes a year later. Programs cannot be rigidly defined by planners but should be flexible systems that leave a wide margin for those working on the ground to adapt to the changing situation. If the system goes so far as to require that workers define evaluation indicators for a particular action ahead of time—matters that vary widely, depending on the moment in which an evaluation is carried out—the system can become a ridiculous and exhausting bureaucratic exercise that produces reports and counterreports full of agreed-upon lies.

In serious social conflicts or emergency situations, evaluation criteria and resource management must be based not on the criteria of development projects under "normal" conditions but on the logic of war and the temporary nature of the situation. Better communication is the only way to make action more effective and to improve relations between different groups.

NGOs were thought up as alternatives that were more horizontal and more oriented toward solidarity and the social emancipation of populations subjected to economic plunder or violence. But are they a "de-ideologized," technocratic form of solidarity, and do they represent more respectable and more efficient versions of voluntarism? Do the programs themselves actually achieve these objectives? Do they help to undo the stereotype that NGOs are the alternative to development, or do they highlight the economic causes of dependency? Obviously, many different organizations exist, with different ideologies, working methods, and organizational models, and analyzing all of these factors is beyond the scope of this book.

One need only take a brief tour of the countries of the South where NGOs form part of the everyday landscape to be reminded that most of the work done by the popular movements and organizations is made possible by the support of their counterparts in the North. Most of the help provided falls within the categories of humanitarian aid and development, but other NGOs work specifically in the field of human rights. Support provided in this field includes the following:

• Training, including access to technical, up-to-date information.
• Networks of attention for victims of violence.
• Distribution of information abroad to promote international pressure.
• Taking on of duties that the locals cannot because of security problems or physical well-being.
• Protection of people, communities, or institutions under threat.

However, together with these forms of aid come significant contradictions. The following table summarizes some of the key issues in the permanent debate on the role of NGOs.

In the last two decades, NGOs have become new agents in the processes of social reconstruction and accompaniment to the people affected by social disasters, managing part of the aid, working closer to the people and with less bureaucracy. However, lack of coordination, competitiveness, and a view focused on funding institutions can make them another mechanism for controlling the people affected by crisis where humanitarian aid intervenes. The experience of multiple disasters highlights the importance of clarifying what is expected of the NGOs, the people, and the state.

NGOs for Humanitarian Aid and Development

Pros	Cons
• *Economic resources.* NGOs provide technical (nonideological) forms of solidarity. They mobilize a large volume of economic resources, unknown in previous decades.	• *Most NGOs do not have their own resources,* which on the one hand guarantees their independence. On the other, however, financing institutions (state agencies for development, local authorities, etc.) decide which countries or types of projects are priorities in accordance with their own interests. Therefore, NGOs may become instruments of government policies, thereby losing their independence and critical abilities.
• *Professionalization of the work.* NGOs have contributed a specific method of working: projects. A project requires prior research, design, a formula, a timetable, a budget, and an evaluation with previously established indicators. Therefore, objectivity is guaranteed when allocating resources, avoiding situations of abuse.	• *Change of internal organization.* Projects have to be presented under a predefined model and style. NGOs have to teach people from the South how to develop projects adequately. This sometimes involves changing the internal workings of the organization.
• *Potential employment for professionals* from countries of the South who otherwise would find it difficult to secure work in social projects, and who may contribute to the reconstruction of basic services.	• *Loss of leadership of popular organizations* as some leaders become agency or NGO workers with the result that local organizations lose talented people in their fight for justice.
• *Promoting development.* NGOs have a more integrated and focused view of the needs of the people.	• *Use of expatriates* means that people from the North work in positions meant for people of the South.
	• *Ethnocentric concept of development.* Development cannot limit itself to exploiting natural resources, providing services, and gathering provisions. Some cultures reject these principles and prefer alternatives that come from their own culture.

Source: Pérez Sales et al. 1999.

Protection of the Population in Danger: Another Role for NGOs

The security of the affected population has to be taken into account during situations of conflict. Normally a divide exists between the NGOs that work specifically in the field of human rights—and thus have a greater concern for the security of the people—and those that manage

> ### The Invervention of Institutions and NGOs:
> ### Reflections on the Nevado del Ruiz Disaster
>
> 1. The lack of coordination between local organizations, state entities, and NGOs caused greater tension from the loss of purpose and effectiveness of the action.
> 2. Lack of a consistent plan of action for situating the aid within the reconstruction process resulted in many NGOs not even able to coordinate themselves.
> 3. The people had exaggerated expectations of state institutions and NGOs. Vertical and paternalistic management caused the victims to have a passive and demanding attitude. NGOs served as a buffer for the tension.
> 4. The NGOs fought for the survival of their projects and took advantage of the disaster as an opportunity to restructure and consolidate themselves.
> 5. The intervention of the NGOs relied on gaining individual support. The projects were technocratic and excluded survivors from decision-making.
> 6. The NGOs' role of advising, accompanying, and supporting groups was relegated to a secondary position.
> 7. The NGOs had to face their own centralized processes of decision-making with little knowledge of the socioeconomic conditions or social and political tendencies of the population.
> 8. A critical conscience was generated in the country with respect to the actions of the NGOs and the necessity that they work in a coordinated way with other NGOs, public powers, and the affected population.

Source: Saavedra 1996.

emergency or development projects. The former are NGOs from the actual country or the international sphere that register complaints (such as Amnesty International) or provide accompaniment (such as Peace Brigades International, PBI). However, there is an increasing demand that the rest of the NGOs and agencies become involved not only in humanitarian aid or development but also in protecting the population. "It's no coincidence that when governments decide to ration aid, they disregard the most critical organizations and tolerate the docile ones. This is what happened in December 1995 when the government of Rwanda expelled thirty-eight NGOs, with the aim of silencing their criticisms of government actions. . . . How can humanitarian organizations respond? One possibility would be to place more emphasis on protection and freedom of speech" (Guest and Saulnier 1996).

The growing recognition of the importance of the protection of a displaced population's human rights highlights a fundamental issue: During a conflict, the violation of human rights is both a cause and

---

The Work of Peace Brigades International in Colombia

Peace Brigades International sends teams of international observers-accompaniers to areas of conflict, when requested by local entities. Since 1994, PBI has had a team in Colombia, where there has been a sustained, internal armed conflict and some of the highest levels of human-rights violations in Latin America.

Because of the PBI mandate, the role of the Colombian entities in the protection of human rights, and degree of local organization, the focus of PBI activity is on protecting the fragile areas of interaction between NGOs and local displaced peoples' organizations. In Colombia, the PBI

1. Provides accompaniment and an international presence through
   a. International accompaniment to NGOs and Colombian entities that concern themselves with the protection of human rights and the problems of displacement.
   b. Participation as international observers in truth commissions and joint negotiations, as a guarantee and reminder of commitment from all sides, especially authorities and armed agents.
2. Lobbies military and civil authorities (on a national and regional level), institutions, diplomatic bodies, and international organizations.
3. Produces and periodically distributes information.
4. Participates in the work of international NGOs in the field of displacement and protection of human rights.
5. Supports the rebuilding of the social fabric through support workshops and training in areas such as psychosocial repair and conflict resolution.

---

consequence of the displacement. Adequate protection of human rights contributes to avoiding displacement, alleviating its consequences, and facilitating the return of the population.

Adequate protection is the responsibility of the state, but very often it is the state that becomes the main source of insecurity. Therefore it becomes necessary for other actors to promote safety and to pressure the state to protect populations in danger. The humanitarian aid mechanisms of the United Nations, however, have not included protection within its mandate (except, in part, the United Nations High Commissioner for Refugees). In reality, what prevails is a conjunction of NGOs and government and intergovernmental entities that monitor the human-rights situation but do not guarantee an effective protection. To carry out the task of protection, NGOs need to broaden their traditional mandates and activities as well as maintain an open and clear relationship with other NGOs focused on human rights.

Despite their enormous limitations in resources and logistic capability, NGOs are able to work in areas of conflict much more easily and

Action to Be Taken in the Case of Human-Rights Violations

1. Document the case well.
2. Keep information in a safe place and keep it confidential.
3. Check the guidelines of the organization on how to treat such situations.
4. Approach local experts on human rights and ask for their advice.
5. Approach, if possible, recognized international or regional organizations to send them information.
6. Inform the victims about what can be done and get their approval.
7. Always keep in mind the safety of the victims and their families.

Source: Amnesty International 1998.

adapt quickly to the terrain. Because they operate outside of governmental structures, NGOs do not call into question the sovereignty of a government, which makes their presence more acceptable and allows for the growing overlap between the work of NGOs and that of international organizations. The tendency for governments to carry out part of their humanitarian aid through NGOs and the greater weight NGOs have on the international stage means that they gain an informal status within local governments.

The accompaniment process and an international presence are both forms of preventive work where transgressors can be seen to be affected by international pressure. The ability of NGO observers to protect depends on the degree of support they receive from international public opinion and governments. The strength of the observers and the NGOs, therefore, lies in an international awakening about the need to protect populations in danger, about their capacity to create friction between governments and public opinion, and about confronting governments over accepted international norms so that they have no choice but to respond to violations. Of course, however, any pressure on a government will be fruitless if it goes against the government's own economic or strategic interests (Eguren and Mahony 1997).

The presence of observers requires a series of specific actions and the training of personnel, which are not included in the regular plans of human-rights or humanitarian NGOs. For example, international observers or accompaniers must maintain a permanent or periodic presence in different settings, they must interview the authorities and other national and international entities regularly, and they must produce information regularly. In this way, the presence of international personnel can become a protective umbrella for the population affected by violence.

Since the conflicts in Bosnia and Kosovo, U.N. missions and other organizations, such as the Organization for Security and Cooperation in Europe (OSCE), have sent teams of international observers to countries in conflict. These observers play a preventive role, but they are also more directly subject to government criteria and political alliances. In the case of Kosovo, the exit of the observers in March 1999 in preparation for the NATO military campaign left the population defenseless against Serbian military plans to deploy fourteen thousand soldiers with the goal of ethnic cleansing. The Serbian army's defiance of the international presence generated very little protest from Western governments (*El País,* April 21, 1999).

Attending to Safety: Managing Dangerous Situations

Preventive action and the management of dangerous situations are now included in the working plans of NGOs in conflict situations. The consideration of security aspects vary according to the NGO, and their policies define contact with armed groups, negotiations with governments, bodyguards, and so forth. Here we discuss the protection of populations in contact with NGOs at different levels: political, organizational, and personal.

The political aspect refers mainly to the coverage or support given to a specific project or action. This may be in the form of prevention when there is a rise in the level of insecurity or as a response to crisis situations. NGOs are increasingly collaborating with social groups, state institutions, or diplomatic representatives that provide them with a support network for dangerous situations and allow them to take preventive action against possible attacks.

The organizational aspect refers to security mechanisms of NGOs, such as political action (maintaining a balance between different sides), work procedures (managing delicate information), and communication (telephone, mail). NGOs should have their own emergency plans for conflicts (for example, what to do with threats to a member of the group or action in crisis situations). To increase the safety of individuals and groups, the NGO must train all members of the team in the criteria and mechanisms for managing these situations.

Key issues are consistency, the internal flow of information, and participation in decision making about what to do after a serious conflict. The workers in the field have direct knowledge of the problems, but they can also become overly involved and lose their capacity to assess danger. It can be just as detrimental to get caught up in the local perspective of the team as it is for the coordination or the central administration of the NGO to make decisions from the outside. NGOs should make sure that risk evaluation and decision-making processes are clearly set out beforehand and that the NGOs consider different perspectives through dialogue and participation.

A project that has structured plans and a political cover should put personal security measures in place. Confidentiality is crucial for building trust with the people, but obstacles exist. On the one hand, many people involved in humanitarian aid come from countries where there are no such security problems and where they have had no experience of serious political conflict. On the other, in many situations the danger may not be apparent. Despite the fact that it is important always to be alert, it is also possible to minimize the danger as a way of alleviating tension. At the other extreme, always focusing on safety over all other issues can result in obsession or paranoia.

Everything has changed dramatically for me. At the beginning, when I arrived, I wasn't scared. It seemed as if things weren't as bad as I had been told. I got used to living in the midst of the situation without being aware of many things. The problems started after my friends were detained and expelled. I walked along the same streets, I did the same work, but everything seemed different, the country had changed. Well, I was the one who had changed. (Volunteer in El Salvador, 1991, in author's field notes)

Changes in routine, being observant, implementing safety measures in the house or workplace, and using caution when going out are just some of the adaptive measures to incorporate into everyday life in violent contexts.

LEVELS OF SECURITY

Political		Organizational	Personal
National Support	*International Support*		
Social groups	Embassies	Support from the	Routines
Institutions	Agencies	organization	Departures
	Support networks	Local support	Risk situations
		network	
		Communication	
		mechanisms	
		Case management:	
		Information	
		Emergency plan	

Working as a Team

Although the teams working in situations of conflict or social disasters are there to carry out specific tasks, the impact of the violence itself, the close relationships that the teams necessarily have to maintain, and the inevitable involvement of personal factors among the performance of the job make the work team also a "life team," which seeks to integrate into its dynamic different aspects of a complex reality.

Teams that Work in Situations of Conflict

- *Full time.* It is often necessary to work and live together. Care should be taken to create a good atmosphere in shared living quarters and a good way of working together.
- *Multicultural environment.* It is important to be flexible and open to cultural differences and to agree on rules for daily life.
- *People change.* It is important to keep continuity and to adopt attitudes that favor integration (respecting the memory of the group and its history).
- A *different country* requires that you get to know it. It is important to understand its different culture and political context and to know how to communicate with the people.
- *Under pressure.* Because of the complexity of the work, the need for continuity, and difficult political situations, it is essential for there to be mutual support within the team.
- *Decision-making.* The demands and delicacy of the situation make it necessary to change plans or have discussions on how to manage the situation.
- *Intense but varied work* requires that one is active, but circumstances may also give rise to feelings of impotence and the work includes bureaucratic activities.

Teams often work in hazardous or disorganized conditions and should strive to accomplish the following to improve their work conditions:

1. The team must have a clear idea of its work to accommodate to potentially complex and ambiguous situations. The objectives of the team's mandate must be made clear and shared by all the members of the team. In situations of violence, it may be necessary to reorganize the type of work that is being done. Threats, fear, or frequent societal changes may require that the team redefine its priorities. "Our work with the displaced was very clearly set out. It was going to be a gradual process of getting closer to the communities and working from their own organizational processes without being directive. However, the mass exodus that took place in the middle of the year made us change our plans. We would like to continue working with our model, but the situation has changed dramatically" (Team working with displaced people, Colombia, 1998, in author's field notes).

2. Teams should be well organized, and they should be clear about the task at hand, the conditions, and the purpose of the work. Teams should be clear about the distribution of functions and responsibilities, including those that are shared. Care should be taken over the decision-making process; this is especially important in tense political situations or when there is limited communication among the members of the team. Flexible planning is essential in unstable situations and in emergencies where immediate response is needed. Of particular importance is the relationship between local teams and central coordinators and keeping in mind not only organizational issues but also the specific characteristics of the local context.

3. Teams should develop the capacity for mutual support and resistance under difficult conditions. Relationships among the members of the team are very important because a climate of trust and acceptance allows people to help each other by exchanging ideas and suggestions, sharing feelings and information, and dealing with difficult experiences and attitudes.

PROBLEMS ASSOCIATED WITH LOCAL AND COORDINATION TEAMS

Field Teams	Coordination Teams
Fewer opportunities available for leisure and "disconnecting."	Stress from lack of local information or a high level of bureaucratic work.
Conflict is nearer, creating a greater sense of action, but with the consequences of decisions seen more clearly.	Greater risk that the team will disperse, that each member will concentrate on his or her own duties, and that criteria will not be unified.
Small cities or communities where groups are related and communicate a lot among themselves, resulting in rumors and problems of confidentiality.	More contact with other groups, which can increase confusion about information.
Small problems can lead to conflict or adversely affect relations. (Individual team members must keep a healthy attitude around the rest of the team.)	Risk of seeing the local team as less significant within the larger context. A task-centered dynamic that affords little attention to relationships.
Feeling of isolation from the center of the organization.	Risk of centralization and not distributing necessary information.

The dynamics of the group became very difficult. The same issues kept coming up and were all related: exhaustion, not giving ourselves space for our own needs, the work always taking priority. . . . We decided to talk about it, committing ourselves to following through with the process however painful (and it was). . . . In some way, we had set ourselves impossible challenges that we had to overcome. We didn't have the strength to do that, so our "challenge" became even more difficult. We didn't realize that the situation in the country had changed a lot, as well as what we could do in the field. When we realized all of this, we were able to help each other to overcome our feelings of helplessness. (PBI Team, El Salvador, 1990, in author's field notes)

Practical Advice for Mutual Support of Team Members

1. Talk openly about the problems affecting the team members to avoid misunderstandings. Talk about the problems or difficulties in the group, however painful such a discussion may be, rather than pretend the problems do not exist.
2. Bring up the problems in such a way so that everyone can contribute to the discussion and put forward his or her point of view.
3. Give each person the chance to say how he or she feels. In this way, the group can rebuild a common vision. If this is not done, the group may lose its internal cohesion.
4. Have a constructive point of view: Think about what to do and how to proceed in order to reinforce the commitment to solidarity.
5. Learn to adapt to new situations, especially when there have been traumatic experiences or an increase in the level of tension. The group should be able to adjust its goals according to the situation.
6. Decide on a process in which everyone can contribute his or her point of view. Such a process provides emotional security and facilitates decision making.
7. Create a common purpose for the group, in which everyone can talk about his or her experiences, rebuild relationships, and get back to work.

Source: Martín Beristain and Riera 1993.

Ethical Issues in Humanitarian Aid

The team put forward many dilemmas: What is the point of our work if it is only relief work and not prevention? Very often you don't know who you are working for, what is behind it all, or what your options are. Also, we are faced with many economic demands that we cannot fulfill. We are here because there is racism and our lives here are worth more than the lives of this country's people.

—*Overseas workers workshop, Guatemala, 1995, in author's field notes*

Some of the situations in which humanitarian aid takes place are ambiguous and this gives rise to increasing ethical dilemmas in overseas work. Humanitarian organizations have long been faced with many difficult practical and ethical dilemmas, and the dilemmas of overseas workers are the same as those faced by humanitarian organizations and are also of a political nature. They include the use of the aid by adversaries in a war; the possibility of becoming accomplices to the atrocities by staying in a certain place or by abandoning a population in need; giving testimony about atrocities or not with the risk of having to abandon the aid; increasing the aid when all this does is allow states to get out of taking political action (Hermet 1993). In some cases, these dilemmas can lead to strong contradictions as, for example, in 1995 when NGOs debated their role in the refugee camps in Zaire at the same time as they were witnessing there the presence and control of the militia preparing for more violence. "Generally, the decision to stay in a country requires three main conditions: security, the state of negotiations, and the involvement of the local community. It is important to learn to say no if these three conditions are not met and not to fall into playing the role of angels or boy scouts. It is also important to respect the agreed-to strategy, refusing to become a money machine and making sure our actions are transparent" (Hirtz 1994).

Also, on a personal level, those who work in humanitarian aid face ethical dilemmas that are rarely discussed openly, such as how to decide, when there is a lack of resources, who receives food or treatment. Such dilemmas can make people ask themselves such questions as, What is the purpose of my role in humanitarian aid? or, What am I doing here? "People who have to leave the country often face ethical dilemmas and feelings of guilt. They may experience feelings of betrayal or a questioning of their very identity. They may find it difficult to talk about these issues with confidence or to understand their circumstances. In other cases, the possibility that the people we work with might suffer a negative consequence because of some action of ours obliges us to act with great precaution" (CADDHHC 1997).

Being present in situations of injustice can provoke moral responsibility and guilt. To deal with these dilemmas, overseas workers can try and find alternatives that range from identifying with the people to keeping themselves locked in their role. From the people's point of view, overseas workers are there to help them, beyond the role defined in humanitarian aid programs. For the overseas workers, this may redefine their role and commit them even more to the people, but it may also create conflicts with the mandate or the criteria of the humanitarian organization. It could also create the need to evaluate realistically the possibilities and the consequences of more involvement.

People who work in humanitarian aid "represent" the Western world, and the populations they work with often approach them to express their suffering, make claims, or protest situations of injustice. This identification with the stereotype of the country of origin, especially when a relationship of trust has yet to be established, can be the source of con-

flict. For example, in the crisis and massacres in Rwanda, Belgian overseas workers working there found themselves the object of anti-Belgian
feelings (Sydor and Philippot 1995). On other occasions, as in certain
moments of the armed conflicts in El Salvador and Chiapas, these prejudices have been used in campaigns against foreigners—for example, the
criminalization of NGOs—as part of strategies to isolate affected populations and to limit solidarity.

In the face of such ethical dilemmas, people can feel powerless given
the magnitude of the problems and the ineffectiveness of those who
have the authority to solve them. In these cases, many may ask themselves the question that ends the following testimony, taken from the
Vietnamese refugee camps in Hong Kong: Who is listening?

At the beginning of 1989, we discussed what our role was in the camp. It was a
constant dilemma: whether it was better that we stay in the camp to provide an
essential but minimal service to the refugees, hoping that this was the best solution. . . . The whole time we had strong feelings about the detention of these
people and the unjust screenings we were witness to. I stayed, of course, but I
used the contacts I had to send information out of Hong Kong to those who
could lobby against what was happening.

The most difficult situation was when the refugees protested by slashing their
stomachs in front of us. A group of agency workers and staff from UNHCR
decided to meet to discuss what could be done. Some of the Vietnamese found
out about the meeting. As they couldn't enter, they slashed their stomachs in
front of the door. I will never forget how I felt as I was being escorted by the
security forces, passing by the injured and the rest of the people from the camp.
You could feel the powerlessness of these people in the air. My heart was full of
despair. What affected me most was that I represented the hope and power of
the West, and yet I was completely powerless.

I will never forget that day in May 1990. One hundred tear gas bombs were
thrown at section 5 of the detention center called White Head. That day we
weren't allowed to enter the camp. When we were finally allowed to enter, I was
showered with requests to communicate to the outside what was happening. I
told many people, but I've just found out that last week, on April 13, 1994, 557
tear gas bombs were thrown. Who is listening? (Maryanne Loughry, Letter to
RSP, April 1994)

Moral dilemmas like these show that humanitarian actors must be bear-
ers of a distinct ethic that pervades all that they do, so that humanitarian
aid respects the dignity of the people it proposes to help (Brauman
1993).

Stress in Humanitarian Aid Work

Humanitarian aid work usually takes place in stressful situations—
stressful both for the affected populations and for the overseas workers.
Violence places a direct threat on those who work in human rights or

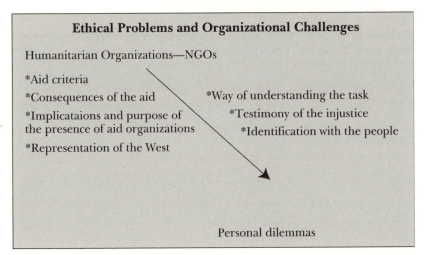

Ethical Problems and Organizational Challenges

Humanitarian Organizations—NGOs

*Aid criteria

*Consequences of the aid   *Way of understanding the task

*Implicataions and purpose of   *Testimony of the injustice
the presence of aid organizations   *Identification with the people

*Representation of the West

Personal dilemmas

development. In humanitarian aid, the following overlapping categories of stress are used: day-to-day stress, accumulated stress, and stress related to suffering and death (CICR 1994). Day-to-day stress is related to the rhythm and volume of the work, frustrations, and the personal difficulties of adapting to a different and often trying situation. This daily stress, within the limits that can be faced on one's own, can act as a stimulus for working and may even be positive for the humanitarian aid experience. Accumulated stress, which can be caused by one's living conditions, threatening situations, the difficulty of finding rest, and the lack of one's usual social support may, over time, result in health problems or emotional difficulties (see the section Effects of Stress later in this chapter). "One of the main factors of tension or stress is powerlessness. We do a lot but always feel helpless over the violence against the civilian population. In many cases, we either doubt the effectiveness of our actions or we are often faced with the insensitivity of the people around us" (CAD-DHHC 1997). (Stress related to suffering and death will be addressed in the next section.)

Dealing with Misery and Pain

Dealing with situations of extreme poverty, suffering, and death is another part of humanitarian work that creates stress and anxiety. It may arise from serious incidents like violence or threats of violence, or from the traumatic situations that workers share with people in the course of performing their daily tasks. All this can lead to feelings of powerlessness, guilt, and sadness.

The brutality that causes so many of the deaths leaves a lasting impression. The aim is to terrorize, and often it tortures the imagination with thoughts of the victim's suffering, which can alter a person's view of reality. Some people prefer not to know the details of some deaths, as they can be especially gruesome. This is a normal reaction, as long as it doesn't become a long-term avoidance of the truth about certain cases. Some of the cases we receive open up old wounds of the pain of other deaths. Each case brings us sadness. The pain is greater when we know the victims. In addition to the direct victims, we also suffer for the surviving orphan children. (Testimony from members of Amnesty International, 1997, in author's field notes)

People who provide humanitarian aid may also have vicarious experiences. This can happen when they see or share the traumatic experiences of the population they are working with, especially if they identify with a person's story or suffering. Listening to traumatic testimonies can also have a physiological effect. Workers may remember or relive their own previous traumatic experiences. In psychoanalytic terms, this is known as countertransference (Wilson and Lindy 1994). All of this implies that those who work with people who suffer should be aware of their own limitations and have their own way of coping with the stress, including following organizational strategies (see the section Organizational Strategies later in this chapter).

All of us were shocked when we listened to the testimonies. For some of us, it was the first time we had ever dealt with such brutal violence. For those who had gone through similar experiences themselves it was even more painful, because it was like reliving the pain and suffering. We had to limit the number of testimonies, reassign some people, and hold meetings once in a while to share our feelings, support each other, and do leisure activities. (Recovery of Historical Memory Project Team, Guatemala, 1998, in author's field notes)

Dealing with death may also reveal other, more positive things: the importance of other aspects of life, the capacity one has to face negative events, what one's priorities are, and the positive attributes one possesses. For example, 35 percent of the members of the rescue team who worked on a derailment said that, as a result of their involvement in the event, they had a more positive view of their own lives (Hodgkinson and Stewart 1991).

Organizational Stress

The structural organization of most groups is quite complex. The groups follow a mandate in which their actions, roles, and tasks are clearly defined. As discussed earlier, this orderliness can help to prevent problems, but organizational structures can themselves become a source of stress. "When supervising and evaluating programs, the different criteria of NGOs and agencies are often a source of organizational stress. The need to adjust projects to the 'fashionable' criteria of the moment means that local NGOs place a huge effort in redefining priorities when there is a change of approach. For the agencies, failure to adhere to deadlines, lack of specific information, and so forth are also sources of stress" (CADDHHC 1997).

Common organizational stress factors include the distance between hierarchies and the inability to make independent decisions; the bureaucratic nature of the work with too many regulations, formalities, and a feeling that the purpose of the action is lost; conflicts with the mandate for being too strict or too ambiguous at times and thus not followed by workers or counterparts. Ambiguity in the role allows space for creativity, but it also means that the person has to expend energy to define his or her daily tasks. A rigidly defined role loses the capacity for innovation and leads to routine monotony. Some key factors in preventing organizational stress are clarity in tasks and responsibilities, as well as participation of workers in decision-making processes and periodic assessments.

Effects of Stress

> How can you work with people who have gone through such horrific experiences? It is not easy. It means becoming completely involved. In the first year, nearly everybody on the team suffered from nightmares. This was especially the case after Tuesdays, the day we received people. Hardly anyone on the team could get up on Wednesday morning.
>
> —R. Mollica, M.D., Director, Indochinese Psychiatric Clinic, Boston, Mass., quoted in Stearns 1993

INDIVIDUALS

Generally, people who work in humanitarian aid have not faced experiences as traumatic as those of the affected population. However, by working and observing in disaster situations, they can sometimes show similar physical, cognitive, emotional, behavioral or spiritual effects (Hodgkinson and Stewart 1991).

Because of the nature of the work, which requires quick decisions and flexibility, people can often feel stress. As a result, people suffer from difficulties concentrating, being flexible, focusing their thoughts on a specific problem, and making evaluations and decisions. Stress has a negative effect on the way work is done. It contributes to absenteeism or taking refuge in easier or more repetitive tasks. Other effects include substance abuse or engaging in other risky behavior. On an emotional level, stress puts people under pressure and makes them lose interest in their work or in the population, which can lead to disappointment, victimization, or distrust (Cherniss 1980). All of these are examples of cumulative stress that should be confronted as soon as they appear. "Such prolonged contact with violence often makes me feel numb. It is a defense mechanism against suffering. I feel emotionally drained. I know it is normal, but I've also realized that it is important not to be hardened by it and therefore lose the capacity to feel solidarity" (J. Martínez, DDHH, NGO, Chiapas, 1998, in author's field notes).

If a person does not perceive these effects or is unable to take measures to confront the situation better, he or she runs the risk of "burning out." Burnout is characterized by fatigue, frustration, low self-esteem and little interest in other people (Rawnsley 1989). A person may go through different stages, such as enthusiasm, feeling numb, frustration, and apathy. The person does not have the energy to face problems or to improve his or her physical or emotional state. The situation becomes unbearable and requires immediate attention. To avoid this, it is necessary to identify cumulative stress early to encourage coping mechanisms and other organizational strategies.

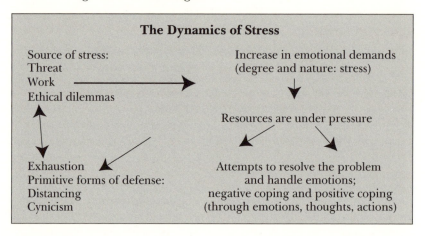

The Dynamics of Stress

Source of stress:
Threat
Work
Ethical dilemmas

Increase in emotional demands
(degree and nature: stress)

Resources are under pressure

Exhaustion
Primitive forms of defense:
Distancing
Cynicism

Attempts to resolve the problem
and handle emotions;
negative coping and positive coping
(through emotions, thoughts, actions)

The Group

Reactions to stress do not occur only within the individual; they occur also in the interactions between people. Tension can cause an increase in verbal aggression or the isolation of some people. The group members may behave negatively to avoid the problem, allowing silence to reign, or may keep busy so they do not have to think. When facing a difficult or an uncertain situation, people may cling to rigid rules or fall back on prejudices. These types of reactions may cause the group to become a source of stress for overseas workers instead of a source of mutual support.

Negative Group Reactions to Stress

- Inflexibility regarding norms or assessment criteria.
- Hyperactivity: group members keep themselves occupied in repetitive tasks or by taking refuge in their work.
- Lack of attention to the infrastructure and climate of the group (housing, food, etc.)
- Silence: group members avoid discussion of issues that cause tension, which increases avoidance behavior and stress.
- Negative emotional climate ("Nothing can be done") or controlled behavior ("You have to be careful what you say").
- Blaming one person: group members focus the problem on one person when the real cause is the uneasiness of the group.
- Constant discussion of work and issues of concern without respecting spaces away from work. Problems are discussed, but not in a way suited to finding solutions.

In long-lasting stressful situations, groups may not find the space to address their problems in a constructive way. In tense situations, otherwise normal group problems such as difficulties getting along with group members or disagreements between members more easily affect the basic rules of operation or the mutual trust within the group. Teams should pay attention to group dynamics and treat it as if it were part of the working agenda.

Coping with Stress: To Share Feelings or Not

The positive or negative ways of coping with stress depend on the moment, the context, and so forth. What might be negative in one situation may actually be effective in another. In addition, individuals have different styles or ways of dealing with negative emotions or stress. In highly stressful or dangerous situations, people often contain their emotions to be able to face the problem and defend themselves from the circumstances. This inhibition can protect the person from feelings of anxiety. However, the suppression of emotion or negative thoughts entails great effort. If it becomes "chronic," it may stimulate unwanted thoughts in addition to the psychological expenditure and psychological fatigue (Pennebaker 1995). When a problem is difficult to control, a person may drop to a "lower level" of thinking (trying not to think, avoiding the problem, oversimplifying, and so on). Sometimes, this is done "automatically"—a person may drop to this level without being aware of it and thus the ability to be aware of what is going wrong also drops. The person becomes a prisoner of a paradox (a person may think something is right when in reality it is wrong). People who inhibit their thoughts or emotions have a "self-repressive" way of coping with problems, which in turn may become a health risk.[1] If everything "goes well" (if their defense mechanisms "work"), people can handle difficult situations; however, when flexibility is needed, people may have more difficulties in adapting. For example, they might find it hard to identify their feelings, listen to other people, change their view of the problem, and so forth. Lower levels of thinking such as addiction to television, religion, and ideologies or religions with rigid forms of thinking may be useful to people because they offer simple answers to senseless tragedies.

Flexible thinking is generally healthier and less stressful than rigid thinking. A lower level of thinking avoids both the problem and the feelings of a lack of control. A higher level of thinking allows for thought about the complexity of the problem. If one has potential control over a problem, it is an advantage to be aware of its different facets and the context that surrounds it. In traumatic experiences, it is important to be flexible, to talk to other people, and to admit one's emotional state. It is also true that uninhibited people may feel more stress if they cannot speak (for fear of reprisals), whereas the inhibited person can adapt more easily to this situation.

Avoiding the Breaking Point

1. People who have experienced very difficult situations often refer to a type of breaking point. This could be the case of a rock climber, for example, who is surprised by his or her own strength, and then suddenly, within minutes, loses his or her grip and falls. This same situation has been described in other highly stressful physical or psychological situations like being in prison or in concentration camps (where people who encourage others and seem to manage well, suddenly "break"). On many other occasions, after having passed the most stressful point and reacted well, the person may become ill or suffer from serious health problems. The person may then suffer from complete exhaustion, both physical and psychological.
2. Even though a person feels very capable, it is important for him or her to act in a balanced and rational way to avoid reaching the breaking point.
3. A person must keep a balanced rhythm regarding sleep and meals. Although a person may not feel hungry or tired, the lack of food, sleep, and basic care weakens one physically and psychologically and can lead to exhaustion.

INDIVIDUAL PATTERNS

The alternatives when facing stress are to act on the source, to decrease its effects, and to change the manner of confronting it. Chapter 5 described the basic aspects of individual coping mechanisms and the importance of social support. Most humanitarian aid workers are from the West and are familiar with some forms of stress management, such as exercising on a regular basis; eating a balanced diet; getting rest, sufficient sleep, and time for relaxation; and engaging in healthy activities.

These are all positive ways to manage stress, but they are difficult to implement. Under precarious conditions, it is not always possible to have a bed, an individual room, or sufficient time to rest. Overseas workers need to be aware of their needs but also of the influence their behavior has on the population. For example, it would be extremely insensitive to drink alcohol when it is banned from use by the local population. Therefore, a flexible and sensitive attitude is needed when adapting to the local context.

Despite the practical limitations, communicating with family and friends helps people to maintain social relationships, share experiences, and avoid focusing endlessly on problems. Also, writing about the traumatic experiences is a positive way of dealing with them, as long as it does not become an intellectual exercise (that avoids one's feelings) or a substitute for action (where writing becomes a way of taking refuge from the demands of the situation).

Attitudes for Coping with Stress within the Group

- Accept your own limitations and do not put moral pressure on others. Increasing pressure on ourselves can be useful in moments of crisis, but later it can cause exhaustion.
- Accept your feelings and do not deny others the right to have feelings. Inhibiting your emotions can help when a certain action is required, but over time this can lead to a loss of energy and lack of communication.
- Look after yourself and avoid self-blame. Identifying problems, errors, or responsibilities is useful, but blame often leads to paralysis.
- Accept any reaction as normal after an extreme situation. If we avoid labeling experiences as pathological, we are more able to accept reactions in ourselves and in others. Nonetheless, we should still pay attention to unusual reactions as they might be a cause for concern.
- Acknowledge the right to rest. Preventive measures are linked to welfare and quality of work.
- Affirm life. Despite the suffering, try to inject the joy of living into every task with the affected population.

Source: CADDHHC 1997.

Mutual support between people working in humanitarian aid helps to improve stress management and gives the experience more meaning. For example, when an important decision is to be made in an ethical dilemma, group discussion and group decision-making helps to reduce guilt. However, competitiveness among organizations working in the same place—say, over who is in charge of carrying out certain actions—may decrease the possibility for mutual support among workers.

ORGANIZATIONAL STRATEGIES

The organizational strategies that can be used to diminish sources of stress or improve workers' stress management include prior training, supervision, changes in the organization of the work, and follow-up support to address worker's experiences. Institutional factors that can improve stress management are the consideration of psychological needs and the degree of flexibility and innovation within the organization.

The training of humanitarian aid workers plays a preventive role. Part of the training is general background (knowledge of the country, the political situation, culture, and so on) and technical preparation (the project, activities, and so on). Another part should be to give greater importance to humanitarian aid work and the experiences involved in it to increase people's ability to handle stress. This is done not only through stress-management training but also by increasing technical competence and knowledge of the situation and clarifying the role of the aid worker.

Supervision entails discussing difficult cases or ways of solving problems with a professional or manager in the organization, who plays a supportive role during the action. Efficient supervision should help to handle difficult situations and improve self-confidence, and should be sensitive to the needs of the worker. Adequate feedback will help to evaluate the work after it is done.

It is especially important to prevent reaching "points of no return," whether of an individual or a political nature. Continuous monitoring of a situation as well as of the individuals and teams responsible for the work will help to evaluate whether the political space is too restricted or if the negative effects of a particular action or the accumulation of stress pose a risk to workers' health or to the work itself.

Another way to diminish stress is to rotate highly stressful jobs and to establish rest periods (CICR 1994), but changes of location often conflict with the continuity of an action and the confidence workers may have gained with a population. A balance is needed between the workers' needs and those of the population, and the objectives of the action, the tasks of the each participant, and communication rules must be clearly defined, as this can help diminish stress in uncertain or ambiguous situations. Mechanisms for self-evaluation and participation in decision-making processes should be part of any humanitarian organization, as these can help to improve the management of the difficulties.

Coping with Critical Incidents

Some experiences are especially difficult to handle. Critical incidents such as threats or being a witness to violence generate high levels of stress. In addition to coping with the initial impact of the experience, the person has also to learn to live with the experience and find ways to increase his or her confidence and go back to working normally in such a situation.

Although all situations are unique, following are some suggestions on how to promote support and improve the energy of a group that has to face disasters.

1. Make something positive from the experience. Keep active when an event is still very close. If the person feels okay, he or she might even be surprised by this and wonder when it will hit, but this is not necessarily going to happen, even if difficulties almost always appear after a few days. The first priority is the mission, its safety, and its coordination. Don't act rashly. Make group decisions, and don't be led by impulse reactions. Engage in joint activities intended to relieve tension and to keep people from constantly focusing on the problem.

2. It is quite common to have sleeping problems and nightmares, to have recurring thoughts about the event, or to find oneself in a permanent state of alert. These reactions will disappear in time and they should not interfere with one's daily work.

3. After a few days, things that do not get included in reports but are very important, such as sensations, experiences, a change in how one sees the work or the world have to be shared with the group. Highly stressful situations may bring the group closer, but they can also make small problems seem much larger. Look after the dynamic of the group and avoid misunderstandings. Pay particular attention to the effect of rumors. Take the time to analyze them, compare information, get opinions from outside, and keep calm.

4. It is most difficult to return to "normal" after the event. Analyze the situation after a few days to see what has changed within the group.

5. Maintain a healthy diet and a healthy working rhythm to be able to cope with this type of situation.
6. Regarding the work, avoid extreme reactions, whether complete paralysis (nothing can be done right now) or acting as if nothing has happened. Make realistic working plans, including time for meetings and rest periods. Do not hold meetings constantly, although some meetings may be inevitable. Try not to dwell on the situation. In moments of confusion, the group may need more time together, but try to add creativity to the meetings to break the routine. Take breaks as necessary.
7. Meet as a group to share information and to make group decisions. All participants should be patient and open. Keep in mind that victims of the threat might find it difficult to explain all the details, or they may feel that others do not really understand their situation.
8. Discuss security, which will probably be an important part of the reorganization of daily life once the extreme event has passed. Take greater precautions, but do not do so obsessively. Maintain group decisions and, if necessary, set dates on which to review them.
9. Avoid constant discussion about the problem, especially at night; each person should have some time for him- or herself before going to bed. Reinforce what has been achieved and avoid being overcome by fear. Keep a sense of humor to distance yourself from the event and put yourself in a good mood. Keep a daily "routine" to stay active, even though it may have to change from week to week. If it is difficult to find time with the group to share experiences, find someone you trust and talk to that person.

Knowing all of these suggestions is not the solution, but following them may make finding the solution easier.

The Difficulty of Returning

The experience or the stress caused by these situations may not be over when workers finish their work and return to their native countries. They might have problems coming to terms with their experiences or reintegrating into society—finding work and reestablishing friendships.

After having worked abroad for a long time or having had difficult experiences, overseas workers may need to share their experiences with people who know them well and understand them (family, friends, colleagues, and so on). However, the different rhythms and styles of life and the differing importance of the experience for workers and for their families and friends may make it difficult to share experiences. Therefore, overseas workers may face two culture shocks: one in the place where they have done their humanitarian work and another on their return because of the banality and the ethnocentrism of the people of their own culture (Moghaddan, Taylor & Wright, 1993). Workers who are returning should be aware of these difficulties, avoiding seeing themselves as victims or overrating themselves, in order to reintegrate more constructively.

Some people may also have experienced critical or traumatic events and need support. In these cases, it may be useful to look for individual help or share these experiences in a support group. With these psychosocial demands, an NGO needs mechanisms in place for people who have been affected by traumatic experiences to be able to ask for help.

However, these forms of support must be meaningful and respond to the needs of the people, especially when these overseas workers have had to leave the country because they were arrested and released or because of an increase in violence or threats. These people may have been more affected and have a sense that their experience is "incomplete." Fear or anxiety for the people who are still there may be another added element. Because the experiences have had a social cause, these people may feel the need to do something positive for the society they have been working in (for example, to give testimony or organize activities) and not just to seek support in resolving their psychological problems.

The people of Sudan are marvelous. The foreigners would go back to the safety of our homes and the warmth of our families and friends, who offered us all their moral support, however difficult that may be. But those people we left behind had no escape and they couldn't go on resisting. Despite their terrible situation, they did everything they could to console me, saying that they accepted their destiny. They only asked one thing of us: that we return home, rest and recover, and then talk about them to our families, friends, countrymen, that we tell the world about them so that they wouldn't forget them. That is why I'll never stop talking about them. (M. Knoppers 1996, 278)

To recover their sense of action in a new context is a challenge for the people when they return home. The importance of committing to changing things from their home and of sharing their experiences unites the need for reintegration and the need for continuing other types of humanitarian aid work, including political action that works to alleviate people's suffering.

Chapter 7
Cross-Cultural Interactions

When John Hardbattle, a Bosquimano-kwe from Kalahari, was a child, his mother talked to him about the variety of populations: "God created all of us. We are all equal. But we are different."

—IWGIA 1992

Cross-cultural interactions are a part of humanitarian aid, whether among relief workers working in another country, populations who have been displaced, or multicultural aid organizations. Those who work in cross-cultural situations must understand their own reactions and the cultural variability in work and social relations. Being aware of other peoples' symbols, ways of life, and modes of communication can help aid workers behave according to the norms of a given place, promote culturally sensitive interventions, and reduce the stress of cross-cultural interactions.

This chapter begins by setting out the basic issues surrounding the interaction between cultures. It then reviews the cultural differences and the difficulties of cultural interaction and finishes by discussing three practical experiences: (1) cultural differences in the framework of cooperation with Latin America, (2) reverse culture shock when relief workers or emigrants return to their countries of origin, and (3) communication between people of Western and Asian cultures.

The Relationship Between Culture and a Context of Domination. Culture is a product of society, and in many countries where there has been political domination, cultural forms of adaptation have arisen. Far from naturalizing social behaviors as part of "the culture," many collective reactions or attitudes are a result of oppressive social contexts. The so-called "Latin American fatalism" or the "culture of poverty" are clichés that do not consider the historic conditions that these peoples have endured. When these attitudes are taken to be natural, the perception of a need for change is lost. For example, according to some writers, the most humble sectors of the Latin American nations often demonstrate social conformism; it is part of the fatalism that leads them to accepting their lives as governed by external powers over which they have no control. According to Martín-Baró (1989), fatalism is a consequence of colonial domination. Coerced conformism was an instrument that reduced the need for physical coercion to maintain power.

Stereotypes and Generalizations. Generalizations about cultural characteristics (for example, "Chilean people are cheerful") should not allow us to lose sight of intracultural variability. Many differences—individual, socioeconomic, ethnic, or geographic—exist within a society.

Political and Social Violence. War and political repression have left many marks on the lives of the people. How they have adapted to violence (for example, silence as a response in many Mayan communities in Mexico or Guatemala) may be more important than cultural differences. To understand the reactions of the people, it is important to bear in mind not only cultural differences but also the context.

The Impact of Cooperation. The significance and impact of the aid influences transcultural interactions. The cultural impact of humanitarian aid—both in its conception and in its actuality—should be part of an evaluation. In particular, it is important to evaluate how it has furthered organizational processes and social emancipation within contexts of cultural difference, such as when, for example, money is introduced into community relations or when priority has been given to one group over another.

Stereotypes, Prejudices, and Discrimination

El pueblo salvadoreño	*The Salvadoran People*
Los hace lo todo	They do it all
los vende lo todo	They sell it all
los come lo todo	They eat it all
—*Roque Dalton*	

Stereotypes and prejudices influence cultural interactions. Stereotypes are ways of organizing information to describe the characteristics of a certain social category. Walter Lippman (1922) defined them as "pictures in our heads." For example, a stereotype of refugees is that they are passive and helpless victims. Stereotypes influence not only interpersonal relationships but also how humanitarian aid is organized. Certain assumptions tend to be made—that there are no professionals among the refugees of a camp, or that, if there are, none of them is competent to help. Therefore, humanitarian aid tends to import professionals instead of using those available locally.

Stereotypes favor selective perception; that is, people are more inclined to perceive events that confirm their stereotypes. During the distribution of food, for example, any difficulties the population may have using unfamiliar scales would confirm their supposed inability to manage food distribution, which leads later to the refugees being described as passive people. Another example: the news of drug trafficking in a marginal neighborhood with high immigration gets turned into a confirmation of the stereotypical association of immigrants with illegal activities.

These images based on partial or biased information contribute to the creation of prejudices. The words *victim*, *passive*, and *helpless* imply both a negative moral judgment and a paternalistic attitude. Negative evaluations become forms of discrimination when they lead to not employing refugees or giving them work below their abilities or under conditions that the aid workers would not accept themselves. The mass media and international organizations providing aid are where we receive the frequent images of miserable, passive victims of large-scale disasters or famine.

Code of Conduct: Images and Messages about the Third World

1. Avoid either catastrophic or idealized images that appeal more to charitable feelings than to serious reflection.
2. Present all people in such a way as to preserve their identity and dignity, with background information on their society, culture, and economic means.
3. Use real testimonies instead of the interpretations of a third party.
4. Highlight people's ability to take care of themselves.
5. Mention internal and external obstacles to development.
6. Underscore interdependence and joint responsibility for underdevelopment.
7. Avoid all kinds of discrimination (racial, sexual, cultural, religious, socioeconomic, etc.).
8. Consult those from "the South" in the creation of any kind of message.
9. When collecting funds, ensure that the recommendations of this code of conduct are respected.

Source: Comité de Enlace ONGD-UE 1989.

Even though the use of stereotypes is often denied, they appear subconsciously within attitudes or in nonverbal behaviors (such as the use of a childlike tone of voice). Not including the local population in decision-making processes, or not allowing members of the local population to participate, is a form of discrimination. This discrimination has been evident, to take one example, in the Comprehensive Plan of

Action in Asia, where decisions were made on the repatriation of asylum seekers in their absence.

Cultural interactions take place amid relationships of power. Power has been defined according to three basic criteria: It is based on the possession of resources, it occurs in social relationships, and it produces effects in that same social relationship (Martín-Baró 1989). The asymmetry of power between NGOs and the affected populations constitutes a form of power that skews cross-cultural interactions toward the dominant perspective. Making the interests of aid fit the needs of the population diminishes this risk.

Collective disasters may also reinforce stereotypes and prejudices between certain social or ethnic groups. The interruption of a common life and cultural exchange in previously multicultural societies can lead to confrontations and justifications of violence, as was the case in the Bosnian War. In other cases, such as in Africa under the effects of colonialism, changes in interethnic relations, promoted by local elites under the control of the metropole, have provoked many wars or outbreaks of violence against civilians.

In this sense, changing the stereotypes within humanitarian aid itself as well as stereotypes about the genesis of conflicts is necessary. According to a survey carried out by NGOs, one out of two people think that the basis of the relationship between so-called first- and third-world countries is based on the need third-world countries have for aid from the richer countries (Comité de Enlace ONGD-UE 1989). The risk of stereotypes is that they encourage people to think that poverty is a fact in itself (as in a "culture of poverty") rather than a consequence of the social system and the international relationships surrounding it. When this contextual framework is forgotten, the demand for change falls not on society or on the system but on the individual.

Cultural Differences and Similarities

> The Europeans don't know. They see a black man and they don't where he from. For them, all Africa the same, all blacks the same. They don't know which country. Europeans speak only colonial language. . . .
>
> —Omar from Ethiopia, in Díaz 1998, 18

Cultural differences also influence cross-cultural interactions. Many different definitions and approaches to culture exist. Kluckhon (1952) found more than one hundred definitions or explanations referring to values, knowledge, rules, ways of understanding life, and so forth. *Culture* thus is a series of behaviors, emotional experiences, and implicit knowledge shared among the members of a group or a community.

Given its taken-for-granted nature, even those people who are familiar with a culture may find it difficult to explain.

The study of values has been a focus of interest in the research on cultural similarities and differences. Hofstede (1980) identified four dimensions in which values manifest themselves: individualism-collectivism, masculinity-femininity, regulation and control, and distances from power or hierarchy. Differences in values explain the different relationships between a person and a group and the different ways of dealing with problems and the uncertainties of life (Díaz-Loving et al. 1981). Relationships between men and women and relationships between individuals and forms of authority (and even nature) are both areas where culture differences in values become evident.

Industrialized societies of the North exhibit more individualistic characteristics—that is, they express the concerns of the individual over those of the group—whereas African, Asian, or Latin American societies exhibit more collectivist values with a more stable relationship between the individual and the informal groups he or she belongs to. Rockeach (in Morales et al. 1994) measured differences between Africans (collectivist) and Europeans (individualist) on a scale of values. The Africans valued a peaceful world, salvation, national security, equality, and social recognition; the Europeans valued true friendship, family security, mature love, a beautiful world, and an exciting life. The comparison between such diverse populations should be treated with care; however, these differences indicate that the Africans have more communal and social values, and the Europeans focus more on the people immediately around them and the meaning of their individual lives. The influence of a community-oriented approach is evident in the way problems are discussed, the process by which decisions are made, and the degree to which experiences are shared. "We call this process [the decision-making process] a qualitative democracy in Naam [an ethnic group in Burkina Faso]. Within the Naam movement, to avoid the drum leaders, we have set up a qualitative democracy as opposed to a quantitative democracy. In the Naam groups, we carry out our elections by consensus. The drum politicians in fact prevent our development. The Naam groups discuss together until they find the adequate person for each position" (testimony from Burkina Faso).

Culture and Emotions

In the study of cultural differences, another point of interest is the experience and expression of emotions. Differences in emotional experience are important for humanitarian aid workers to consider because such differences determine how an event is experienced collectively, how dif-

FOUNDATIONS FOR THE DESCRIPTION OF A CULTURE

Subjective Culture	Objective
1. Beliefs, norms, and values are based on Relationship with authority Relationship between the individual and the group Relationship between men and women Family models Management of conflicts Relationship between individual and nature Concept of work Concept of time Death and religion Concept of ownership 2. Important roles within the social structure, defined positions, expected conduct, and punishable behaviors for people. 3. Symbols and rituals	1. Production patterns 2. Habitat 3. Language

ferent individuals respond in crisis situations, and whether mental-health problems appear.

A cross-cultural similarity exists in facial expressions, perceived bodily changes, and inclinations toward action. The way people show sadness, happiness, anger, or fear is similar across cultures. However, the verbal expression of these emotions and how they are dealt with varies (Mesquita and Frijda 1992). In collectivist cultures, for example, people may feel worse because they are alone and cannot see their family; they may tend to look for the support of the community or carry out certain group activities or celebrations, more than in other cultures (Basabe et al. 1999).

In one culture, psychological suffering may be considered normal, but in another it may be considered embarrassing or abnormal. The person may be afraid of his or her own reactions, reject them, or even be unable to establish a link between the problem and the experience. In many cultures, suffering may be expressed "indirectly," such as through physiological problems. In others, the expression of emotions may be mediated by a series of factors such as culture, pain management, or gender roles.

"I didn't feel anything. He just died. What can you do? . . . I went to warn him. I met the police on the way. They hit me with a stick and asked me where I lived

	Individualist Culture	Collectivist Culture
Self-concept	• Individual, independent, assertive, self-confident	• Harmonious with others, modest, relational
Communication	• Verbal and direct, openly expresses affection and needs	• Nonverbal, indirect, expresses affection by fulfilling obligations
Doctor/patient relationship	• On equal level, little involvement	• Hierarchy, with deference; doctor is concerned about patient
Meaning of illness	• Illness means failure and one has to fight against it	• Illness means bad luck; it is normal, the result of things from the past and less avoidable

Source: Adapted from Nilchaitovit, Hill, and Holland 1993.

and where I was going. I was going to warn him, but he didn't pay attention . . ." [begins to cry]. The wife intervenes: "How can you say you didn't cry? You did cry over your brother." He says: "What's the use of crying? You are weak if you cry." (Testimony of relatives of detained or missing Mapuches, in Pérez Sales et al. 1998)

Another example of this variability in emotional aspects is in the concepts or ways of symbolizing and living one's experience. For example, an emotional state such as sadness is described and experienced very differently depending on the culture. In Western countries, we speak of "depression" and the causes and symptoms are similar. In Asian countries, however, sadness is not expressed so much in terms of subjective emotional reactions as it is in a wide variety of external, bodily symptoms (Marsella 1978). It is because of these differences that those who work in humanitarian aid need to develop a cultural awareness to improve their understanding and their ability to give support. "From an ethnolinguistic viewpoint, the Mapuche Mapuzugun have various words to define sadness. The term *Ürkuyawlu* seems to be the closest to the meaning of depression. The literal translation would be 'he who is tired.' The term *jazkün* is defined as sadness in some areas and in other parts of the region it is anger or rage" (Pérez Sales et al. 1998, 193).

If we consider some of the emotional aspects associated with the experiences of suffering and trauma in populations affected by violence, we find some of the following important differences:

- In rural and indigenous cultures, the suffering caused by traumatic experiences is often expressed through a somatic reaction and is conceptualized as "getting sick."
- In indigenous cultures, traditional explanations may be different from those in Western cultures and are likely to have consequences in how problems are handled. For example, in the Mayan culture trauma is associated with a "fright" that has to "taken out of the body."
- Certain everyday experiences such as dreams also have a different meaning. In indigenous cultures, dreams are considered a form of communication with ancestors or a premonition, and nightmares may not be considered the traumatic experiences they are in Western cultures.
- The presence of the deceased is part of everyday life in indigenous cultures, which makes the observance of rituals and ceremonies very important and which provides other explanations for the uncertainties of life.
- Many collectivist cultures have their own creative expression through dance or music, such as in black communities where music is a part of the grieving process and social relationship.

Concepts of Time and Space

Humanitarian interventions bring with them certain concepts of time and space, which influence both organizational criteria and the interaction with the population. Humanitarian aid is based on a Western concept of time, wherein time is something to be divided, segmented, and used in terms of speed and productivity. According to Grossin (1969), industrialization changed the relationship between time and work in Western societies. People do not eat when they are hungry; they eat because it is time to eat. Time is money, the saying goes, and it has to be used in the best way possible. Conversely, collectivist cultures have a more comprehensive vision of time; it passes more slowly and is used in terms of sociability. In many rural cultures, the concept of time is linked to the cycles of nature. This could mean, for example, that when there is to be a return of refugees, the NGOs are more concerned with the calendar and the population more concerned with the harvest and when they can start working the land.

Time is perceived as "slower" in Latin America than in North America (Zubieta et al. 1999). For example, the decision-making processes that a certain community is accustomed to may not reflect the urgency or short-term efficiency planned by the relief agency and workers. Without a certain cultural sensitivity, it is possible that a short-term project, even if it intends to have members of the local population participate in it, may establish a dynamic in which the people are not really able to take part, therefore becoming a subtle form of imposition. "Nobody decides for us. We have to consult. We have to think seriously about it. Time is the child of the earth, of the culture, of resistance. An NGO offered a lot of material to the communities of the Sierra for a school. We had to say yes or no within twenty-four hours because the person was going abroad. The decision took two months. They said: 'It's not possible. If we say yes, we cannot take the responsbility because it's [the NGO's] time, not ours" (Martín Beristain 1997, 90).

On an interpersonal level, this may mean that relief workers have to learn to take this concept of time into account and adapt themselves to the situation when they have informal encounters or meetings. In a place where nobody wears a watch or where schedules are part of formal communication and established norms (that is, punctual but the important thing is to arrive; to arrive "about an hour" after the agreed time, and so on), an excessive preoccupation with time is pointless and can be a source of stress.

Other cultural differences that may be important for daily life are those related to space and privacy. In indigenous cultures, physical closeness or touching between men and women may be seen as a sign of sexual interest and not as a form of support. People of other cultures, might be more tolerant of touching between men and women. People who work in the poor, rural communities of collectivist cultures may find their private space limited and their sense of privacy challenged when living in an open space. The concept of privacy in a place where there are no doors is indeed different, but that does not mean that it does not exist. It will help relief workers to observe and respect people's notions of space and ways of relating spatially to others in order to help to avoid conflicts.

The Role of Communication

Communication is a part of humanitarian aid, from managing information to teaching skills, whether in personal or work relationships. Humanitarian aid workers must bear in mind the needs of the population by establishing communication mechanisms and channels that allow for feedback from the people.

Anthropological studies have revealed that in communication between two people who do not share the same cultural framework, a higher probability exists that a misunderstanding will occur. Culture allows you to go from what you say to what you want to say (Bateson 1976). In many cultures, to consent does not always mean to agree; it can mean to avoid upsetting the other person. As opposed to the Western custom of asking directly, in Asia people tend to agree even if they do not, as a way of adapting to the situation or being friendly. People who work in humanitarian aid should learn about these behaviors; otherwise, they risk creating misunderstandings or conflicts.

"Yesterday, in the bar, lots of Moroccans, lots of them," Sergio tells me.

"You are like the Spanish, even though you are from Senegal," I said laughing. "I'm sure there were only a few Moroccans, but you say there were a lot, like the Spanish say."

"We Africans say that when the Spanish speak, they exaggerate. If a Spanish person speaks, they might say: Ah! There are many black people there, many! And maybe there's only one black man!" (Djili, Gambia, Díaz 1998, 138)

Communication is also a process of exchange. Humanitarian aid workers should keep in mind the exchange patterns and the meaning they acquire in the society in which they are working. For example, giving and receiving food is a form of communication, which might signify support or be seen as the maintenance of dependence. In the case of a therapeutic relationship, an intimate conversation between a therapist and patient is seen to be strange in some traditional societies. It would be more common to talk in the presence of family or friends who not only listen but also give their opinions. Talking about personal matters in a first interview may disturb people, so, especially in traditional cultures, a prior informal meeting is usually necessary to have a drink, talk about other aspects of life, and get to know each other before going on to other, more difficult issues. Nonverbal communication is another factor in this process. Whereas visual contact is common in Western cultures, in many cultures it may be common for people to look the other way while talking to you, as a sign of respect.

When communicating with someone, it is important to consider the relational aspects of the conversation. Too much concern for the content of what is being said without noticing how it is being said might lead to communication problems and conflict. This can happen in all cultures, but it is more likely to happen in collectivist cultures where interaction is centered not so much on goals as on keeping harmony in relationships and the cohesion of the group.

In his analysis of communication, Habermas (1989) has defined four key points to help interpret communication difficulties: lack of intelligibility, disagreement about the problem, unacceptable behavior, and distrust and lack of sincerity in the relationship. These four points are not static. Rather, they can help us to understand how a problem that starts with the lack of clarity (misunderstanding of an opinion) can be interpreted as a disagreement (to be against the idea) or how a behavior that is not acceptable (to speak loudly and abruptly) can be seen as a person acting in his own interests. All of these possible misunderstandings are more probable in cross-cultural interactions, given that the language, codes, and meanings are all different.

Keys for Communication

Intelligibility: Refers to the semantic-linguistic comprehension.

Truth: Refers to whether what is said is consistent with reality or with the shared references of reality.

Rectitude: Certain rules of communication should be adhered to.

Sincerity: There is an intention behind the communication: the person's credibility is at stake.

Source: Adapted from Habermas 1989.

Cultural differences, emotional climates of fear or tension, lack of knowledge of the language, and difficulties of working with translators—all of these factors may distort the communication process in the distribution of humanitarian aid. At the same time, communication is a key instrument in the work of humanitarian organizations that can help people to work together better and resolve everyday conflicts.

A translator is necessary when there are language barriers. Despite the obvious problems, some of which are summarized in the following table, the involvement of translators may help to ease communication as well as translate cultural concepts and ways of understanding things. (Chapter 8 discusses the difference between bicultural workers and translators). Translation can help aid workers to understand the forms of expression and the values of the people with whom they are working, and translators are often motivated to become more deeply involved in their work. Some of the NGOs that participated in mental-health programs in Bosnia-Herzegovina report that after a few weeks the translators knew the questions that were routinely made so well that they themselves became more deeply involved and were making fairly precise diagnoses.[1]

Working Relationships and Organizational Culture

The framework of humanitarian aid and cooperation, and the meaning that it has for both "sides," also influences cross-cultural interactions. As mentioned earlier, the possession of resources constitutes a form of power that can influence cross-cultural interactions. In addition, many agencies and NGOs have their own organizational culture—ways of

WORKING WITH TRANSLATORS

Potential Problems	Recommendations
• Ethnic origin that does not inspire confidence in local population • Incomplete knowledge of both languages. • Nature of the translation (censure or content changes, questions much longer than the original, etc.) • Effects of personal traumatic experiences of the translator.	• The translator should speak in first person (in the same way as the person who is speaking: *I was followed . . .*). • The translator must have empathy for the person. • The translator should have basic knowledge about what is being discussed. • The translator cannot have been overly affected by the situation. • The questions should be brief and precise.

organizing the work, rules and regulations, mandates, and so on—that not only makes up part of its internal methodology but also forms the basis for interacting with the population. Organizational cultures should try and adapt to the local context, rather than asking that the population adapt to the methods and criteria of the aid organizations.

When working with disadvantaged populations, workers require personal commitment, in addition to professionalism, to develop and carry out plans. Clear rules and guidelines that work to avoid patronage relationships, dependency, and personal overinvolvement are also necessary.

Concepts used in the North should be exchanged for ones used in the South. Most development and humanitarian aid projects (but also to some extent scientific exchanges) are one-directional in their conception and design, but, one cannot transfer the same child-development patterns used in, say, Sweden to rural communities in Honduras where children learn how to use a machete at a very early age.

Sometimes even progressive groups from the North have little cultural awareness. In the last years of the war in El Salvador, some feminist solidarity groups carried out campaigns on body awareness and contraception that clashed with the perceptions and ideas that local women had about themselves, and, in fact, were in accordance with the birth-control campaigns of the far right government.

Very often actions are designed "here" to be carried out "there," and the concepts used are those poular at the time in development agencies or government offices. Therefore, purported "counterparts" are obliged to learn the organizational culture of the North and lay out their priorities in terms of what is acceptable to those with the resources, even when this may not correspond to their real needs. One year, agencies might be able to finance projects "for women," as others promote "social participation" or "sustainable development" projects that have to be written following a particular "logical framework." The effect is that the needs of the "donor" precede and mediate those of the people. For example, the organizational culture that works based on short-term contracts rooted in institutional politics (with frequent rotations of staff) penetrates through to the local situation.

Peltzer (1996) analyzed the expectations for the operation of a center for torture victims in Malawi and found marked differences between the Europeans who supervised the project and the local professionals from Malawi, as summarized in the following list:

Supervisors from the North	*Local Staff from the South*
• Expect initiative, goals from local staff.	• Expect to follow a working guideline.
• Expect a personal commitment to the program.	• Expect understanding toward their personal and family situations.
• Wish to see a gradual transfer of responsibility from the North to the local staff of the South.	• Are not motivated by more responsibility; prefer a system of reinforcement through sanctions.
• See all workers as "equal."	
• Consider that research should be an essential part of the center.	• See everyone's social origin as different; believe that castes and status should be respected.
• See work as an important source of personal development.	• Expect research to be carried out under the close supervision of the director.
• Believe that decisions should be made by consensus in an assembly.	• See the center as a way to earn a living with good working conditions.
	• Decisions were later changed by a person who consulted with a closed circle of people.

As shown in this list, the respective expectations do not match because of cultural differences. For example, the European approach to relationships of power, ways of making decisions, and collective and personal goals is different from the African approach. This implies the existence of different organizational cultures. Sometimes it is difficult to break the relationship pattern that exists between NGOs from the North and

South. In some way, the relationship of dependency that often arises in refugee populations is a result not only of the suffering and trauma they have faced, but also of the type of "donor-receiver" relationship that the NGOs and humanitarian aid agencies have established for years. All of this can easily lead to irritation and mutual rejection.

Development or aid programs should take into account the violence and disasters that a population has suffered. Despite enormous suffering, people and communities have developed survival mechanisms and creative ways of coping with problems, which have a cultural basis. Part of the task of development work is not only to provide assistance but to support these mechanisms and organizational processes.

In a deeper sense, the consideration of cultural aspects should bring about mutual learning and enrichment, both personal and collective. Many communal values—such as a respect for nature—not only are traditional values in many cultures but also may form the basis for reinventing a future for everybody.

"Why do you speak to the Earth, give it water, burn sugar and incense, and take flowers?" many ask me.

And I answer: "Where do you think your clothes come from? Those clothes are made of cotton and they come from the coast; where does your food come from, vegetables. What does the chicken eat? The Earth gives everything to us and we have to be grateful, we have to talk to the Earth and that's why we say *nan*. Where do you spit, where do you bathe? The Earth gives you everything and that's why you should appreciate it, and the Moon because it gives us light, and the Sun because it gives warmth to the plants. (Ajanel, in Solares 1993)

Culture Shock and Acculturative Stress

When people move around, they confront another culture, and the differences between cultures become obvious. This interaction can create ambiguity, communication problems, and the need to learn to live in another culture. In the case of refugees, these problems will appear especially in the settlement stages. The problems depend on the cultural identity, the attitude of the receiving population, and the relationships that are established (Berry 1991). The ease with which the Karen refugees, escaping from Myanmar (formerly Burma), integrated into the Thai population was due to the cultural proximity of the populations, the good relations while living together, and the receiving population's attitude of solidarity—in addition to the possibility of self-organizing in small camps (Bowles 1998).

Cultural interactions can be a positive learning experience or they can entail a degree of stress, called culture shock or acculturative stress. The concept of *culture shock* was developed by Oberg (1961), who defined it as a generalized state of depression, frustration, and disorientation that people experience when they are in a new culture. Culture shock generally occurs when there is a loss of familiar reference points, which generates a state of confusion.

Culture shock is characterized by the following symptoms: stress or fatigue caused by the effort of adapting to a new culture, a sense of loss and feelings of nostalgia, rejection of the receiving population or vice versa, confusion about roles and role expectations, a sometimes painful awareness of the differences between cultures, and a feeling of helplessness because one is not able to act competently (Taft 1977).

The concepts of acculturative stress and culture shock overlap. The acculturation process may mean that people have to confront new sources of stress and activate new mechanisms to cope with it. The stress produced by culture shock is greater when the cultural interaction has been forced, such as in the case of displaced people and refugees.

For immigrants or refugees, especially those who move to countries of the North, the culture shock may entail a series of stages corresponding to time, expectations, financial resources, and capabilities (Páez et al. 1997):

1. The first stage would be marked by euphoria or relief at having overcome the danger or the obstacles of the journey. A person arrives in a new place where he or she can fulfill his or her dreams. The person may become overactive in looking for work, housing, and support from others

2. Gradually the person may see things more realistically as he or she starts to face financial problems or discrimination. Communication problems, difficulty in contacting family members, and a yearning for what they have left behind can develop.

3. Later, a person may begin to experience anger because he or she is failing in attempts to be understood in the new culture (people laugh at the difficulties with the language, he or she is treated coldly, and so on).

4. Depression may appear six to nine months after arrival, when the person feels that he or she has not been successful in his or her efforts, that he or she cannot integrate or be accepted, and that what he or she has left behind cannot be replaced in the new country.

5. Finally, the person begins a gradual process of acceptance, during which the person begins to integrate, developing adaptive strategies. This is the start of a period of transition that can lead to different situations, as shown in the following table.

Assimilation occurs when one's previous cultural identity is lost and the new culture is taken on as one's own. Those who assimilate are those

MODELS OF CULTURAL INTERACTION

Identification with the receiving culture	Maintaining the Culture of Origin	
	Yes	No
Yes	Integration	Assimilation
No	Segregation	Marginalization

who avoid their compatriots, speak pejoratively about their country of origin, and try to integrate into Western society as quickly as possible. *Integration* is the maintenance of the culture of origin at the same time as acceptance of the differences of the receiving culture. This response corresponds to a bicultural identity. *Segregation* is when the culture of origin is maintained and the new culture is rejected. It is a superficial form of adaptation; for example, the person learns the language and how to manage housing, economic support, and so forth, but avoids all social contact and strongly rejects the values of the new culture. Finally, *marginalization* is the rejection of the culture of origin as well as the new culture (a lumpen proletariat isolated from the two cultures).

Research in places like Canada, France, and Spain confirms that the most common attitude is integration followed by assimilation and then segregation. Those who are marginalized suffer the most stress, but the people who accept assimilation into the dominant culture also tend to have lower self-esteem. Discrimination from the dominant culture explains both this stress and the low self-esteem. In general, the process of constructing a bicultural identity is very stressful, especially when there is little contact with the dominant culture, when people face discriminatory behavior, and when they have to accept low social status.

In addition to the personal differences, immigration or refugee policies in the receiving countries influence these models of interaction. Many people have to live with segregation or marginalization because they do not have documents to achieve legal immigrant status or are persecuted by the police and sent back to their home countries. Also, dispersion policies (to which refugees are sometimes subjected) do not encourage integration. It becomes more difficult for the person to integrate if he or she is isolated from people in the same situation. If possible, people should be grouped together or it should be made easy for them to contact or meet other people in the same situation so that each person can integrate at his or her own pace. Nonetheless, the receiving countries should accept that the refugee may reject certain steps toward integration because they expect to return to their countries of origin as soon as possible. This should not cause any conflicts or denigrate the value of the aid. Rather, it should be seen as a logical process to be followed until the person is better able to redefine his or her life.

Conflicts between generations may be common among the refugee population itself, given differing capacities and strategies for acculturation. Children and young people may have a stronger capacity and more opportunities to learn adaptation strategies, even though they face the difficulty of forging their identity in a cross-cultural context. Adolescent Guatemalan refugees in Mexico often had more contact and higher expectations regarding Mexican society and culture. The return to Guatemala gave rise to more difficulties and family separations precisely because of these different strategies for cultural adaptation. The following testimony taken from Latin American refugees in Europe illustrates this process:

Yes, the young people are "becoming" European and they are forgetting about their country. They do not identify with the ideology that mobilized their parents' generation because of the exile. . . . It's the parents' fault because they did not oppose the integration into a highly developed "capitalist" country, and they are not concerned about developing their ideology. Many parents experience this rupture and they do not see it as a sign of normal psychological development. (Vázquez and Araujo 1990, 122)

Cross-cultural interactions also have an active influence on the new culture. In the case of displaced populations, settling in a certain place may have a cultural impact on the local population. Sometimes the actual humanitarian aid, such as the creation of refugee camps, will instigate population movements and cultural interactions because of the precariousness of local living conditions, as was the case in the Mwenw Ditu transit camp in Zaire (Boulvain et al. 1994). Dealing with the suffering of the displaced population may encourage welcoming behavior in the locals, but it might also provoke competitiveness over available jobs and perceptions that international organizations consider the displaced more highly than the receiving population. The aid should help to improve the situation for the refugees and their local relationships. This means, for example, that the receiving populations should also benefit somewhat from the services and be encouraged to participate in training and education.

Improving Cultural Interactions

Humanitarian aid may also have a cultural impact on the very communities where it is being carried out. Living together with people from other countries, the presence of international organizations, and the deployment of resources at a given time may likely contrast with the situation of poverty or with the culture of the people. Another problem may be how to involve the local population in the aid effort. The advisability of speaking directly to the women of an Afghan refugee community about the prevention of diarrhea cannot be evaluated using Western criteria without bearing in mind the social structure of the Afghan community, how to involve men, and the general context of an Islamic culture (Sondorp 1992). In that case, a certain cultural sensitivity on the part of humanitarian aid workers can prevent family conflicts by involving men in the spread of information on how to care for the children.

Improving cultural interactions should be a goal of humanitarian aid. Aid workers and organizations should be aware of the differences, have knowledge of the culture, and acquire skills to manage themselves within it. The first step is to be aware that workers take for granted the implicit matters that make up Western culture (Pedersen 1988). Among these are concepts of what is normal, a belief that the individual is the basis of society, speaking in abstract terms, linear thinking of cause and effect, a direct approach to solving problems, placing greater importance on the resolution of problems than on keeping harmony and good relations in a group, and a belief that it is better to be helped by specialized systems than by informal relationships. Only when one is aware of the differences between cultures can one be open to change.

On a personal level, the following suggestions show how to decrease the distance between cultures and how to improve communication:

1. Know the language, keeping in mind nonverbal communication, and be aware of stereotypes and prejudices.
2. Know the social, political, and historical context of the place and its basic behavioral norms.
3. Develop the necessary communication skills for the particular cultural context through education and a positive attitude toward those with whom you are working.

This chapter ends with three examples for training in the management of cross-cultural interactions: (1) cultural differences in Latin America, (2) reverse culture shock, and (3) communication problems between people from individualist cultures and collective cultures.

Example 1: Cross-cultural Interaction in Latin America[2]

Some central areas of daily life in which cultural differences will appear in Latin America are respect and conduct in relationships, climate and sociability, forms of communication, conflict management, time management, and social differences. Even though some of them appear as problems, they are also a way to learn different kinds of interaction as well as the values on which different groups and societies are based.

RESPECT AND CONDUCT IN RELATIONSHIPS

Generally, in Latin American cultures people treat each other more formally than in the North and place greater value on being deferential to others in daily life, both in greetings (for example, in a meeting, people introduce themselves with their full name, shaking hands with everyone present) and in personal treatment (for example, people frequently use the polite *usted* form of address, even within the family). This type of formal treatment with gestures of kindness also appears in written communication, where interest in the person's situation is expressed before talking about the matter at hand.

Ignoring these factors leads to the impression that people from the North are disrespectful. Formal behavior is not, however, contradictory to sociability patterns in the more individualist countries of the North. However, such "impolite" behavior does correspond to a relationship of power—an acceptance of hierarchy and social formal relations, even in groups that are considered to hold horizontal values (like NGOs and human-rights groups). In Latin America, respect is shown depending on social status, age, or gender, and therefore it is important to show more respect toward parents and the elderly than is done in individualist cultures.

CLIMATE AND SOCIABILITY

In Latin American cultures, it is more common to share one's space by inviting others home, say, for dinner than it is in individualist cultures. In Latin America, meeting in a bar is considered cold and distant. To Latin Americans, it is important to be friendly and to please the other person by showing interest and a positive feeling about the relationship. However, sometimes expressions of this friendliness can be taken to mean something else. For example, addressing someone with affectionate phrases may be perceived in the West as a sign of amorous interest when they are intended as common signs of friendliness. Insignificant gestures such as a small gift from a foreigner to an indigenous woman may be perceived by the community as a proposition. Accepting to be the godmother or godfather at a baptism is not only an act of assistance at a social function but the establishment of a future relationship and promising support for the child.

Even though it is relatively easy to adapt to these displays of positive sociability, it is also easy not to give them much importance. Therefore, it is just as important to manage the climate within a working relationship as it is to carry out the appointed tasks. Too much emphasis on goals will confirm the stereotype that people from Europe, Canada, and the United States are cold and unfriendly. Bodily contact is also more common in Latin American cultures. Men and women normally touch or hug each other during dances or parties. This does not mean, however, that there are not certain boundaries that should be respected and conduct to be avoided. Gender roles are far more rigidly defined and behavior is largely based on masculine and feminine stereotypes.

Finally, because Latin American cultures tend to be more collectivist, Europeans and North Americans often mistakenly think that where there is little privacy (as in the allocation of space in a house), there is no intimacy. However, just because conditions of poverty may not allow for doors in a house does not mean that there is no intimacy in the house. Not taking these boundaries into account may suggest a disrespectful attitude.

FORMS OF COMMUNICATION

Latin Americans use predominantly an indirect style of communication, especially when discussing problems or giving criticisms or emotionally charged comments. A direct "no" is not normally used, and forms of denial are usually softer; for example, instead of "no," one would say, "more or less" or "maybe that's not a good idea," and so forth. Denial is often seen as a way of rejecting the other person, and this tends to be avoided. The meaning of certain expressions may be different, too. In Central America "enough" (*bastante*) means "a lot," and "average" (*regular*) means "bad."

These examples suggest that more attention should be paid to the context of words and phrases and to nonverbal communication, which is often the real transmitter of meaning. Latin Americans tend to believe that how they say something delivers a lot of information to the people listening and that it is easy to understand what the speaker wants to say. Other differences are the speed at which people talk—for example, Spaniards generally speak much more quickly than Latin Americans— and the manner of discussing problems, as when everyone has to speak in a meeting both in order to approve of the debate and to express their personal opinion. Many indigenous people, for example, end by saying, "That is my opinion" or "That is what I have to say."

The image that the people may have of the aid worker or group may encourage as well indirect communication—For example, not saying "no" to those who have the resources or who want to help. However, other misunderstandings may be mistakenly attributed to the culture, such as a lack of collaboration—for example, refusing to hand out a questionnaire at a university, which cannot be done because of a lack of resources for photocopying, may be interpreted as a lack of interest.

Another problem may be the interventionist attitude of individualist goal-centered cultures, where people tend to give their opinions about everything and risk being considered domineering. On some occasions, it may be preferable not to insist on offering solutions and to respect the rhythm of the people, even when things could be done better another way. These attitudes are all part of development work.

CONFLICT MANAGEMENT

Ways of managing conflict also vary in different cultures. Outbursts with a negative emotional charge are looked down upon in Latin America with its more indirect style in confronting disagreement. This indirect style may also become a source of conflict, because a dynamic of avoidance makes it difficult to approach the problem. Outbursts will acquire different meanings for people of different cultures—a "row" could be seen by one person as someone's need to unload and by another as a break in trust. Latin Americans are generally less willing to compete openly and competitiveness in others is seen as something threatening.

It is also important not to do anything that might harm the social image of the speaker. In collectivist cultures, more than in individualist cultures, image is linked to one's role in a group. Any criticism made in front of other people could damage a person's image and would be considered enormously disrespectful. It is essential to choose the right moment to speak and to avoid openly or subtly disqualifying the other person.

TIME MANAGEMENT

The concept of time management is more flexible in Latin American cultures and relates to sociability. This means that schedules are more flexible and notions of punctuality have more latitude. For those who are accustomed to strict timekeeping, delays or long periods of waiting may be frustrating (in Mexico, "now" means "in a bit"). What for some people is a fixed time is for others an approximation.

More flexible time management also suggests less competitiveness (which does not mean a complete lack of competitiveness, it means that competitiveness can be expressed in other ways). Often when Latin Americans have to adapt to European cultures, they feel more competition and that everyone is rushing from one place to another.

In rural communities, time management is linked to the rhythm of nature. In addition to the flexibility regarding schedules, these different rhythms influence daily concerns. For example, the refugee communities in Mexico planned their return to Guatemala in 1992 by taking into account the rhythms of the agricultural cycle and the weather. Humanitarian organizations overlooked this because they were more concerned with organizational schedules and politics.

In indigenous cultures, time is a circular and not a linear concept. The distinction of any sequence between the past, the present, and the future is unclear. For example, the Mayan population (in Guatemala and Mexico) and the Mapuches (in Chile) speak of the time of violence as a cycle that could repeat itself and is related to previous natural or political disasters they have experienced. They also speak about their ancestors as if they were part of the recent past, a concept related to their collective memory.

The two extremes in the different concepts of time management are the imposition of timetables and schedules by NGOs and development agencies, and delays and excessive nonchalance regarding deadlines by local populations. Useful mechanisms to handle these problems include adapting projects to the realistic possibilities of the population in question, exhibiting more sensitivity toward historical and cultural processes, and establishing a consensus on work methods and greater personal flexibility.

SOCIAL DIFFERENCES

Poverty is part of daily life in many Latin American countries, especially in the places where development work is most often carried out. The division between the rich and poor is obvious not only in rural communities but also between neighborhoods of the same city. Living in a context of such glaring inequality requires many forms of adaptation among middle-class, professional people. However, these situations were also present in Europe and North America after the war and there are still areas of social exclusion or marginal neighborhoods in the countries of the North.

Despite the collectivist culture, class differences and socioeconomic status often stem from segregation from other groups. Racism and social exclusion toward indigenous people (for example, in Guatemala), black populations (in Colombia), and disadvantaged groups (street children in Brazil) are evident on the part of dominant socioeconomic and ethnic groups.

There is also an ambivalent attitude toward Europeans and North Americans. On the one hand, their capabilities, interests, and resources are viewed positively. On the other, however, their individualist ("selfish") tendency is viewed negatively (recalling, for example, the Spanish conquistadors or U.S. policies or political responsibility). Nonetheless, the actual aid and resources mobilized by humanitarian aid can mediate

---

Guidelines for Latin Americans Regarding Cross-Cultural Interaction with People from the North

1. Be aware that some European and North American cultures appear less deferential and respectful. Generally, people do not speak in a polite or respectful manner, nor is it as important for them to recognize the status of other people. People do not treat each other with as much respect as in Latin America.
2. Be more direct and say clearly what you want to say. The Northern cultures are more direct so it is better to say things directly. The indigenous, in greater measure than other Latin Americans, need communication to be more open, explicit, and abstract.
3. Do not expect people to be as polite or "well brought up" as in Latin America. People in other countries make criticisms more openly and do not treat others as politely. A criticism or disagreement is far less relevant here than in Latin America. It is common to shout or argue, and often it is of no great importance.
4. People from the North will not normally invite you to their homes. This is not a sign of contempt. Social contact normally takes place in public.
5. People are more individualistic and express pride over what they do, in such a way that would be considered exaggerated or immodest in Latin America.
6. Compared with Latin Americans, people from the North are not as attached to their extended families. They would probably feel uncomfortable with the Latin way of involving "all the family" and would find it difficult to show the same sort of respect to parents and the elderly as would be considered normal in Latin America.
7. People from Northern cultures are more willing to compete openly, and they are not so threatened by competitiveness.
8. Europeans, Canadians, and Americans find it less important to maintain harmony in relationships than do Latin Americas. It is normal to criticize and to make relatively negative comments.
9. In the North, people are very focused on their specific group of friends or partners. After superficial contact, people from the North are less likely to continue the relationship than are Latin Americans.

Source: Adapted from Páez et al. 1997.

---

these social differences and have a cultural impact. The display of resources in contrast with the poverty of many populations may assign aid workers a new status, which requires that these social differences be handled consistently with development principles and the people's dignity. Relief efforts must be adapted to local criteria with the participation of the local population and provided with clarity and transparency.

Example 2: Reverse Culture Shock[3]

The return was a day of celebration, but then I felt like a foreigner in my own country. I felt lost. I couldn't recognize myself. I felt terrible. I felt like I had disowned my past, a part of myself. What was I going to do with everything I had experienced in Europe? How could I talk about it? How could I give meaning to my life?

—*Vázquez and Araujo 1990, 228*

Just as emigrants who have spent a long time away from their home country, aid workers may find themselves suffering from a reverse culture shock on their return home. Despite returning to the familiarity of their native countries, they may suffer from cultural stress from the return to their daily lives, from a change in their expectations, and from others' reaction to their presence. The five basic problems to consider about reverse culture shock are changes in self-concept, frustrated expectations of self, frustrated expectations of others, sense of loss, and change in values.

CHANGES IN SELF-CONCEPT

Before returning home, many aid workers realize that the image they had of themselves is different after the experience of the trip and their work abroad. Some of the most common things that may change in their self-concept are the sense of belonging to a group or nation (which can lead to a certain loss of "identity"), acquisition of nonverbal communication skills (new ways of expressing and comporting themselves); and new verbal communication skills (speaking new languages and the access to the new concepts and cultural values that come with them). The person may realize that his or her *old self* would not have tolerated many of the behaviors or ideas of his or her *current self,* and this may generate contradictions: It may also help a person to be more tolerant in some respects and less tolerant in others.

The people who remained in the country of origin will also have changed. Those who return feel forced to conform to the cultural values of their society of origin. The new values acquired abroad—such as a sudden interest in politics or the type of work that is sought—may not be understood. This may provoke a critical reaction. It is often difficult to understand the experience of the person who returns, and he or she may feel isolated as the family waits for him or her to "get back to normal." All of this generates feelings of isolation and loneliness once back "home." The person may feel that he or she belongs neither "here nor there" but somewhere in between. The person may also feel that he or she fits completely neither in one place because it is not his or her culture nor the other because the person no longer identifies with its values or customs.

FRUSTRATED EXPECTATIONS OF THE PERSON WHO RETURNS

Even though people expect to suffer from culture shock when they arrive in a new country, very few expect a culture shock when they return home. This unexpectedness makes the situation more difficult. Sometimes people have unrealistic expectations of their return, which stems from an idealized image of their country of origin. This is especially so in those people who found it hard to overcome the initial culture shock—for example, those who had doubts about leaving their country or who did so in order to accompany a partner out of a sense of duty. To overcome the initial culture shock, they idealized what they had left behind and would often think about the time when they would return. That idealized image eventually turns against them.

Expectations regarding personal relationships are especially problematic: relationships sometimes seem more solid from a distance than they are in reality, those returning sometimes expect to be respected (even admired) by certain people, people who remained can seem distant and preoccupied with other interests, and the person who expects that a friendship will pick up where it left off may be disappointed to find that the relationship is no longer as important to the person who remained.

FRUSTRATED EXPECTATIONS OF OTHERS

Sometimes family members, friends, or work colleagues have their own, sometimes unrealistic, expectations of what a person will say; want to do, see, and eat; and how the first reunion will be. Family and friends may feel frustrated when they see that the newly returned person does not seem to be particularly happy or does not seem to appreciate what they do for him or her. They do not expect, for example, to receive sharp comments or criticisms about their lives. When a person turns down an invitation to a party given by friends, the friends may take this as an insult, without realizing that this is a normal process. Sometimes they may want to surprise the person with local news and are surprised when he or she does not seem very interested.

SENSE OF LOSS

Returning people often express a sense of loss. They have had to say goodbye to friends they may never see again and who are in danger, and they have left a place that they have learned to love, a project that was

> **Questions to Consider before Returning Home**
>
> - Among your family and friends, whom would you like to see immediately and whom would you prefer to see later?
> - With whom will you have to redefine your relationship? How should you prepare for that reencounter?
> - What would you like to share with your family and what wouldn't you not like to share?
> - From among your new values, which might cause tension or misunderstandings?
> - How do you think that what you left behind will have repercussions once you return home?
> - What ties would you like to keep with the organization?
> - What are your plans for employment?
> - What are you going to miss about the place you are leaving?

fulfilling, and close colleagues. All of this entails a grieving process. If the person had a position of responsibility and was a "foreign expert," he or she now returns to becoming just one among many professionals. And, for some, returning means going back to a financially difficult situation or unemployment.

Going home may be seen as a return to routine and thus boredom. The city of origin may have more resources, leisure activities, and so forth, but it may also be a colder and more distant urban lifestyle— where everybody seems too busy to spend time with their friends—so that one feels a loss of group cohesion.

Change in Values

For the person who returns, the main challenge is to *recognize* the changes in his or her values or attitudes and to *decide* which ones he or she wants to maintain for personal growth and to make part of the life to which he or she has returned. It is important to understand the issues that must be confronted:

- Accepting that the integration process is mutual and that there is a need for affection and understanding instead of criticisms toward the people around you.
- To continue supporting the projects you left behind, be aware of the limitations and have realistic expectations of what can and cannot be achieved.
- Decide whether you would like to integrate your experience into your career plans for the future.

- Consider how to integrate your new awareness and values to life in your country of origin.

FACTORS INFLUENCING REVERSE CULTURE SHOCK

Studies show that reverse culture shock is more common in women than in men, and that the risk decreases proportionally in line with the frequency of trips back and forth and the amount of contact with home during the period abroad. Research also shows that whereas family relationships are strengthened during the separation, friendships tend to suffer during the return and intimate relationships are often endangered. The returnee should be prepared to avoid some of these difficulties.

Following is some practical advice to improve the process of return for the returnee, family, friends, and NGOs

1. From the organization or NGO
   a. Provide information during the training and initial preparation on the importance of considering the return and provide additional relevant information about it at the time of return.
   b. Take the time to receive the person once he or she has returned, giving the person the opportunity to talk about the experience as the person gives reports, and so forth. Express your recognition on behalf of the institution for the person's work and effort. The first contact should not be in passing— "How did it go over there?"—but an allotted time for the person to summarize his or her experiences.
   c. Try to provide opportunities for the person to meet other people who have come back from the same country, such as in a working group or other support group. Provide information, support projects, and ways of keeping in contact.
2. For the returnee
   Before Returning
   a. Prepare those who are expecting you back. Write and explain all the things that are concerning you, and what you expect or do not expect on your return. Write about the changes you have experienced in yourself, the most important experiences you have had, what you miss most about your country, and what you expect to see when you get back. Allow others to prepare for your return and to express their expectations about it.
   b. Prepare yourself in the same way as if you were traveling to a new country: Ask friends what is new, read the news, evaluate the changes in the employment market, and so forth.

Once You Are Home
  a. Take into account that the return is a long process. After a few years' absence, it may be advisable to take your time in looking for work, perhaps a couple of months to decide what kind of work you would like to do and where you would like to live.
  b. Do not confuse jet lag with the frustration of returning. During the first week it is normal to be tired, irritable, and down.
  c. It may be advisable to spend a week or ten days at a friend's house and gradually meet up with other friends, to avoid saturation. The integration should be done in two stages: first to the country, the food, the political situation; and later to friends and relationships. Decide who you will call and in what order. There should be no problems if your family or friends explain that you are back and you feel fine but that you would rather not see too many people until you are situated. You need time before meeting up with people again and talking about your experiences.
  d. Look for people to talk to. It is useful to talk to people from the organization who have spent long periods of time abroad because they will understand your feelings and the contradictions that you feel and they can support you with their own experiences.
  e. Try and keep your moral commitment to the country and the people you were working with, looking for ways to continue your support.
  f. Tell yourself that this is an experience of cultural interaction, and both worlds are just as real. Try and observe your own culture through the eyes of an anthropologist and feel privileged that you have had the opportunity to experience other cultures.
3. Family and friends
  a. Listen without making judgments. Try and keep the communication going and try not to take things personally or as a personal affront. Encourage the person who arrives to talk as much as he or she wants.
  b. Try and protect him or her from having too many people around. If he or she isolates him- or herself too much, however, suggest activities, while respecting the person's right to be alone if that is what he or she wants.
  c. Accept changes in tastes, preferences, activities, and so forth.

Example 3: Communication between Cultures[4]

The following example shows how two people acting in good faith interact in a "culture-centric" way, causing mutual confusion and irritation.

As is usually the case, in this situation there is a conflict of interest between the two people.

Mrs. Robertson is a British woman teaching English in an Asian country. She has not been living in the country for very long. Mr. Chi is one of Mrs. Robertson's students and has failed his final exam. Mrs. Robertson has asked him to come to her office at 12:00 P.M. to discuss the results. She has arranged to meet a Mr. Davis for lunch at 12:30. At 12:20, Mr. Chi knocks on her door and enters without waiting for a reply, which surprises Mrs. Robertson. Mr. Chi picks up a chair, puts it down very close to her, sits down, and asks her with a smile: "Have you had lunch, Miss?"

Mrs. Robertson answers sharply: "Sit down over there, Mr. Chi!" pointing to a chair a couple feet away from her, "and explain to me why you are twenty minutes late."

Mr. Chi hesitates and partly lies: "The train was delayed and I couldn't take the bus, so I had to walk" (the last part is true).

"Well, I can see you are capable of saying almost anything," she says, disturbed by his lies. "Your final exam was not good at all. Why did you do so badly, Mr. Chi?"

Mr. Chi sneezes violently twice.

"Do you have a cold, Mr. Chi?" she asks.

"No, it's because of your bad smell," says Mr. Chi, referring to her perfume. Mrs. Robertson is amazed at his insolent response.

Noticing the reaction that his answer has provoked, Mr. Chi goes back to talking about the English course and answers the previous question on why he did so badly: "I don't know. I tried really hard and I read the book about four times, Miss. Anyway, we all thought the exam was very difficult."

"You shouldn't hide behind your classmates. You are responsible for the results. Trying hard is not enough to pass," answers Mrs. Robertson.

"But thanks to you my English has improved a lot. Your course was wonderful, Miss. I need to pass this course to go on to the upper level," says Mr. Chi.

She answers: "That is not my problem, Mr. Chi. We assess your ability in English and it is low. You have been absent a lot and that hasn't helped."

"My mother was in the hospital this semester, Miss, and I had to visit her every day."

"Your first responsibility is to your studies, Mr. Chi. Why didn't you visit her in the afternoons or evenings?"

"But, Miss, who would cook and help my little sister in the afternoon?"

"You can't expect to get a good mark with that piece of rubbish," says Mrs. Robertson, to which he responds, to her surprise:

"Yes, Miss."

Mrs. Robertson is becoming more annoyed as the conversation goes on: "I have an appointment now, Mr. Chi, so you have to go."

"Can't you give me a pass through compassion, the kindness of your heart? I really need to pass this course."

"What? Through the kindness of my heart? I've never heard anything like it! Mr. Chi, I have to go. Call me if you want me to give you an answer on doing the exam again," she says, opening the door. Mr. Chi walks out feeling sad and confused.

"And next time don't arrive late, Mr. Chi. If you're not here on time, don't expect to find me here," she says, ending the interview.

When Mrs. Robertson meets Mr. Davis for lunch she complains about the arrogant and irresponsible nature of the students she has. She is quite angry.

Mr. Chi, a little depressed, tells his sister that his teacher is not very friendly, behaves aggressively when there is a problem, and is too strict when it comes to giving marks. The girl is not surprised at these negative comments, even though she is a little surprised at the forcefulness of his comments, as she has often heard him say that he understands only about half of what his teacher says.

SOURCES OF CONFLICT

Linguistic

> *"You can't expect to get a good mark with that piece of rubbish," says Mrs. Robertson, to which Mr. Chi responds, to her surprise: "Yes, Miss."*

It is obvious that because of his poor English, Mr. Chi has not understood the negative in the sentence. Also, the use of colloquial words makes understanding between cultures even more difficult. "Piece of rubbish" does not mean anything to Mr. Chi. Care must to be taken to speak slowly and in the standard language when communicating with people from another culture.

Rules for Physical Interaction

> *When Mr. Chi knocks on the door and enters without waiting for an answer, this surprises Mrs. Robertson. Mr. Chi picks up a chair, places it very close to her, sits down, and Mrs. Robertson tells him to sit further away from her.*

The conflict between the Western and the collectivist cultures is evident over rules for interaction. The desirable distance for interaction is much less in Africa, Asia, and Latin America than in the United States and Europe. For Mr. Chi, it is surprising to sit so far away from someone you are talking to, whereas for Mrs. Robertson to speak sitting so close to someone is only appropriate for intimate relationships. Also, in individualist countries personal space and doors often mark the boundaries. To knock and enter without waiting for an answer is impolite. In Asian countries, the established rules on personal space and doors are more flexible. Mr. Chi knows that Mrs. Robertson is waiting for him, so he knocks and enters immediately. By doing this, he is questioning the authority, status, and self-esteem of Mrs. Robertson without realizing it, which leads the teacher to repeatedly make clear his position relative to hers.

Rules of Time and Respect

> *Mr. Chi arrives twenty minutes late and after a few minutes Mrs. Robertson ends the meeting. The first action surprises and irritates the teacher and the second surprises the student.*

People from individualist cultures plan their time and their personal relationships on a strict personal timetable. People from collectivist cultures have a much more flexible concept of time and appointments. An appointment at twelve means "more or less at twelve." By arriving twenty minutes late, Mr. Chi has put Mrs. Robertson in a difficult position and has made her feel rushed as she has a lunch appointment ten minutes later. However, by ending the meeting abruptly, which in Mr. Chi's eyes is unjustified, she has not respected him as a person, and he feels dishonored.

Self-Concept and Causal Explanations

> "I tried really hard and I read the book about four times, Miss. Anyway, we all thought the exam was difficult," says Mr. Chi referring to his classmates.
> "You shouldn't hide behind your classmates. You are responsible for the results. Trying hard is not enough to pass," answers Mrs. Robertson.

Mr. Chi's explanation, "I've tried really hard" is dismissed by Mrs. Robertson, but it is a common and legitimate explanation in Asian collectivist cultures. Effort is highly valued, but Mrs. Robertson emphasizes Mr. Chi's lack of ability and poor results because in individualist cultures individual performance is very important.

Mr. Chi places a lot of importance on the fact that the whole class thinks that the exam was difficult. Attributing a poor result to external causes is a way of defending his self-esteem, but Mr. Chi insists that he is not so different from the rest of the group. In collectivist cultures, self-image is based on relationship and conformity with the group, not in the differentiation of the individual with others. When the teacher says to him: "You shouldn't hide behind your classmates. You are responsible for the results. Trying hard is not enough to pass," she bases her statement on the concept of a person as an independent individual and the importance not of the effort made but of the proven ability. Mr. Chi's explanation is based on effort and the similarity between his self-image and that of his peers.

The explanation that Mr. Chi gives for his absences (looking after his mother and sister) is dismissed by the teacher, who tells him that his main concern should be his studies and she probably thinks that he is lying again—which is not the case. Placing individual achievement before relationships and family duties is accepted in individualist cultures, even though the main source of stress is family problems and family losses. However, in collectivist cultures, priority is given to personal relationships, especially family, over individual achievement.

Management of Conflict and Lying

When Mr. Chi justifies having arrived late because of the bus and train, the teacher gets annoyed and accuses him directly of lying ("Well, I can see you are capable of saying almost anything").

In collectivist cultures, negative events are normally explained by external causes to avoid an open conflict between superiors and subordinates. To avoid questioning the self-image, "white lies" are often accepted when they are used to avoid a conflict. Even though these lies are sometimes obvious, they are accepted to keep the peace and avoid embarrassment. In individualist cultures, lies constitute a rupture in a desirable relationship, and people express conflict more openly. That doesn't mean that people from individualist cultures are not reluctant to give bad news or bend the truth in some situations, just that conflict is far more frequent and even acceptable.

Respect for Authority, Compassion, and Compliments

Mr. Chi's compliments ("Your course was wonderful") and appealing to the teacher's kindness and compassion (he has a difficult family situation and asks for compassion) are clear sources of conflict. His compliments have no effect on Mrs. Robertson, who interprets his attempts as "corruption."

In individualist cultures, basic criteria have been established and are the "legitimate" basis for making decisions. It is supposed that subordinates and superiors know these criteria and are guided by them. However, in collectivist cultures, where there is more distance from power, people of a high status have considerable authority and power to exercise at their discretion. Subordinates try and show respect to their superiors through compliments and appealing to their kindness. It is legitimate for Mr. Chi to appeal to the teacher's kindness (showing respect and recognizing her power). For Mrs. Robertson, to pass someone out of compassion would be to question her professional integrity and betray the methods of assessment.

Rules for Emotional Expression

Mrs. Robertson openly expresses her anger toward Mr. Chi—sharply telling him to sit away from her, opening the door for him to leave, and criticizing him directly—Mr. Chi subtly criticizes her in front of his sister but does not show irritability or depression in front of the teacher.

In individualist cultures, emotions are linked to the image of oneself and they are expressed more directly. Anger is more frequent and acceptable if your rights or status are being questioned illegitimately. In collectivist cultures, emotions (especially negative ones) are not expressed directly to others and never to people of a higher status or to superiors. Chi probably felt embarrassed and reached the conclusion that the teacher is a typical rude Westerner, clueless about interpersonal relationships, who has caused an unpleasant incident that he has had the misfortune to be involved in without having wanted to be.

Rules for Communication

> Mr. Chi asks the teacher if she has had lunch, he tells her about his family situation, the importance this exam has for him, and problems with public transport. Robertson talks only about the main issue: the exam and the results.

People from collectivist cultures talk indirectly, about everything and nothing, showing an interest in the person and his or her situation. People from individualist cultures talk directly and in an abstract and specific way on one issue.

In individualist cultures, it is common to talk to people on the same level, which is why the teacher uses the surname of the student when she addresses him. However, Mr. Chi does not use her name or surname when addressing her and uses the polite form "Miss," which is a sign of respect in Asia. Communication is more formal and aimed at showing deference and respect toward superiors.

Chapter 8

Reconstructing the Social Fabric: Psychosocial Care

It may be the first time that the psychological and spiritual needs, and not just the physical or material needs, of the traumatized people have been taken into account on a large scale.

—Arcel 1994, 20

This quotation from a book on the aftermath of the wars in the former Yugoslavia underscores the social and political context of psychosocial interventions. Why did it have to be a European war in which the psychological needs were finally included on the humanitarian aid agenda? Because the war was no longer something happening far away and the victims were part of our very selves. In 1995 in Croatia and Bosnia-Herzegovina, there were around 185 psychosocial programs, most of them foreign, and over the last several years there has been an increase in these types of programs for all types of disasters. Despite this, the majority of programs continue to follow an individually based, medical-model approach with little cultural sensitivity.

The appearance of a psychosocial component in humanitarian aid improves the relationship between NGOs and the population at the same time as it opens up a new debate: How can we avoid "psychologizing" humanitarian aid, which would be only a new version of the "medicalization" of human suffering,[1] but rather have it become an element of prevention, a stimulus to local resources and the rebuilding of social networks?

Prevention as a Social and Political Activity

The main objective regarding mental health should be prevention aimed at identifying possible risks, instead of waiting and responding only after difficulties appear. Prevention is based on eliminating or reducing the conditions that cause mental-health problems and stimu-lating support mechanisms.

Improved health can be achieved first by reducing conflicts, social injustice, poverty, and forced displacement. Criss and Johnson (1994) argue that the concept of peace has to be rethought, starting from the reduction of conflict to the active promotion of peace through social justice. Because most of the mental-health problems that appear in emergency situations are caused by social or political reasons, its pre-vention is both a political activity and a health-related activity. How-ever, these prevention measures are not limited to the political sphere. Prevention depends on greater understanding and greater political commitment, as well as a more active role from overseas workers, mental-health workers, defenders of human rights, and pressure groups from their countries of origin.

Some of the stress factors of the affected populations could be under the control of international or governmental agencies or NGOs. For example, the conditions under which a repatriation is carried out could cause fear in the refugees about how they will be treated on their return to their country of origin, insecurity because of a lack of information, and uncertainty about how they will work, among other things. Some of these factors could be reduced if international agencies or governments anticipated these problems instead of basing their decisions on eco-nomic criteria or political interests.

This preventive action presents a challenge as well to those who inter-vene in conflict situations. In many cases, people may see that those who are officially protecting them are closer than they think to those who are attacking them, or that they are not really committed beyond their political declarations.[2]

Also, the way in which humanitarian aid is conceptualized and imple-mented on an organizational and social scale can either promote health or be a health risk. For example, the reuniting of families and school education is beneficial for children and this should be taken into account from the beginning. Activities that promote social integration and encourage refugees to take an active part in the organization of their lives, will help them to overcome the state of "limbo" that often arises in provisional circumstances.[3]

A psychosocial approach should be based on a realistic analysis of the problems and needs of the population and an ability to adjust the aid to the specific situation. For example, a demilitarization project cannot simply be a disarmament process accompanied by economic aid. Take the example of the social reintegration of boy soldiers. This process should take into account the fact that these boys are returning to areas in which there are no basic services and their return will mean an extra burden for their families. In rebuilding their own identity (from soldier and guerrilla fighter to peasant) and their relationships with others, both children and families will change how they see life, how they cope with conflicts, how they view the war, and more.

**Psychosocial Perspective of Civilian Reintegration:
Issues to Take into Account**

- Attitudes and social reaction (degree of polarization, prejudices, family, etc.).
- Management of fear and traumatic experiences brought on by the new situation.
- Hierarchy and dependency habits.
- Loss of expectations: despair, resentment, meaning of experience.
- Need to feel useful and part of an active process.
- Habit of resorting to violence.
- Documentation, legal issues, etc.
- Financial needs.

It is necessary to change attitudes in the receiving country that may have been influenced by military propaganda so that people do not behave according to ethnic or political stereotypes. For example, in the return of Guatemalan refugees from Mexico, the educational work carried out by popular organizations and human-rights and religious groups on encouraging a positive attitude toward the refugees was very important because they were considered a hostile population by the army and had been accused of being subversives in many communities.

Mental-Health Programs

As part of a comprehensive approach for humanitarian actions, a psychosocial approach should include interventions specifically oriented toward the mental health of the affected population. These mental-health programs should include prevention and cure. Normally a distinction exists between primary, secondary, and tertiary prevention.

Primary prevention refers to reducing risky situations to prevent problems from occurring. *Secondary prevention* is aimed at more vulnerable populations and refers to identifying problems early. *Tertiary prevention* refers to preventing complications in people and populations most affected. At a primary level, the most common activities would be providing clothing, games, and activities for adolescents; providing health services, nurseries, educational programs, and recreation centers; creating jobs for heads of families; and lending support to the community leaders.

The secondary level would consist of the early identification of mental-health problems through encouraging medical visits, and training health professionals or social figures (such as teachers) to identify problematic cases. The tertiary level could include initiatives such as creating a health center led by a professional, developing a network of mental-health workers for children, and offering support workshops for the most affected people. Even though mental-health programs combine different approaches, they differ between having a clinical-therapeutic focus and a community focus.

The Community Approach to Mental Health

An approach to mental health that focuses on the community and favors social support and community integration may often be more appropriate than psychotherapeutic interventions. Summerfield (1996) questions the use of individual psychological treatment for problems that are clearly collective and that have social and political causes. In such diverse places as Mexico or Bosnia, as people were struggling to survive amid violent conditions, the local population clearly rejected NGO research questionnaires that focused on individual psychological problems.

Most mental-health problems can be treated and most psychosocial support needs met at the closest health service to the community. During the postwar period in Bosnia, the director of the psychiatric hospital in Sarajevo confirmed that 70 percent of mental-health problems could be treated at the primary health-care or community level (Jones 1995). In many cases, mental-health services are based on an individual clinical perspective, and therefore it is necessary to advance toward a more interdisciplinary approach based on the community.

Ager (1995) describes the community-centered approach as a set of preventive and curative actions based on sharing and discussing experiences within the group, providing practical assistance in areas such as child care and finding employment, and providing more individual care to those who need it.

In addition to programs that address a community's needs, it is important to consider groups that may be at more risk. These more vulnerable cases may be caused by prior psychological problems, families that have lost a member, people who have directly experienced violent situations, and less-experienced people who have fewer personal resources or social support.

Many issues may not present themselves as mental-health problems. Listening to what people say in social contexts and talking to local leaders or people who are an important reference in the community provide

Steps for Mental-Health Community Work

1. Evaluate the work.
   - Demand
   - Risks
   - Needs (time, monitoring)
   - Criteria
2. Identify leaders.
   - Type of leadership
   - Skills (mobilization, integration, etc.)
   - Perception of the problem
   - Limitations
3. Know the context and the community.
   - Culture/values/beliefs
   - Behavioral norms
   - Groups
4. Develop network strategies.
   - Multiplying agents, leaders, groups
   - Training, social activities, memories, celebrations
5. Monitor and evaluate.
   - Two-way exchange of information
   - Thoughts on the process
   - Evaluation of results
6. Establish a link with local health services.
   - Education
   - Referrals
   - Support-supervision
7. Stimulate positive factors.
   - Social support
   - Cultural, ideological, and religious factors
   - Coping mechanisms
   - Time for the group and community
8. Identify risk situations.
   - Social disintegration
   - Acculturation-identity
   - Impact of experiences
   - Personal and social vulnerability
9. Provide strategies for people who require more care.
   - Employment networking
   - Local health services
   - Traditional healers
   - External support

the building blocks for the community approach. This way, problems that people face can be understood better and the community can become more involved. Teacher training on trauma-related issues is a possible strategy for identifying problems, and it also offers support to the children as shown in the following case from Guatemala.

> ## MIR[4] Program for the Sociocultural Integration of Bosnian Refugees in Switzerland
>
> *Promotion of identity.* The expression and reconstruction of cultural identity is important for the welfare of the population through activities that promote social relations and collective and cultural expression: gatherings, trips, sports, and cultural activities.
>
> *Psychosocial welfare.* Stress prevention and support after traumatic events, through individual meetings to discuss problems, sharing experiences in groups, educational activities, supervision, and support to the professionals involved.
>
> *More activity.* One of the problems for refugees is the lack of activity. Passivity and dependency arising from the situation and the difficulty of integrating reinforce the feeling of incompetence and lack of control over their own lives. To tackle this problem, occupational activities, activities with the children, workshops, and the sale of handmade products are needed.

Source: Loncaveric 1996.

When the school term ended, it was the orphans who were affected the most, they felt lonely so we did specific activities with them. The children were motivated to participate in these activities out of their desire to play but also their search for adults in a positive context. During these activities, the children found opportunities for expressing their feelings about events and the suffering they had caused. They also exhibited feelings of resistance and distrust, which caused difficulties in their relationships with others. About two-thirds of the orphan children between the ages of six and fourteen participated in these workshops, together with other children who were not directly affected but who joined in of their own accord. (Cabrera et al. 1998, 85)

The community approach should also underscore existing positive strategies for facing ideological, cultural, and religious issues. It does not necessarily have to focus on trauma. Work in conflict situations can also help to overcome stereotypes, improve communication skills, and create positive social attitudes. "The groups really started to work well when instead of talking about 'traumatic experiences' they talked about problems in the refugee camps, conflicts with the director of the camp or with the time-table, the political situation, and especially resuming control of their daily lives and focusing on collective or individual resolutions to immediate problems" (Jones 1995).

SOCIAL INDICATORS

It is important to take social indicators into account when providing support to communities affected by social or political disasters, as these often display the difficulties the population is facing.[5] Very often, suffering is not always expressed and demands for care are not always received through the normal channels such as medical visits.

Certain social indicators, such as family or group conflicts, difficulties at school, aggression, and drug or alcohol abuse, may be considered indicators of a community going through difficulties. Paying attention to these indicators and listening to the demands of the people can be a way of identifying these problems. These indicators were used in the case of the community of Xamán to diagnose and monitor the effect of the massacre (Cabrera et al. 1998). They were used to try and understand the progress and continuing problems that the community faced and to make decisions on the type of support to provide. Continuing problems included (1) the mass grieving process, which especially affected the families of the victims but also the community as a whole; (2) the impact of the threats, fear, and reliving the experience because the community had survived other massacres in the 1980s; (3) the criminalization and blame the community was subject to from outside and the search for a meaning to the tragedy within the community; (4) the organizational impact and the emergence of new leaders and structure; (5) conflicts, in part worsened by the humanitarian aid and different opinions on the type of aid program needed; and (6) the impact of impunity and the legal investigation on the fear and expectations of the community.

However, other social indicators may be a sign of the welfare or recovery of the community. Sometimes there are signs that the community has gone back to its daily life—for example, positive rituals such as the harvest ceremony, commemoration of the birth of the community (as in the case of the refugees from Guatemala in Mexico), or the reconstruction of the social organizations that have been destroyed. These signs of the welfare of the community help to affirm its identity. Also, some people or groups, when faced with an extreme situation, react by increasing social cohesion and forming a defense against suffering and social destruction.

Working with Community Partners: The Multiplying Effect

One of the strategies of the community approach is training and working alongside the "multipliers" of the affected community—leaders, group representatives, teachers, and so forth. Multipliers can help to identify problems and available resources, and through more training and experience they support the most affected individuals and communities. Work with multipliers encourages an authentic intercultural exchange, provides a trusting relationship with the communities, facilitates the continuity of the work, and reinforces the social fabric and existing support networks in the community.

Problems with "Multiplication" Work

Despite what would appear to be the ease of working with multipliers under the community approach, in practice we find some constraints:

1. Availability of time. Many people in these positions are already overloaded with work. In addition, psychosocially oriented activities are rarely considered a priority given the grave social needs of the people.
2. Lack of collaboration from authorities or leaders, who constitute the entry point for the work with groups and communities.
3. Effect of the disaster on the multipliers. The multipliers may themselves be affected, which diminishes their ability to cope with other people's suffering.
4. Unclear criteria or inadequate selection of people.
5. Financial and social needs that place limitations on time or activity.
6. Possible perception from people or groups that the work is for a specific group or NGO.
7. Security problems. Under threatening situations, the work of the multipliers may be considered dangerous and subject to repression.
8. Need for recognition (moral, material, or economic) of their role in the community. This may support them but it can also be a source of conflict.

In 1991, ECPROSAM, a training program in mental health, received people for training from all over El Salvador. Resources were available to these people with traveling expenses to attend the training. A large number of health promoters were trained over a period of three years. They were trained without a clear idea of where they would work or the sustainability of the initiative. The increasing number of health promoters began to demand a recognized qualification from the Health Ministry and a position in the health system. To which the ministry replied that the training had not been provided by them and that they did not have the financial capacity to employ them, not even with a symbolic fee. In the end, the Canadian finance company withdrew its funding and ECPROSAM disappeared (Pérez Sales 1999).

Positive Experiences and Resources in Working with Multipliers

1. The systematization of experiences and the use of basic materials, working guides, and so forth facilitate community activities.

2. Accompanying the multipliers in their first few tasks can increase the perception of security and self-confidence. In the case of problematic experiences, this accompanying process opens the possibility for discussion and adjustment and diminishes a negative self-appraisal ("I can't do it").

3. Teaching of multiplication techniques in the last stages of the training increases the ability and confidence of the multipliers.

4. Providing areas for mutual support among multipliers helps to share experiences, learn new ideas, and give a collective purpose to the work without depending on the arrival of an external manager.

5. Focus the work on tasks that the multipliers normally do with a reference group (women, young people, and so on) and have them adapt the contents.

6. Mobilize personal resources such as time or dedication through prior political or religious commitments.

7. Specify selection criteria: availability, sensitivity, leadership ability, and so forth.

We decided to ask the community to assign a promoter to us, with a signed contract in which the organization commits to training the promoter and providing him or her with supplies (basic medicine, medicinal plants, stationery, and so on). In turn, the organization agrees to provide the promoters either with material compensation or by working their land while they are working for the community. In this system, the community feels that the promoter is working for them and they can ask him or her to fulfill certain responsibilities, clearing the way for collective management based on revolving funds. The problem arises when the community is not well-organized and cannot guarantee it will fulfill its side of the agreement. As far as possible, the sustainability will also depend on the involvement of public authorities, as long as they are not involved in the violence. (Pérez Sales et al. 1999)

THERAPEUTIC APPROACHES

Programs with a therapeutic approach focus on a cure and cater to the people or families who are most affected. They all share a common element: to recall or reconstruct the traumatic experience.[6]

In general, these programs recognize that expressing and reconstructing the experience helps the person to feel better. Therapy with children uses different techniques such as games, pictures, and dramatizations. Working with nonverbal techniques such as art or theater can spur creative communication.

The testimony (Cienfuegos and Monelli 1983) or account of the trauma (Mollica 1987) involves a written account of the events, through a process of recording and editing, in which the person can keep a permanent record of what happened for personal or public use. When the therapeutic process transforms the personal suffering into social testimony, it seems to diminish the effects (Becker and Lira 1989). For many people, sharing their experiences can also have a social purpose, such as helping others who have the same difficulties.

> We had suffered because we had been tortured, but also because of the lies of those who had concealed it and the lack of opportunities to talk about it and start the healing process. The objective of the group was to support each other but not only to share our experiences among ourselves. We also hoped that we could contribute to helping other people or groups who have to cope with the consequences of violence. In the beginning, the group talked about personal experiences, analyzing the effects of repression on individuals and collectives and ways of coping with fear and resisting torture. Later on, we discussed the consequences on our lives and constructive ways of coping with these problems. (Mutual support group; Sarea 1994)

The person becomes an active part of the therapy, and the role of the therapist is to clarify, encourage, and act as witness. Further into the testimony, psychological reactions such as guilt for having given names of friends or family members are seen as inevitable reactions to pain and helplessness (McIvor and Turner 1995). Reconstructing one's own identity can be an important objective after traumatic experiences such as rape or torture and disrupted grieving processes (Barudy 1989; Vesti and Bojlom 1990).

Over the last two decades, various clinics have offered specialized treatment for victims of violence or social disasters. Despite the advantages of this specialized help, in many countries where the traumatic events affected the enitre population, more of a stigma is attached to this help. In countries where means are scarce, these clinics could be considered as catering only to the "elite" of the affected population. "In Chile, for example, whereas the majority of the population in different regions never had access to mental-health care, CINTRAS [Center of Mental Health and Human Rights] carried out long-term individual psychoanalysis for a select group of twenty-five people. Including people in work-therapy programs, rehabilitation, and family groups, CINTRAS had a budget in 1994 of over \$400,000" (Pérez Sales 1999).

Traditional and Local Health Systems

For more continuous support of those most affected, it is helpful if someone from the person's family or social group accompanies him or her to the therapist and carries out a part of the subsequent follow-up.

When working with people from other cultures, bicultural workers are essential and should be distinguished from translators as shown in the following list (Pérez Sales 1999):

Translators	*Bicultural Workers*
• Their work involves bridging the *language barrier*.	• Their work involves bridging the *cultural barrier*, by proposing areas for work, suggesting or facilitating contacts with people or community authorities, and contributing to the working program as they take local elements into account.
• They are expected to be faithful to the original text.	• More than changing one language into another, they are expected to reinterpret the key elements from one culture to another.
• They do not intervene in the diagnostic or therapeutic process. A minimal distortion of the information is expected.	• They are an active part of the diagnostic or therapeutic process. They can take charge of the session, freely asking questions and looking for diagnostic elements that are specific to the culture.
• The Western therapist decides on the therapeutic process.	• The session may be interrupted for the exchange of opinions between the therapist and the bicultural worker. Each may formulate his or her therapeutic proposals from the cultural context and decide together which strategy to follow.

The therapeutic elements used are based on Khmer thinking and culture schemes. The work is carried out in teams of co-therapists with a local bilingual mental-health worker and a Western therapist who discuss and prepare the sessions, or they can interrupt the session to discuss how the interview is going and how to continue. Both decide on the best approach for the patient based on the KCBM[7] philosophy, resorting to traditional therapists or Buddhist monks who live in the refugee camps. Despite the collectivist nature of Asian societies, the traditional Buddhist model understands suffering and tragedy as a result of the individual *karma*, related to previous lives and events. This means that the suppression of anger and conformity of the individual is favored more than collective and organized support, which in many cases calls for individual treatment and not group treatment preferred by other cultures. (Lavelle et al. 1996)

The World Health Organization and UNHCR make recommendations on how to relate to traditional systems in the field of mental health with displaced populations (UNHCR and WHO 1992). However, Ager (1995) points out that attempts to reconcile Western medicine and traditional approaches are often carried out as a symbolic interpretation of traditional practices in a decontextualized form. They fail to take into account the social function of these practices in non-Western societies and thus do not recognize the same social function in Western medicine. The risk also exists that the predominance of Western medicine will perpetuate the colonial status of the Third World (Berry et al. 1992).

A young soldier consults a healer because he feels that the spirits of those he has killed are following him. The healer decides to hold a ceremony in which the parents of the soldier should be present, and in which the spirits will speak through him. The young man can listen to them and ask them for forgiveness. The deceased asks for material compensation and that the soldier help the families of the survivors. The soldier accepts and subsequently feels much better. (Mozambique, in Efraime 1993)

Traditional healers are better able to understand culturally determining factors and to have their own therapeutic resources. In many cases, they have broad experience and demonstrated efficiency. They also apply criteria from other therapeutic processes, such as trust, respect, understanding of suffering, and an ability to help. However, in some countries certain forms of traditional healing may have been involved in the violence. In an effort to favor local therapists, refugees from Rwanda found themselves in the hands of those who had been responsible for the genocide in their village a few months before (Efraime 1993).

WORKING WITH TRADITIONAL HEALERS

Advantages	Disadvantages
1. Work from within the culture. Use therapeutic strategies that are not accessible to a Western therapist.	1. Attribution of unforeseen causality.
	2. Different objectives.
2. Ethically more respectful.	3. Some practices may not respect human rights.
3. Proven effectiveness.	
4. Reinforce the adaptive strategies of the culture.	4. Healers may sometimes be allies with sources of power.
5. No language barrier; no need for translators.	5. Must distinguish between authentic traditional healers and untrained therapists or charlatans.

Source: Pérez Sales 1999.

Also, the presence of local professionals can help to overcome problems that are inherent in the intercultural community, which underscores the importance of the participation of traditional healers in the health system. The participation of midwives in Bangladesh and traditional healers in Thailand have made various projects successful because of their prestige and their having the trust of the population, as well as providing continuity in the treatment (UNDP 1994).

Last, after a disaster one of the main priorities should be the reconstruction of existing health services as a way of reinforcing local resources and participation (Zwi and Ugalde 1989). This supports the local professionals and provides continuity. With the creation of parallel health services, though, there is a risk that it may decrease public efforts to attract professionals to provide these services, therefore weakening the reconstruction effort. This happened with APRONUC (Provisional Authority of the United Nations in Cambodia) in Cambodia, where the higher salaries meant that professionals left their jobs and joined the international organizations (Biberson and Goemaere 1993).

The Experience of the PRAIS Program in Chile: As part of the Repair Bill passed by the government and in compliance with the demands of the Association of Relatives of the Missing, Detained, and Victims of Political Violence and mental-health organizations, the state took as its own obligation medical care for the victims. In order to do this, it created health teams in all the regions and installed them in all the hospitals of the public-health system, run by a multidisciplinary team of general practitioners, psychologists, psychiatrists, and social workers. The program has been widely accepted because of its location and also because the mental-health medical attention is indistinguishable from all the rest. (Prais 2006)

Intervention in Crisis Situations

PSYCHOSOCIAL CARE IN DISASTERS

During disasters, it may be necessary to integrate therapeutic elements with community work. Psychosocial support services should offer an accompanying process from the first stages, striving to avoid labeling a person as a victim or sick person. Teams should base their work on the following basic attitudes:

1. *Listening and supporting.* A listening, accepting, and supportive attitude is fundamental at the time of contact with survivors.
2. *Helping to cope with what has happened.* The people must be helped to understand their experience, offered support that will allow them to restore their sense of control over their fear—"Nobody could foresee what happened." "The majority of people would have done the same as you."—in a way that does not make them feel victimized by a random and threatening world.
3. *Understanding the emotional reactions.* Reassure the survivors that the strong emotional reactions that they have experienced, or that

overwhelm them, are common and that they are normal reactions after a disaster. These are some of the common reactions: fear, feeling of despair, sorrow, nostalgia for those who are no longer with them, feeling of guilt, sense of shame, anger, wondering why they survived, memories, and systematic reminiscence of the people they have lost. These feelings are stronger if many people have died, if the deaths were sudden or violent, if the bodies have not been found, if there was a close relationship with the deceased, or if the relationship with the deceased was troubled. Time, accompaniment, and solidarity are needed to cope with the impact of the disaster.

4. *Normalizing physical symptoms.* Fatigue, lack of sleep, nightmares, loss of memory, difficulty concentrating, palpitations, trembling, difficulty breathing, diarrhea, tension that can produce headaches or backache, menstrual irregularity, and changes in sexual interest are all common physical reactions brought on by stress. It is important not only to see them as an expression of suffering but also to pay attention to the worst-affected people, helping to reduce their symptoms but without medicalizing the suffering. When people find themselves bewildered by the emotional shock, dealing with the physical symptoms could be a useful way of doing something, establishing a good relationship, and improving their well-being.

5. *Appreciating changes in social relations.* Help survivors to identify the changes experienced in family and social relationships, including actions of solidarity, new friendships, and support groups. Initially, the force of the impact may prevail, but these changes may be seen and later reevaluated as part of the resources for reconstruction.

6. *Foreseeing subsequent tensions* that can appear in social relations. The survivors may feel disappointed by the lack of support and understanding that surrounds them. Furthermore, many former problems might resurface in the form of conflicts, especially during the reconstruction phase. Accidents tend to be more frequent after episodes of severe stress. It is, therefore, important to restructure people's daily lives as soon as possible and organize support. Prevention and handling of conflicts can be a support strategy in contexts of social disorganization or where conflicts or problems with aid management have occurred.

7. *Taking the following actions:*
   a. Favoring activities to stay active and help others, as this helps to lift people's spirits. However, overactivity is negative and prevents people from helping themselves.
   b. When people feel ready, confronting reality, attending funerals,

and inspecting the losses may help them to cope with what has happened.

c. Receiving help from others is positive, as well as being able to talk about what has happened. Even though advice about trying to forget and moving on can be full of good intentions, most of the time it will have a negative effect as it involves an impossible task and suggests a lack of understanding.

d. A certain degree of privacy to cope with feelings is important, taking cultural differences into account at all times.

8. *Providing support teams that act as a witness.* Victims can talk about what happened so that the witness accepts it and validates their experience. In some cases, it is a way of making a formal complaint or having the opportunity to explain what has happened. This is especially important in the case of socio-political disasters. This attitude can help to make sharing their experiences more meaningful to the survivors at the same time as it leaves a testimony with a social value. However, an excessive display of means in contrast with the misery of the people, or an overactive role that relegates the victims to a lesser role, may give rise to the teams becoming the center of attention and creating distance from the people affected. All this creates a challenge for professionals, as it means going beyond the usual framework of their jobs with a stronger commitment toward the affected population (Hodgkinson and Stewart 1991; ILAS 1996).

9. *Controlling the impact of humanitarian aid.* Some ways of assessing and controlling the negative effects of providing humanitarian aid, particularly the reaction to dependency and conflicts, are taking into account the local impact of the aid in relationships of power, the increase in social differences, and so on; establishing a clear consensus on the criteria for aid; seeing to people's demands and encouraging the participation of the affected population; supporting self-organization; guaranteeing an effective control of the aid; and promoting mutual support systems and solidarity networks, instead of creating dependency (ODHAG 1998).

PARTICIPATION AND SELF-HELP: GAINING POWER OVER ONE'S OWN LIFE

The aim of support programs should be to stimulate people's initiative and responsibility over their own affairs. Although many programs declare that their main objective is to encourage people to gain control over their own lives (*empowerment*), in reality it is often a case of how to make people participate in programs that have been designed by others.

Programs based on a philosophy of helping often see people as passive: receivers of the aid or beneficiaries of the program. In some pro-

> ### Should Victims Be Encouraged to Talk?
>
> Many people believe that it is always good to talk after going through a traumatic or difficult experience. A frequently used technique consists of interviewing very soon after the event (debriefing). In the interview, the affected person should (a) describe what happened from his or her perspective, (b) express what he or she believes to be most relevant about what happened, and (c) say what the worst thing was about the experience. In this way, supposedly, the mental-health problems associated with the traumatic impact may be prevented (PTSD).
>
> However, research shows that talking about the traumatic event immediately after it has occurred does not have the desired effect, because: (a) talking about emotional experiences of traumatic events is psychologically exhausting; (b) talking about what has happened has a positive effect on physical health in the long term, but it can have an immediate negative effect on mood and the physiological state; and (c) encouraging people to talk about their experiences immediately after the event is not positive. Nonetheless, taking part in emergency committees or support groups can help people participate, solve their problems, and share their experiences in a more relaxed way with other people.
>
> In short, talking is positive if you include emotions and reappraisals, if you are able to distance yourself psychologically, if it is not done in a repetitive way, and if the person is willing. Although it is true that supressing your emotions is negative, being forced to talk is not necessarily beneficial. Furthermore, cultural differences should also be considered when expressing or sharing emotions.

Source: Pennebaker 1995; Rimé et al. 1998.

grams, participation is seen as something instrumental: a basic requirement for the delivery of the aid or counting on the people to carry out the programmed activities. However, in community participation oriented toward increasing the empowerment of the people and their communities, people are considered the most important part of the process. Community participation increases social support and the capacity to rebuild the social fabric. It should, therefore, be seen as an indicator of the quality of the programs and the reliability of the decision-making (Gedalof 1991).

In this context, the concept of self-help refers to how people can improve their situation by sharing their needs and problems, learning from the positive experiences of others, and offering mutual support for change. Research on traumatic events and the analysis of social trends has demonstrated the value of peer communication.

From a psychological perspective, mutual aid processes include objectivity and an analysis of the situation; mutual support; the recognition of hidden feelings and experiences; the generalization of experiences;

finding solutions and integration; the development of common actions to cope with problems; and the development of gratifying social activities (Heap 1985).

Group Resources for Mutual Support

Make sense of what has happened. Objectify the events; make sense of what has happened from an ideological, religious, and symbolic viewpoint.

Make an area to meet and relax. Enjoy socially and culturally significant activities.

Give mutual support. "Lend each other strength" to generate the necessary energy to support each other and work together.

Control impulsive reactions. The group can help its members not get carried away with reactions that have not been thought through or feelings that have not been confronted, thus avoiding an excessive emotional release, favoring instead a more "regulated" reaction trying to understand others.

Identify feelings. Share and make sense of feelings that have remained hidden or denied because they were considered to be negative, whether from shame or social prejudice, or because they did not conform to the moral values of the person.

Generalize experiences. This helps people to "open up" and free the altered image they may have of themselves. This also helps to restructure the implicit rules, making them more liberal.

Implement solutions. Decisions or solutions discussed and proposed in a group are adopted more easily by everybody.

Develop collective power. The individual capabilities and the potential summoned by the group help it to actively confront problems. This can be especially valuable in the last stages of the group process.

Encourage communication. The culturally acceptable behavior of symbolizing the experience (through group rituals, celebrations, etc.) can make expression and collective identification easier and encourages the reconstruction of a sense of identity.

These mutual support groups can also provide the opportunity for a social meeting place and personal growth that does not necessarily focus on traumatic experiences. For example, in Bosnia, Marie Stopes International set up a network of centers and self-help groups for women, where the main purpose was not to focus on traumatic stress but to enjoy regular meetings in a pleasant environment to discuss issues brought up by the women, such as: Are husbands the boss? Do you have to get married to have a child? It showed that, as in other wars, one of the most significant psychosocial effects is how women change the way they think about themselves (Jones 1995).

Similarly, in the postwar period in El Salvador, the main reason for setting up women's groups as mutual support groups was to discuss questions such as: What will happen to us after the war? (Garaizabal and Vázquez 1992). "I'm returning to El Salvador, which has progressed a little bit since the war. I'm going because I feel like going and because Sandra has invited me to go and support her women's group. They found themselves searching for places where people like themselves, previously organized by the FMLN [Frente Farabundo Martí de Liberación Nacional, Salvadoran guerillas during the 1980s], can find help. They get together, celebrate, search, cry, and try to fill their new lives with color in a country that they sometimes don't recognize as their own" (Martín Beristain 1997).

Working in groups has profound meaning given the social nature of the experiences and the communal sense of the rebuilding process. However, this should not become another way of isolating people or of overemphasizing their status as the "affected population." Groups that focus on a particular event are more effective when the event was experienced by a group; when the people do not have any other opportunity to share their problems and find solutions; and when people can benefit from sharing experiences with others. The importance of overcoming the risk of stigmatization or being considered "the special ones" must be kept in mind.

Assessing Group Interventions

Assessments of some group treatment programs for people who suffer from collective traumatic events show that people tend to assess the programs positively but that there was no marked impact on symptoms. In other words, even when people assess a group positively, there is not always a reduction of symptoms (Hodgkinson and Stewart 1991). However, a review of research into the efficiency of self-help group interventions showed a positive overall effect (Lieberman 1993).[8]

Most of the research shows that group work has a positive effect, particularly among those people who were in danger of developing pathological grief. Studies also show that people who took part in the groups were healthier and recovered more quickly than those who did not. Interventions focused on the individual are more effective at the beginning of the grieving process, whereas interventions involving the reinsertion of the affected population are more appropriate later on.

Models for Work with Community Mental-Health Groups

Mental-health groups are based on different work models depending on the use of time (extensive or intensive models), the continuity of the members' participation in the group (open and closed models), as well as the focus on the content of the process of sharing experiences (educational or socialization models). Following is a prototypical scheme for a mutual support group.

1. Methodological conditions
   - Necessary organizational conditions.[9]
   - Small-sized groups (6 to 12 people), but this can vary.
   - Between 4 and 10 sessions, lasting 2 to 3 hours each (depending on the context and type of group).
2. Support and identification
   - Combine the necessary conditions of trust with the wealth of experiences and the type and origin of the participants.
   - Similar conditions of problems and feelings of stress.
   - A reciprocal identity among the participants allows them to create ties within the group based on the type of experience (prison, loss of family member) and social characteristics (ethnic group, gender, etc.)
3. Ways of working
   - Work on common cores of experience: fear management, personal experience, family difficulties, reintegration into groups, etc.

In terms of time, in an extensive model, work takes place over a longer period of time and with less frequency (for example, twice a month). In an intensive model, work takes place for a shorter period and more frequently (for example, two to three hours once a week).

MODELS IN MENTAL-HEALTH GROUPS: TIME AND PROCESSES

Extensive	Intensive
• Allows each person to take on specific commitments and to have enough time to carry them out.	• Allows a gradual learning process.
	• Provides stronger group support and motivation.
• Provides more attention at the beginning when the group process is activated.	• Result of missing a day is less problematic.
	• Self-help
• Requires less travel and involves fewer security problems.	• Skills training
• Multiplication	• Local communities
• Isolated areas	

Regarding the participants' continuity in a group, an open model structures the group as a means for getting together, discussing, and participating, in which people come and go. In contrast, in a closed model, the group is formed on a particular date with a certain number of people over a certain period of time; new members will not be accepted halfway through the process.

GROUP MODELS: OPEN AND CLOSED

Open	Closed
• People who have been in the group longer become models for those who have just arrived (internal transfer of experience and knowledge). • Is more dynamic, but the working rhythm may be disrupted. • Results in a lesser degree of trust.	• The sensation of always starting again is avoided. • Roles are identified more easily. • More care is taken over the group process. • Greater difficulties arise for the concluding phase of the group.

The educational model establishes a place for discussing and sharing experiences where behavior guidelines are recommended. The aim is to understand problems and to learn new attitudes. The coordinator intervenes more with explanations and interpretations of people's experiences. The socialization model puts the focus on the socialization of experiences, with participants freely sharing experiences. The group process prevails over the learning process. The coordinator hardly takes part, except to suggest a topic for discussion or to redirect the discussion if the point has been lost.

Following are the factors that determine the type of group model to be used:

- the objectives of the group
- the time available
- the experience of the coordinator

When in doubt, start with the extensive, closed, and educational models because they are easier to coordinate. With them, there should be fewer problems dealing with negative emotional outbursts, and it is easier to create an atmosphere of security and trust among the group's members.

MITIGATING THE DAMAGE: PSYCHOSOCIAL REPAIR

To rebuild the social fabric of a community, active measures are needed to help improve the situation of the victims such as alleviating the damage and providing economic and moral compensation. In addition to projects for victims, some governments, humanitarian agencies, and cooperation and solidarity organizations have implemented psychosocial projects with different aims, including economic compensation, development projects, commemorations and monuments.[10] In practice, however, very little real assessment of the internal logic, conception, and effect of these actions has taken place.

Even though these projects may help to solve the problems of the affected families and communities, the direct impact of the aid given for living conditions cannot be assessed without considering the impact on the dignity of these people. Support organizations for families of the arrested and the disappeared in countries of the Southern Cone of Latin America have made this claim as have studies assessing compensation measures.

A study of the impact of the measures mentioned earlier on the Mapuche families of the arrested and disappeared in Chile has demonstrated the limitations of this economic approach from an ethnic perspective. Economic compensation given to the families of victims caused serious inequality among families, internal conflicts, and difficulties in understanding the administrative aspects of the Reparation Law (Pérez Sales et al. 1998). In other countries in which the state has assumed responsibility for some of the massacres, such as the cases of Xamán (Guatemala, 1995) and Trujillo (Colombia, 1989–92), the aid management caused conflicts and was based on legitimization criteria determined by the state. Furthermore, all these compensatory measures cannot be separated from other necessary measures such as those concerning collective memory or the demands for truth and justice.

Any reparation action should be based on the following concerns: the participation of the affected population, the capacity of the affected population for decision-making; the clarity and fairness of the criteria, and the recognition of a contribution to—not a substitution for—the need for justice. The following table lists the variables that influence the internal logic of the psychosocial repair processes. These should be governed by the logic of repairing the social fabric and not by the logic of control, often used by the state.

Memory and Reconstruction Processes

Experience has shown us that it is amnesia that makes history repeat itself over and over again. Having a good memory allows us to learn from the past, because the only reason for recovering the past is to use it to transform life in the present.

—Eduardo Galeano (1996)

REPARATION LOGIC

Repair . . . What?	Frequent Problems in State Logic	Reconstruction of the Social Fabric
Return dignity to people and their families.	Increase social control with aid (militarization, etc.)	Consider the local impact and the demands of the people.
Prevent the causes so the problem is not repeated; value collective memory.	Divert the attention of the justice system (give economic compensation to avoid legal procedures). Allow anonymous memories (without culprits) or a clichéd version of the events.	Keep the restoration of dignity present in every action, based on the values of human rights.
Rebuild neighbor and family ties (the social fabric).	Ignore whether aid is increasing social differences or community divisions.	Help to face the consequences of war and repression; respond to real problems.
Provide security and trust.	Allow deception, on some occasions, with certain forms of aid (unfulfilled promises, low quality of aid).	Support the people's own organizations (not the creation of new structures, unknown to the people)
Reestablish a moral conscience in society.	Increase the legitimization of the state (populism, electoral patronage, keeping up appearances amid international pressure).	Give the people control of the aid. Provide effective control systems for aid management. Avoid corruption.
Reconsider plans for the future (individual and collective).	Control aid and repair processes (increase in dependency, costly procedures, imposition on how to use the aid, etc.).	Make an ethnical commitment. The people who work on these programs identify with the suffering of the victims and their struggle for dignity. Give collective boards or recognized authorities the capacity to make decisions on reparation. Increase the capacity for organization and mutual support.

Collective memory is the result of members of a group rebuilding their past based on their interests and references in the present. For people affected by violence and social disasters, memory provides therapeutic value and the value of justice and social recognition and can therefore play a preventive role in psychological, social, and political matters.

In the contexts of war and political repression, the victims have not had the opportunity to identify those responsible, have not benefited from social recognition of the events or their suffering, and have not had reparations based on justice. In addition, memory is often tied up by fear, social devaluation, or even criminalization of the affected population. All this has a negative effect on the individual and social identities of those affected, as well as other wider social effects that derive from impunity.

THE CELEBRATION OF MEMORIES

Collective memory is a way of recognizing that events occurred, that they were unjust, and that they should never be repeated (Jodelet 1992). For the victims and their families, the main motivation is to know the truth and to gain public recognition of their unheard story. This implicit demand for dignity is strongly linked to the recognition of injustice, to the claim by victims and their families as people whose dignity has been violated, and to the demand for social sanctions for the perpetrators. These types of memories contribute to a collective elaboration of the trauma, recognizing that it is in the past, substituting a psychological simultaneity (continuing to relive the traumatic experiences of the past) for a past-present sequence, and slowly dislodging the pain and resentment.

The commemoration of past events allows for public recognition and the attribution of meaning, but even when this cannot be accomplished, the memory may still remain through habits, oral traditions, and historical archives (Ibañez 1992).

Talking about what happened also led to reporting illegal cemeteries, to holding ceremonies as in Sahakok (Alta Verapaz), where the elderly people had dreamed of installing a cross at the top of the hill where so many of their brothers and sisters had been left without a burial. Twenty-eight communities organized themselves to make this dream come true. The people inscribed the names of the 916 people whose remains were on the mountain. (Martín Beristain 1997)

Ceremonies and public recognition are valuable because they dignify people's sacrifices. Much more than a mystification of suffering or the turning of the deceased into heroes, memory and giving dignity to the dead are also ways of giving meaning to their participation in society or the significance they gave to their groups and communities. For many people, that memory also brings about a social conscience and a stimulus for their lives.

The dictionary says that "to bury" means to place a dead body under the ground. Raquel wants to have a funeral and bury David, and we all go to accompany her. She has finally obtained the necessary papers: once again fighting against the bureaucracy of the living that also applies to the dead. Marta says she doesn't want to bury the ideals of the people or what they did. Between us we write the words of our dictionaries of life. Where it says "bury," it will say "break the silence" and "to rescue our name and dignity." Bury means "to care for." (El Salvador; Martín Beristain 1997)

The search for the truth also has an impact on the grieving process, as in demands for exhumation to determine the circumstances of a death. These exhumations are not carried out for only political or practical reasons. Respect for the memory of the dead and the dignity of the survivors must form part of the activities that involve confronting the pain. Activities such as exhumations and the collection of testimonies should be carried out with the participation of those affected and their communities,[11] and must be endorsed by laws that make procedures easier and help coordinate the efforts of the institutions and groups that take part.

Attempts to support the processes of collective memory must take into account that the memories of the traumatic events evoke intense emotions in people who give testimony or who find themselves linked strongly to the victims. The people who collect those testimonies and memories need good listening skills and an attitude of respect, and they must provide support afterward, not just formal organizational criteria. Bureaucratic attitudes and obstacles also form part of impunity, which brings about added suffering for the victims and their families. Attention should be paid to local processes and respect given to the rhythm of the affected communities so that the legal and technical processes do not become another obstacle.

Celebrations and commemorations should remember not only the pain but also the solidarity. It is important for families to reflect on positive memories, pleasant events, achievements, and affection, all of which may make the loss more tolerable and help the survivors recover their own self-confidence.

Confronting the Pain

Nonetheless, even the survivors of massacres may have as much desire to forget about what happened as to talk about how much they have suf-

The Memory of Moral Harm: Aurora Community, Xamán, 1996

Six months after the massacre, the community became involved in the reconstruction of collective memory. We call this work "the memory of moral harm." This initiative arose from the need to evaluate the moral harm done to the whole community by the massacre, and to present it as part of the petition in the judicial process. The methodological design of this proposal, which involved the participation of all community groups and sectors, was carried out by a mental-health team and a group of representatives from the community.

1. Workshops were developed with the leaders and representatives of all the sectors of the community to reconstruct the consequences of the events and the coping mechanisms used: production, relations with the neighboring villages, culture and religion, health and education, etc.
2. Subsequently, the leaders increased those workshops: they collected narratives, paintings, murals, letters, and summaries of the effects and how the situation was confronted. All the sectors of the community took part (five hundred people from twelve different social groups), including children, adults, and the elderly.
3. Later, an exhibition was set up in the community with all the testimonies and material collected in those workshops, and national and international organizations took part. The exhibition recreated the events, the impact on the people, the response from the groups, who the victims were, and the demands of the community.

This collective memory was used to develop working material and to publish a pamphlet that would serve as useful testimony for other communities and future generations.

Source: Cabrera et al. 1998.

fered. Traumatic events tend to be avoided or inhibited, whether because of the threatening and painful nature of the memory, because of the stigma and rejection that they may cause, or to protect those close to them. Memory generates pain, but at the same time, because of its impact, events may keep reappearing so that victims cannot forget. Therefore, the context does not favor the assimilation of these traumatic events nor the search for a meaning to what has occurred. "I would like to tell you how much this hurt me. Before I started talking, I was very tense and still feel like this due to thinking about all these things. But I now see it from a different perspective, it doesn't hurt so much although I have experienced it again in another way, and sometimes I feel resentment and think about who I have to get even with" (ODHAG 1998, 8).

Self-censorship or imposed silence has been described as a deep scar, a violent suppression of many years that is a testimony to the suffering of a penetrating wound. However, despite this public inhibition, the

---

Reconstruction of Collective Memory:
The Value of the Testimony

The testimonies are treasures, the fundamental basis for the reconstruction of the historical memory, but they may also produce some biases because of the following:

1. The time elapsed since the events (e.g., reliability of dates).
2. The traumatic impact of the violence and its possible effects.
3. The interviewer's supposed evaluation of political participation (it is especially difficult in an initial interview to admit to a relationship with a guerilla when there was danger).
4. The organization of memory—initial simplification; exaggeration of some events; a conventional version adapted to the needs of the present—which may make certain issues appear, especially with regard to political struggle or people's hopes ("They tricked us").
5. The cultural context in which they are read. Cultural context frames subjective ideas such as time (e.g., a chain of events) and forms of expression (envy in traditional societies, etc.).

Source: ODHAG 1998.

strongest community memories are those that belong to the groups under threat, who are associated with a higher level of thinking and sharing among those closest to them. In a threatened community, memories serve above all to emphasize a sense of common identity. In this way, episodes of division and conflict are often left behind (Thompson 1988).

DISTORTION OF MEMORY

Many examples exist throughout history of a tendency to rebuild memory in a distorted way, to the point of blaming the victims. For example, according to some surveys, the majority of the German population over forty believes, fifty years on, that the Jews were partly responsible for the Holocaust (Daniel 1992). Another common tendency is silence. In Germany after the war, the reigning attitude was to not talk about it or to not accept being judged for past involvement with Nazism. In the period following Salazar's dictatorship in Portugal, the reaction was similar, with a generalized silence about active participation in the former regime.

Official versions often suggest it is necessary to "turn the page of history to rebuild society." Reconstruction must be built over a forced amnesia, as if the event had no important consequences. Those responsible suggest their own version of events, where the avoidance of remembering or a conventionalized memory predominates, thus maintaining a coherent image of themselves. As in the case of the dirty war in Spain (Batallón Vasco-Español and Grupos Antiterroristas de Liberación, both rightist, extremist armed groups), the responsible politicians recalled the violence as that which was defensively necessary ("Those were hard times"), but it did not explain the events.

In other cases, the unwillingness of the victims to recall also plays a role in the distortion of memory. In Chile, for example, this type of "conspiracy of silence" has had an ideological impact: to legitimize the present situation. The arrest of the ex-dictator Augusto Pinochet initially brought about a continued polarization because of the lack of information, the ideological justification, and the distortion of the recollection of the crimes committed against humanity by the Policía Política de la Dictadura (the political arm of the police during the dictatorship in Chile).

This example also shows that in recent traumatic events, sharing thoughts about the past leads to a polarization of attitudes or at least a more negative attitude toward the current situation. The impact of the events experienced in Chile and the demands for justice and repair that were not listened to cannot be ignored. Therefore, the collective memory of events may make an underlying conflict more explicit in the effort to achieve a new social equilibrium. In countries with fewer conflicts about the traumas of the past, however, a reappraisal usually delivers an improved image of the society.

I am surprised by the lateness of the discovery of this fracture and even more so by the confusion about the causes. It is clear that there is a deep social fracture in Chile. How else could it be in a society that doesn't know the whereabouts of three thousand of its citizens, that has seen its fundamental rights denied, that has put up with terror, torture, injustice, the murder of opponents inside and outside its borders, and the exile of hundreds of thousands? There wasn't enough strength to put up a resistance, and it wasn't worth opposing because it was protected by eternal impunity. (Sepúlveda 1998)

The distortion of collective memory and the lack of social recognition of the events have an effect on survivors, such as "privatizing" the damage, not restoring dignity to the victims, and losing support for the people most affected, who find themselves without a social framework to give their experience positive meaning. Some of these distortions are initiated deliberately, such as the attempts by totalitarian regimes to rewrite history. For example, the Augusto Pinochet Foundation runs the Institute of the History of Chile, which is writing a contemporary history based on its own interests. Distortions may also result from efforts to hide episodes considered embarrassing. Finally, others could be well-intentioned changes to provide a true account of past events. The following box shows the processes of the distortion of memory, which include multiple mechanisms to make the recollection conventional.

Distortion of Collective Memory: Strategies and Mechanisms

Selective omission: Thomas Jefferson, who wrote "all men are created equal" in the U.S. Declaration of Independence, was the owner of many slaves.

Manipulating the association of events. The United States[12] tends to see the Iraqi invasion as a response to the September 11 attacks.

Exaggeration and embellishment. While the Red Army carried the full weight of the allied victory in World War II, it was the Normandy invasion that was magnified.

Blaming the enemy. The German bombings of Freiberg and Guernica were carried out by the Luftwaffe, but the French and the Republican armies, respectively, were blamed.

Holding the circumstances responsible. During the Spanish and Portuguese conquests, the annihilation of Native American populations was attributed to illness.

Stressing one causal event over others. The Crusades were a "noble attempt to guarantee the rights of the pilgrims," leaving out the religious fanaticism and the conquest of territories.

Social labeling. The war of Portugal against Angola, Mozambique, and Guinea-Bissau was not a "colonial" war, but an "overseas" war. This social labeling has ideological and justifying effects.

Identifying with the winners. In Italy there is a popular joke that when Mussolini was forced to resign, the Italians went to bed as fascists and woke up the following day as antifascists.

Sources: Braumeister and Hastings 1997; Marqués et al. 1997.

COMING TO TERMS WITH THE TRUTH IN FRACTURED SOCIETIES

At the end of conflicts or dictatorships, many societies have considered the need to know about the past by allowing the victims whose experience had been silenced or manipulated to speak out and by encouraging the entire society, a large part of which had been witness to the atrocities, to admit what had happened. Truth commissions are officially responsible for a thorough investigation into the events and will recognize the victims and propose forms of reparation for past harms and prevention of future atrocities.

These attempts have not been free of obstacles. The detractors of these processes, who are largely those responsible for the violence and in general the "official story," have tried to encourage the distribution of blame, prescribing amnesia as the formula for reconstruction. The struggle for the truth is not an easy path; it is subject to all possible social contradictions. According to John Berger (1986), "history instills hope for the desperate or exploited people who are fighting for justice. However, in the world of the relatively rich, the only insatiable demand for history is to forget."

The aim of the unending task of reconstructing the social fabric is to join together what life has separated, what violence has torn apart. We cannot repair the losses, but we can challenge the space that separates.

The effects are disastrous: We are deteriorating bit by bit, in a society where we are not allowed to live. I haven't recovered my life. Especially because so many of our expectations were destroyed. I think our hope is that the great sacrifice they made was not made in vain.

We need to know what happened, to be sure that at some point they died, and to shed light on the guilt of those who are responsible. We cannot ask for revenge, but we can set a precedent so that it doesn't happen again. (Testimony, in ODHAG 1998, 4: 483)

The work of truth commissions brought about a new framework of hope in many countries. However, there has been disappointment in many places because of the expectations that people had for them. Despite including recommendations for the prevention of violence, demilitarization, and so forth, in most cases the conclusions of the truth commissions were not binding and the issue of justice was not included on the agenda. Their duty was not to transform the military or to make the perpetrators admit the truth. The mandate of the commissions habitually includes helping to establish the truth about the past, offering a public platform to the victims, informing and catalyzing the public debate, and recommending repairs for victims as necessary legal and institutional reforms (Hayner 2001). While recognizing the suffering of the victims and shedding light on some cases, the commissions have been able only to hope to reduce the number of lies that were circulating without anybody denying them (Ignatieff 1999); establishing the truth is not always easy.

In most cases, these commissions have worked in an environment where the former killers still had a strong degree of control in the political process or were threatening to destabilize the situation. In Latin America, the experience of the search for the truth has shown the military's resistance to change, as in Chile and Argentina, where the elected governments were forced to choose between justice and their own survival. The military and the police have survived investigations, even with their legitimacy undermined, and have kept their power intact in an exercise of false reconciliation.

Nonetheless, impunity is not inevitable even though it is frequently seen as the only possible outcome. In the case of South Africa's Truth and Reconciliation Commission, the perpetrators had to present themselves voluntarily to be investigated by the Commission to be able to receive an individual pardon; if they did not do this, they would be investigated and eventually punished by the justice system.

In my opinion, we shouldn't consider the healing of South Africa as completed, but as a process, and the Commission has contributed to it magnificently in that now the victims of the atrocities know what happened to their loved ones and some of them have proved to be magnanimous: They have been able to listen to the confessions of the apartheid agents and have even said they forgive them. Others, of course, are so bitter that they find it impossible to forget the pain of losing those they loved. But I believe that in general the Commission has done a wonderful job and has helped us to move away from the past and concentrate on the present and the future. (Mandela 1998)

In societies where a solid political consensus has been added to the truth and reconciliation process, as in South Africa, truth commissions have a greater chance of being successful (Ignatieff 1999). In other cases, however, such as El Salvador's immediate announcement of amnesty or Guatemala's lack of response to the commission's recommendations, have meant serious official obstacles for reconciliation.

Accepting the truth in fractured societies is the result of a complex process. The publishing of reports on the truth is only the first step. Once the silence is broken, it is likely that other incidents and evidence will appear that will contribute to accepting the truth. Human-rights groups and humanitarian organizations have to bear in mind that support for the affected population does not end once the facts are made public. Further steps are necessary to avoid the truth simply becoming a confirmation of the damage.

In multiethnic societies a reinforcement of attributes may be linked to the identity of the victims after a war. These movements are normal responses in communities badly hit by violence. However, the reinforcement of ethnic stereotypes and the adoption of more rigid identities (for example, an identity based only on one ethnic background) can make "the other one" become an enemy. In many places, such as Rwanda or Kosovo, fear has become a unifying factor in groups that believe they will be protected in the new situation only if they stay together. Later, this becomes an obstacle for living together. In these cases, the aggression that keeps the group united is not only aimed at the outside but also within the group, with the goal of removing anything that separates

From Truth to Reconciliation

The investigation for the truth is an important step in dignifying the victims and in the search for a common history. However, different factors influence the results of this task as part of the reconstruction of the social fabric. Reconciliation is more difficult:

1. In societies with a strong polarization over the past.
2. When there is no new social consensus after the war.
3. If the new framework for living together is presided over by the former leaders or by new, excluding forces.
4. When the existing communities are strongly consolidated around their own truth.
5. When the fear of one group consolidates the identity of another group.

the individual from the group. However, the reappraisal of multiple identities can build bridges where profound separations exist.

MEMORY FOR THE FUTURE

The phenomena of distortion and amnesia have important psychosocial consequences for the future. In one way or another, future generations will be affected by the traumatic experiences of the past. Children of Holocaust survivors, for example, have been characterized as being more preoccupied with death, suffering more from anxiety in dealing with negative events, and being more ambivalent when faced with aggression (Solomon 1990).

For new generations, valuing the memories of relatives is of great importance. In the same way that children born in a refugee camp need to know their history to be able to make sense of their experience, the children of murdered or disappeared relatives need to understand their own situation as part of a wider collective process that avoids stigma and reaffirms their identity. In a more social sense, family members reassert the value of collective memory to pass on to new generations a form of learning from their ancestors' experience to avoid repeating the violence they suffered.

Reconstructing memory cannot be seen as a process that looks only to the past but one that relates to problems of the present. In Guatemala, for example, even fifteen years after the reported incidents and the signing of a peace agreement between the government and the guerrillas, people were still scared because those who benefited from the war and the repressive forces responsible for the atrocities were still in power. They feared living with the murderers in their communities, reprisals for giving testimony, and the worsening of deep social conflicts (that the violence would return). This shows that despite the end of armed conflict, the consequences of war continue and they threaten the future. At the front line of postwar priorities is to put an end to impunity and the need to confront the origin of social problems.

How the distortion of memory has an impact in the future can be seen in the current trend in Latin America to return repressive figures to power; the increase in extreme right movements and racism in Europe; the fact that leaders who in the past collaborated with Nazism or Stalinist repression are now representatives of new nationalisms, and the transformation over time of instigators of war becoming "defenders of peace."

Until a few years ago, these military men had presided over bloody dictatorships or had taken part in them prominently, but then they entered the democratic contest with surprising popularity. General Ríos Montt, exterminating angel of the indigenous population of Guatemala, led the polls when his candidacy for the presidency was banned. A similar thing occurred with General Oviedo in Paraguay. General Bussi, who deposited his hard-earned money in Swiss bank accounts while he killed suspects, was elected and reelected governor of the Argentinean province of Tucumán. Another uniformed murderer, General Banzer, was rewarded with the presidency of Bolivia. (Galeano 1998, 84)

All this reveals the risk of the atrocities of the past being repeated (Páez and Basabe 1993). The following text from a song by the German group Endsieg, "Final Victory," dedicated to the Turkish community, demonstrates this in a brutal way:

> They chew garlic, they come to Germany
> To dirty everything they touch.
> Let's put them in jail
> Let's put them in
> Concentration camps (Baeza 1994)

The frustration caused by impunity, the disappointment of social expectations, and postwar political changes lead to new problems that add to the impact of the traumatic experiences of the war. In addition, the implementation of neoliberal economic policies has worsened living conditions in many parts of the world.

In the postwar context, the large number of people educated in violence through recruitment or paramilitary groups brings about a risk that the consequences of militarization will have an even longer-term impact, given its influence in the change of values and behavior patterns and the maintenance of networks of power. Many countries experience an increase in everyday social violence (assaults, homicide) after a war. Some communities, however, find ways of bringing about justice and encouraging forms of social repair. "In the San Antonio community one man killed another, but they didn't lynch him. Rather, they got together to discuss what to do. The community thought about it a lot and decided the person had to repair the damage he had done. Juan's life couldn't be given back to him, so they decided the man would be responsible for the needs of Juan's wife and children until they were older" (Martín Beristain 1997).

Work on collective memory should be used to develop an educational process that will help to transform the values imposed by militarization: the disregard of the value of other people's lives and the normalization of violence as a way of exerting control over others or of dealing with conflict. According to Hannah Arendt, "the terrible originality of totalitarianism isn't due to the entrance of a new 'idea' into the world, but to the fact that their actions break with all our traditions; they have literally pulverized our categories of political thinking and our criteria of moral judgment" (Arendt 1995, 30). Totalitarianism doesn't mean that you do not forgive anything, but that you become reconciled with a world where such things are possible. Memory, therefore, has a clear preventive purpose. To avoid a repetition of tragedy depends greatly on dismantling the mechanisms that made the horror possible.

Restoring Justice

Maintaining impunity helps those who have power to impose their own version of history—frequently separating the violators of the truth from their own acts—and a social order based on their own interests. For this reason, a number of human-rights organizations, victims' groups, NGOs, and even humanitarian agencies are creating pressure to take those responsible for the atrocities to court and restore justice as a means of prevention.

Justice can also make many of those responsible for violence settle their debts with the past. The possibility of giving evidence under conditions of security and trust, recognizing the dignity of the victims, taking part in the reparation activities for survivors, and being subjected to social sanction are key elements for the ethical restructuring and social reintegration of murderers.

Despite all the difficulties, the experience of various countries has shown how the walls of silence following military dictatorships and armed conflicts can gradually be knocked down. In 1995, former Argentinean captain Alfredo Scilingo, who could no longer sleep without alcohol or drugs, decided to make a public confession, saying he had thrown thirty people into the sea. He reported that in the years of the military dictatorship, between 1,500 and 2,000 political prisoners had been

> ### The Psychosocial Implications of Impunity
>
> - Impunity threatens the belief in a democratic society and is a continuation of oppression and lack of freedom.
> - Impunity creates confusion and social ambiguity. It embodies a lack of respect for ethics and justice.
> - Lies and denials are institutionalized and defended by the justice system of the country.
> - Impunity leads to people looking for their own justice.
> - Impunity invalidates and denies the events and limits the possibility of an effective communication between citizens: traumas, barriers between people, and difficulties with reconciliation.
> - Impunity causes impotence, guilt, and shame in the victims.
> - Impunity affects one's ability to believe in the future and can exclude many people from history.

Source: Sveass 1995.

thrown into the sea by the Argentinean Navy. In 1998, the former Argentinean dictator Jorge Videla was imprisoned. He was not sentenced for genocide but for the theft of babies born to women prisoners in concentration camps, who were murdered shortly after giving birth (Galeano 1998).

Neither Scilingo's crisis nor the investigation of the theft of the babies would probably have gone ahead without the people who were committed and obstinate enough to fight for years against impunity. The memories of the mothers and grandmothers have constituted what Canetti (1966) called a "glass of the mass," that is, a small persistent group that kept the memory alive. Thanks to those people, memory may, on some occasions, become an *open memory* in a *mass network* that draws everything toward justice. Some people thought the trial for Klaus Barbie[13] was pointless given that the incidents were already known by the public; those people felt the memory of Nazism was bing raised artifically. Other people, however, said that "the trial against Barbie represented the possibility of returning to real life, a living lesson of the way a society can go back in a tremendous way" (Jodelet 1992). In the same way, the trial against Pinochet has opened the door to recognition of the suffering and demands of the victims and constitutes a step toward vindicating the past and overcoming the military's abduction of the Chilean transition.

The aim of the court is to make individuals responsible given that guilt cannot be transferred to groups. The trials help transform guilt into shame because they are done publicly and are a moral punishment for the incidents and those responsible for them. The involvement of society itself is a condition for its internal effectiveness. According to

The Ethics of Memory: Trial of Klaus Barbie, Head of the Gestapo in Lyon, France

The custom in my country dictated that a dead child had to be buried in a white shroud, given that white is a symbol of innocence and any death of a child is a disgrace for humanity. This is the message that you must echo outside our own borders. It has to reach South Africa, where children are in prison and in danger; to the Middle East, where they are scared because of the bombs; in Argentina, where the Plaza de Mayo Mothers claimed their loved ones in vain. We will leave this place the same way we came in. After a few days you will dream, like the others, about going on holiday. But, after a few weeks, why can't I look at the children who come out of our schools in the same way as before? I ask you, therefore, that in your diaries, on today's date, July 3, 1987, that you leave the page blank, a symbol of the purity your judgment will have, and when later somebody asks you the meaning of this blank page, you can simply answer: It is the shroud of the children of Izieu.

Source: R. Dumas, lawyer for the people, in Jodelet 1997, 2.

Ignatieff, ". . . for many Germans the Nuremberg trials were the typical justice of the victorious. Only when the German courts judged the war crimes in the sixties did the German people find themselves forced to confront their responsibility for the Holocaust; the verdicts of the German courts were much more legitimate" (Ignatieff 1999, 170).

However, in many places the judicial systems do not offer even minimum guarantees, and impunity is disguised as bureaucracy and legal arguments. In these contexts, the trials also produce an enormous collection of obstacles that the victims and their relatives have to face, from proving the incidents to identifying the culprits, from complying with the slow and complicated procedures to confronting the complicity or contempt of the accused, the judges, and the lawyers.

In the trial for the Xamán massacre in Guatemala, despite evidence of the events, the community was made to suffer threats, confusion strategies, intimidation of their witnesses, slow and complicated procedures, expenses of time and money for travel and gathering evidence, as well as a lack of impartiality when considering the evidence (FRMT 1998).

In addition to the truth and criminal sanctions, other possible goals are social sanctions such as dismissal, elimination of privileges, and a ban from public office. The aim is to take power away from those most responsible for the violence against the population, promote the rebuilding of society, and avoid false reconciliation processes. All of this requires a long and arduous process. The decision of whether to initiate certain judicial processes is a complex one. Families should not be given false expectations that will only lead to more frustration and worsen the situation. However, only through social and political pressure and appropriate legal proceedings will the value of justice be restored.

THE IMPORTANCE OF JUSTICE

The importance of trials can be assessed on different levels:

1. *Legal.* Those responsible receive a fair trial.
2. *Moral.* This is proof that justice is a valid principle. The difference between good and bad is restored by the official public position.
3. *Truth.* Facts are established and secrets are revealed, resulting in public confirmation of the violations.
4. *History.* A new process of rehabilitation and reconciliation may begin, allowing for the possibility of creating a common history.
5. *Ritual.* Trials are public rituals that set the foundations for the transition from dictatorship to democracy.
6. *Political.* Some trials may highlight a legitimacy crisis, which can facilitate legal and political changes.[14]

THE PROCESS OF RECONCILIATION

Nations do not reach reconciliation in the same way that people do. Genuine public gestures are needed that will dignify the victims, bury the dead, and make the past distant. Political leaders can influence this difficult process, which will help people come to terms with a painful collective past. Governments and authorities must be willing to go through this process, and they must have the strength and coherence to overcome stereotypes and attitudes between different social groups or political opposition. Without this change in political culture, there is less chance of joining forces to provoke social change and a risk of more confrontations and divisions that could seriously affect the social fabric.[15] In the words of Ignatieff, ". . . to be reconciled means to break the spiral of revenge between generations, to substitute the vicious descending spiral of violence with the virtuous ascending spiral of mutual respect. Reconciliation can break the circle of revenge as long as there is respect for the dead. To deny them is to allow them to become a nightmare. Without an apologia, or a recognition of the facts, the past will never be reconciled and the ghosts will lie in wait for us (Ignatieff 1999, 179). This means being able to cry for the dead, to share what they have taught us, to be aware that violence does not bring back life, and to honor the dead and missing by struggling to stay alive.

According to Páez et al. (1997), for collective memory to fulfill this role, it must (1) be shared and expressed in rituals and with monuments; (2) be placed in the past and the future of the group; (3) be explained and clarified as far as possible; (4) draw lessons and conclusions for the present; (5) give meaning and rebuild on what has happened by underlining the positive aspects for social identity; (6) avoid a fixation on the past, obsessive repetition, and stigmatization of survivors as victims; (7) go beyond the reconstruction of the facts to become a moral judgment that ethically disqualifies the perpetrators; and (8) if this cannot be done, care should be taken not to let damaging measures or approaches interfere with the process of collective memory.

Conclusion

This chapter has discussed the importance of taking the psychosocial needs of the populations affected by disasters into account. It is necessary to focus on prevention in the approach of aid intervention and specific mental-health programs. The conceptualization of mental health should avoid victimization or the isolation of people, either through a community approach or with different types of therapeutic interventions. This chapter prevents various suggestions regarding accompanying victims and developing measures that consider the organization and resources of the population. The work on collective memory at a social or group level is part of an intervention aimed at supporting the reconstruction efforts of victims and societies affected by war or dictatorial regimes. Restoring truth and a sense of justice form part of the psychosocial needs for reconstructing the social fabric.

Epilogue

> *It is freedom of speech that guarantees the rights of individuals, minorities, groups, or communities. To state that freedom of speech is a luxury of the West is an insult to the historic struggle of individuals and communities all over the world who have fought for the dignity and well-being of their people, the fulfillment of social aspirations, equal opportunities, equal distribution of resources, and access to shelter, food, and healthy living conditions. Statements like these are an attempt to degrade us as human beings, to reduce us to a marginalized existence even within our own communities. They are a vote in favor of Power against the community of Freedom.*
>
> —Wole Soyinka

During a collective disaster, whole populations find themselves in a social emergency. The first step in trying to attend to the needs of the affected population is to understand the individual and collective needs as a whole.

Humanitarian aid takes place in a specific social and historical context, and therefore has psychosocial implications. In addition to the provision of resources, humanitarian aid can also affect family communication, basic living conditions, and legal situations, which are linked to the hopes and needs of the people. Listening to these hopes and attending to these needs is one way of changing the system of humanitarian aid.

A psychosocial approach highlights the risks of the political or military interests involved, the ethical components of the intervention, and the value of justice. Although psychology is usually associated with an individualistic clinical approach, this book tries to focus on the community, emphasizing stimulating the coping strategies of the affected population and supporting available services.

In crisis situations, the psychosocial approach needs to focus mainly on prevention, not just on the treatment of and support for the victims. Education about risks, how to treat information in order to avoid prejudices or panic, and how to develop mutual support are some of the contributions the psychosocial approach can make to populations and workers.

Emergency situations, especially those caused by political crises, present moral and practical dilemmas. Humanitarian intervention takes place in a historical context where conflicts, such as wars, not only break out but are planned and have global implications. Ideological inflexibility, militarization, and ethnic prejudices are part of this initial phase and generate human-rights violations. The psychosocial approach helps to increase awareness about the mechanisms involved in the lead up to a war. Humanitarian aid cannot only intervene after the event to support victims, but as a defense of human rights, it is also a form of prevention.

Finally, this critical approach is intended to help readers reflect on the reality of the specific countries where humanitarian intervention occurs. It is here that stereotypes about humanitarian aid held by local governments, agencies, and volunteers must change so that aid can meet the needs of the people. The people need not only aid but justice.

Notes

Introduction

1. Testimony in Martín Beristain 1997.
2. This book is based on initial work published by the Pedro Arrupe Institute of Human Rights. See Carlos Martín Beristain and Giorgia Dona, *A Psychosocial Approach to Humanitarian Aid* (Bilbao: University of Deusto, 1997).
3. *Expatriate* is the term normally used by NGOs to refer to workers from other countries.
4. For more in-depth discussion of these issues, refer to the articles and books listed in the Bibliography.
5. This hierarchy of needs is not recognized worldwide. For example, in the language of Burundi, the same word is used for spiritual and material wealth (*chanta*) and poverty (*hsinye*).
6. A ration card is often used in refugee camps to identify families for the distribution of humanitarian aid.

Chapter 1

1. We refer here to the 1984 accident at a Union Carbide chemical factory in Bhopal, India—the worst industrial disaster in human history. The chemical leak killed seven thousand people and harmed hundreds of thousands more. The company had not applied the same safety measures in India that are required in the United States (Galeano 1998).
2. The main reason for famine during the 1980s was war rather than drought. Of the thirty-one countries affected by drought in sub-Saharan Africa at the beginning of the decade, only five of them suffered from famine, but all were at war: Mozambique, Angola, Sudan, Chad, and Ethiopia (Moore and Collins 1998, 17).
3. We use the terms "South" and "North" not from a geographic point of view, but from an economic and geopolitical view to refer to poor countries and wealthy countries, or "underdeveloped" and "developed" countries. We reject the latter terms because they do not question the development model; we use the terms nonetheless because they are part of the standard language in the discipline and, to date, a better substitute has not been arrived at.
4. This tragedy was attributed to contaminated oil that had been falsely sold as olive oil.
5. A review of natural disasters showed a 17 percent increase in those who present with symptoms after a disaster (Rubonis and Bickman 1991; Bravo et al. 1990).
6. A review of the impact of traumatic events confirmed this in sixteen of the nineteen studies analyzed (Davidson and Foa 1991).

Chapter 2

1. Frequency of people's responses in the very moment of the catastrophic event: felt fear, 38 percent; thought that the other felt fear, 58 percent; felt trapped, 50.5 percent; believed that their life was in danger, 54.7 percent; asked for help and received it, 68 percent; helped others, 62 percent; thought that there was no solution and resigned themselves to this, 43.8 percent.

Chapter 4

1. See the section titled The Impact of Traumatic Events in Chapter 1.
2. See Chapter 5, The Strength of the People.
3. Programa de Reparación y Asistencia Integral en Salud para las Víctimas de la Represión y sus Familiares (Program for Reparation and Legal Advice for Victims of Repression and Their Family Members).
4. Guilt can affect anybody, but two types of people are especially vulnerable: (1) people with high self-esteem or who are very strict with themselves—the behavior generating the guilt casts doubt on the image of perfection to which they aspire; and (2) people with low self-esteem who are anxious, insecure, and fear ridicule—the negative image they have of themselves is reinforced.
5. From this model of cultural grief, the intervention should be carried out on three levels: (1) allow the natural expression of grief in the language of the refugee, (2) give refugees sufficient time to adapt to the new culture, and (3) teach refugees survival techniques for the new culture.
6. In effect, a review of the follow-up studies on disasters found similar levels of psychological disorders in people who have suffered natural and human disasters after one year. However, after this time, symptoms tend to persist in people affected by human disasters.
7. People who have been victims of natural disasters tend to believe that the world does not make sense, but victims of human-created disasters perceive the world more negatively and with less benevolence; they also have a more negative self-image. (See Chapter 1.)

Chapter 5

1. Schwarzer and Leppin (cited in Stroebe et al. 1993) synthesized eighty epidemiological studies and found that objective, subjective, or functional social support was linked to a lower rate of depression as well as a lower death rate.
2. Catecholamines function as hormones and are involved in responding to stress (as are adrenaline, noradrenaline, etc.).
3. In an open account, 12 compared to 7.6 percent and 24 compared to 15 percent, respectively. The differences were statistically significant (ODHAG 1998).

Chapter 6

1. We need to point out the risk of the increase in use of terminology such as "beneficiaries" or "IDPs" (internally displaced people) when referring to a

population affected by violence or disasters, as these terms show little sensitivity to the situation of the victims.

2. Goffman describes the processes and rituals of disidentification from internment in closed institutions (prisons, hospitals, psychiatric hospitals, etc.), which entail, among other things, a lack of intimacy, regulation of daily life, loss of an adult role, a new personal identity, an inability to make decisions for oneself, and so forth.

3. These conscious or subconscious forms of denying feelings or experiences may be useful when nothing can be done to alleviate the pain, allowing for a reduction in activity and time to think about solutions to the problem. Denial or inhibition may also be a form of rejection as a protection against pain or guilt.

Chapter 7

1. Observations (personal testimony) of the mental-health team Médicos del Mundo (Doctors of the World) in 1997.

2. Adapted from C. Martín Beristain, "Crosscultural Interaction in Development Work in Latin America," a summer course on crosscultural psychology given at the Universidad del País Vasco in San Sebastian, Spain, 1988.

3. Taken from P. Pérez Sales, *El Choque Cultural Inverso* (Seville: International Health Cooperation, Medicos del Mundo-Spain, 1998).

4. Adapted from Smith and Bond 1993.

Chapter 8

1. The *medicalization* of suffering refers to understanding a person's experience solely as a medical problem. This can be negative when it turns what is a political or structural social problem into a technical matter, or when it decontextualizes the stress of a population. Victims are seen as passive sufferers (*patients*) instead of active participants in a process in which there are health problems.

2. The rejection by the Bosnian people of the role played by the U.N. mission UNPROFOR (United Nations Protections Force) was based, among other things, on the lack of protection from such slaughters as the Sbrebenica massacre, which took place in a U.N.-protected city, and on the lack of serious intent to arrest well-known war criminals. Before the NATO intervention, the Organization for Security and Cooperation in Europe mission chief in Kosovo, William Walker, reported the massacre of dozens of civilians by Serbian police and declared his shock at such a crime. This same person supported the El Salvadoran army as U.S. ambassador in 1989.

3. In addition to providing the basic needs of food, clothing, health care, and decent living conditions, other important aspects in psychosocial care are (1) managing the settlement (Are the refugees represented and do they take part in the decision-making process?), (2) ensuring personal and group security, (3) documenting and recognizing refugee status (mobility, etc.), (4) providing access to information on family members (organization of the regrouping, means of communication, etc.), and (5) encouraging community participation (meetings, community activities, activities with the children, collaboration in common tasks, etc).

4. MIR is an acronym from Serbo-Croatian for "peace" and "inner tranquility."

5. Individual indicators such as symptoms, feelings, and personal experiences are discussed in Chapters 2 and 3.

6. The many different therapeutic approaches for working with survivors of torture or organized violence include testimonial, psychodynamic, cognitive-behavioral, pharmacological, and family or group therapy, among others.

7. KCBM is an acronym for *kruu Khmer, counseling, Buddhism, and medication. Kruu* means traditional healer.

8. Four out of the six studies included a control group.

9. The location must be adequate for people to feel comfortable and be able to make eye contact. The coordinator may have assistants to help in moments of tension, who can contribute to subsequent assessments and collect some shared experiences. Notes on the group experiences can be useful, but in other contexts may not be recommended or could even be dangerous. Maintain an informal atmosphere (with breaks for coffee, etc.).

10. According to the Human Rights Commission of the United Nations, reparation has to cover all the damages suffered by the victim: measures of restoration (to previous levels), compensation (for damages), social rehabilitation (through medical or legal assistance) and general reparations (official declarations, monuments, tributes, etc.), including the guarantee that there will be no more violation of human rights. (The Right to Reparation. E/CN.4/sSub.2/1996/18. Human Rights Commission. The U.N. Economic and Social Council.)

11. See the box in Chapter 4 titled "Principles of Accompaniment during Exhumations."

12. The 1992 invasion of Somalia tended to be seen as a response to the problem of famine, and the war and economic embargo on Iraq (1993–2003) as a way of helping the Iraqi people free themselves of a dictator, occluding in both cases the economic and strategic interests of the United States.

13. Lieutenant in the secret police and head of the gestapo in Lyon, Barbie oversaw the anti-Jewish repression and the "enemies of the Reich." He was nicknamed the Butcher of Lyon because of the cruelty of his methods. He became famous from the case of Jean Moulin, the head of the French Resistance, whom he arrested and tortured to death. Despite being tried and convicted in his absence, Barbie was subsequently protected by the American Counter Intelligence Corps. In 1984, he was arrested in Bolivia and extradited to France where he was tried for the torture and deportation to concentration camps of more than six hundred people.

14. After the arrest of Pinochet, the Chilean military's worries about the possibility of more trials for its participation in an operation called the Caravan of Death has led Jorge Arancibia, head of the navy, to create a mechanism for reaching an agreement on the issue of the missing people during the dictatorship (*El País*, June 19, 1999).

15. An example of these problems in Guatemala has been the conflicts in the community of Ixcán, where, in the mid 1990s, the militarization and political divisions between the Unión Revolucionaria Nacional Guatemalteca (URNG) and the Permanent Commission of Refugees led to discord and violent conflict in the community, which threatened the ability of the various communities of returnees to live together.

Bibliography

ACAFADE. *Florecerás Guatemala.* Costa Rica: ACAFADE, 1990.

ACAT. *Que fais-tu de ton frère?* Bordeaux: Fayard, 1987.

AFP. "El SIDA obliga a los africanos a romper sus tradiciones funerarias." *El País* (Madrid), December 21, 1998, p. 33.

African Rights. *Rwanda: Death, Despair, and Defiance.* London: African Rights, 1995.

Ager, A. *Mental Health Issues in Refugee Populations: A Review.* Mimeograph. Harvard Medical School, Harvard University, Cambridge, Mass., 1994.

———. "Dislocation." In R. Desjarlais, L. Eisenberg, B. Good, and A. Kleinman, eds., *World Mental Health: Problems and Priorities in Low-Income Countries.* Oxford: Oxford University Press, 1995.

Agger, I. "Longing for Sarajevo: Understanding the Trauma of Humanitarian Aid Workers." In I. Agger, S. Vuk, and J. Mimica, eds., *Theory and Practice of Psychosocial Projects under War Conditions, in Bosnia-Herzegovina and Croatia.* Zagreb. ECHO & ECTF, 1995.

Amnesty International. "Manual de entrevista para investigación en derechos humanos." Draft. Madrid, 1998.

———. *Recomendaciones para la recogida de testimonios sobre violaciones a los DDHH.* Madrid: Documento interno, 1998.

Appe, J. "Refugees in Europe." *Refugee Participation Network* 14 (1993).

Arcel, L. T. "War Victims, Trauma and Psychosocial Care." In L. T. Arcel, ed., *War Victims, Trauma and Psychosocial Care.* Zagreb: Nakladnistov Lumin, 1994.

Arendt, H. *De la historia a la acción.* Barcelona: Paidós, 1995.

Bacic, R., et al. *Memorias recientes de mi pueblo (1973–1990), Araucanía.* Temuco: Centro de Estudios Socioculturales, Universidad Católica de Temuco, 1997.

Baer, J. W. "Study of Sixty Patients with AIDS or AIDS-Related Complex Requiring Psychiatric Hospitalization." *American Journal of Psychiatry* 146 (1989): 1285–88.

Baeza, P. "Xenofobia: ¿recaída o enfermedad crónica?" *Mujeres en Acción* 1 (1994): [23–26].

Barudy, J. "A Programme of Mental Health for Political Refugees: Dealing with the Invisible Pain of Political Exile." *Social Science and Medicine* 28 (1989): 715–27.

Basabe, N., et al. "El anclaje sociocultural de la experiencia emocional de las naciones: Un análisis Colectivo." *Boletín de Psicología* (1999).

Bateson, G. *Steps to an Ecology of Mind.* Paladin Books, 1973

Becker, D., and E. Lira. *Derechos humanos: Todo es según el dolor con que se mire.* Santiago: ILAS, 1989.

Becker, D., et al. "Muerte y duelo: Los familiares de ejecutados y su psicoterapia." In I. Martín-Baró, ed., *Psicología social de la guerra.* San Salvador: UCA, 1990.

Benoist, J., B. Piquard, and F. Voitura. *Anthropology in Humanitarian Assistance.* Luxemburg: Network on Humanitarian Assistance, 1997.

Berger, J. *And Our Faces, My Heart, Brief as Photos.* London: Bloomsbury Paperback, 2005.

Berry, J. W. "Refugee Adaptation in Settlement Countries: An Overview with an Emphasis on Primary Prevention." In F. L. Aharn and J. J. Athey, eds., *Refugee Children: Theory, Research, and Services.* Baltimore, Md.: Johns Hopkins University Press, 1991.

Berry, J. W., et al. *Cross-Cultural Psychology: Research and Applications.* Cambridge: Cambridge University Press, 1992.

Bettelheim, B. The Informed Heart: Autonomy in a Mass Age. New York: Free Press, 1964.

Biberson, P., and E. Goemaere. "La reconstrucción de los sistemas sanitarios." In Doctors without Borders, *Escenarios de crisis.* Madrid: Acento, 1993.

Bonnet, C. *Childhood Interrupted by War.* Paris: Bayard Press, Doctors without Borders, 1994.

Boothby, N., P. Upton, and A. Sultan. *Children of Mozambique: The Cost of Survival.* Washington, D.C.: Committee for Refugees, 1991.

Boulvain, M., et al. "Difficultés de gestion dans un camps de transit, Mwenw Ditu, Zaire, 1993." *Medical News* 3 (1994): 24–30.

Bowlby, J. "Attachment and Loss." In *Loss, Sadness, and Depression*, vol. 3. London: Hogarth Press, 1980.

Bowles, E. "From Village to Camp: Refugee Camp Life in Transition in the Thailand-Burma border." In *Forced Migrations.* The Refugee Studies Programme in association with the Global IDP Survey. No. 2. Oxford: University of Oxford, 1998, pp. 11–14.

Bracken, P. J., J. E. Giller, and D. Summerfield. "Psychological Responses to War and Atrocity: The Limitations of Current Concepts." *Social Science and Medicine* 40 (1995): 1073–82.

Brauman, R. "Los medios de comunicación ante las crisis." In Doctors without Borders, *Escenarios de crisis.* Madrid: Acento, 1993.

Braumeister, R. F., and S. Hastings, "Distorsiones de la memoria colectiva: De cómo los grupos se adulan y engañan a sí mismos." In D. Páez et al., eds., *Memoria Colectiva de Procesos Culturales y Políticos.* Lejona: Editorial de la Universidad del País Vasco, 1997.

Bravo, J., et al. "The Psychological Sequelae of Disaster Stress Prospectively and Retrospectively Evaluated." *American Journal of Community Psychology* 18 (1990): 661–80.

Bromet, E. J., H. C. Schulberg, and L. O. Dunn. "Reactions of Psychiatric Patients to the Three Mile Island Nuclear Accident." *Archives General Psychiatry* 39 (1982): 725–30.

Burger, J. M., and M. L. Palmer. "Changes in and Generalization of Unrealistic Optimism Following Experiences with Stressful Events: Reactions to the 1989 California Earthquake." *Personality and Social Psychology Bulletin* 18 (1992): 39–43.

Cabanas, A. *Los sueños perseguidos.* Donusita: Gakoa, 2000.

Cabrera, M. L., C. Martín Beristain, and J. Albizu Beristain. *Esa tarde perdimos el sentido: La masacre de Xamán.* Guatemala: Office of Human Rights of the Archdiocese of Guatemala, 1998.

CADDHHC (Coordinación Alemana de DDHH por Colombia). *Los derechos humanos en Colombia: Memorias del Taller Europeo.* Bendorff: Rhin, 1997.

Canetti, E. *Crowds and Power.* New York: Farrar, Straus and Giroux, 1966.

CICR. *Le Facteur Stress.* Geneva: CICR, 1994.

Cienfuegos, A. J., and A. R. Monelli. "The Testimony of Political Repression as a Therapeutic Instrument." *American Journal of Orthopsychiatry* 53 (1983): 43–51.

COLAT (Colectivo Latinoamericano de Trabajo Psicosocial). *Psicopatología de la tortura y del exilio.* Madrid: Fundamentos, 1982.

Comité de Enlace ONGD-UE. *Código de conducta.* Madrid: Coordinadora de ONGD, 1989.

Cherniss, C. *Staff Burnout: Job Stress in Human Service.* Beverly Hills, Calif.: Sage, 1980.

Choussudovsky, M. "Comment on fabrique une famine." *Le Monde Diplomatique* 1 (1993): 3–5.

Criss, J. E., and P. B. Johnson. "Community Psychology Applied to Peace Studies." In K. S. Larsen, ed., *Conflict and Social Psychology.* London: Sage, 1994.

Daniel, J. "Acerca del pesimismo." *El País* (Madrid), February 1, 1992, p. 11.

Davidson, J. T., and E. A. Foa. "Diagnostic Issues in Post-Traumatic Stress Disorder." *Journal of Abnormal Psychology* 100 (1991): 346–55.

De Girolamo, G., and A. C. McFarlane. "The Epidemiology of TEPT: A Comprehensive Review of the International Literature." In A. J. Marsella et al., eds., *Ethnocultural Aspects of Post-traumatic Stress Disorder.* Washington, D.C.: American Psychological Association, 1997.

Delumeau, J. *La Peur en Occident.* Paris: Fayard, 1993.

De Rivera, J. "Emotional Climate: Social Structure and Emotional Dynamics." In K.T. Strongman, ed., *International Review of Studies on Emotion,* vol. 2. Chichester, England: John Wiley, 1992.

De Waal, A. "The Sanatory Factor: Expatriate Behaviour on African Relief Porgrammes." *RSO Network Paper* 2b (May 1987).

———. "Dangerous Precedents? Famine Relief in Somalia, 1991–1993." In J. MacRae and A. Zwi, eds., *War and Hunger: Rethinking International Relief to Complex Emergencies.* London: Zed Books and Save the Children Foundation, 1994.

Díaz, B. *Todo negro no igual: Voces de inmigrantes.* Barcelona: Virus, 1998.

Díaz-Loving, R., et al. "Comparación transcultural y análsis psicométrico de una medida de rasgos masculinos (instrumentales) y femeninos (expresivos)." *Revista de la Asociación Latinoamericana de Psicología Social* 1 (1981): 3–37.

———. "Contributions of Mexican Ethnopsychology to the Resolution of the Eticemic Dilemma in Personality." *Journal of Cross-Cultural Psychology* 29 (1998): 104–18.

Doctors without Borders. *Escenarios de Crisis.* Madrid: Acento, 1993.

Durkheim, E. *The Elementary Forms of the Religious Life.* New York: Free Press, 1967.

Efraime, B. *Erleben und verarbeiten von Kriegsereignissen bei mosambikanischen Kindern.* Berlin: Humboldt Universität Diplomarbeit, 1993.

Eguren, E., and L. Mahony. *Unarmed Bodyguards: International Accompaniment for the Protection of Human Rights.* Bloomfield, Conn.: Kumarian Press, 1997.

Eisenbruch, M., "Cultural Bereavement and Homesickness." In S. Fisher and C. I. Cooper, eds., *On the Move: The Psychology of Change and Transition.* Chichester: John Wiley, 1990.

———. "The Ritual Space of Patients and Transitional Healers in Cambodia." *BEFEO* 72 (1992): 283–316.

Faúndez, H. "El lenguaje del miedo: Dinámicas colectivas de la comunicación bajo el terror en Chile." In H. Riquelme, ed., *Era de tinieblas: Derechos humanos, terrorismo de estado y salud psicosocial en América Latina.* Caracas: Nueva Sociedad, 1994.

Fernández, I., C. Martín Beristain, and D. Páez. "Emociones y conductas colectivas en catástrofes: Ansiedad y rumor, miedo y conductas de pánico." In J. Apalategi, ed., *Movimientos sociales.* Valencia: Promolibro, 1999.

Fisas, V. *El desafío de Naciones Unidas ante un mundo en crisis.* Barcelona: Icaria, 1994.

Friedman, M., and J. Jaranson. "The Applicability of the Posttraumatic Stress Disorder Concept of Refugees." In A. J. Marsella, T. Bornemann, S. Ekblad, and J. Orley, eds., *Amidst Peril and Pain: The Mental Health and Well-Being of the World's Refugees.* Washington, D.C.: American Psychological Association, 1994.

FRMT. *El juicio Xamán: Un caso más de impunidad: Cronología y detalle de las principales violaciones al debido proceso.* Mimeograph. Guatemala, 1998.

Galeano, E. "La memoria subversiva." in *Tiempo: Reencuentro y esperanza.* Guatemala: ODHAG, 1996.

———. *Patas arriba: La escuela del mundo al revés.* Madrid: Siglo XXI, 1998.

Garaizabal, C., and N. Vázquez. *El dolor invisible: Una experiencia de grupos de autoapoyo con mujeres salvadoreñas.* Madrid: Talas, 1992.

Gedalof, E. "Refugee participation." In D. Tolfree, *Refugee Children in Malawi: A Study of the Implementations of the UNHCR Guidelines on Refugee Children.* Geneva: International Save the Children Alliance, 1991.

Giraldo, C. A., J. Abad, and D. Pérez. *Relatos e imágenes: El desplazamiento en Colombia.* Bogotá: CINEP, 1997.

Goffman, E. *Asylums: Essays on the Social Situation of Mental Patients and Other Inmates.* New York: Anchor Books, 1961.

Grossin, W. *Le travail et le temps.* Paris: Anthrophos, 1969.

Guest, I., and F. Saulnier. "Derecho internacional y realidad: Las lagunas de la protección." *El mundo en crisis.* Madrid: Acento, 1996.

Habermas, J. *Teoría de la acción comunicativa: Complementos y estudios previos.* Madrid: Catedra, 1989.

Harrell-Bond, B. *Imposing Aid: Emergency Assistance to Refugees.* Oxford: Oxford University Press, 1986.

Hauff, E., and P. Vaglum. *Organized Violence and Stress of Exile: Predictors of Mental Health in a Community Cohort of Vietnamese Refugees Three Years after Resettlement.* In C. Martín Beristain and G. Donà, *Enfoque psicosocial de la ayuda humanitaria.* Bilbao: University of Deusto, 1995.

Hayner, P. *Unspeakable Truths: Confronting State Terror and Atrocity.* New York: Routledge, 2001.

Heap, K. *La practica del lavoro sociale con i gruppi.* Rome: Astrolabio, 1985.

Hermet, G. "La acción humanitaria en el desorden mundial." In Doctors without Borders, *Poblaciones en peligro.* Madrid: Acento, 1993.

Hirtz, P. "Una doble responsabilidad." In *Ingerencias: El precio del testimonio: ¿quedarse? ¿irse?* Mimeograph. Médicins du Monde, París, 1994.

Hodgkinson, P. E., and M. Stewart. *Coping with Catastrophe: A Handbook of Disaster Management.* London: Routledge, 1991.

Hofstede, G. *Culture's Consequences.* Beverly Hills, Calif.: Sage, 1980.

Horowitz, M. *Stress Response Syndrome.* Northvale, N.J.: Aronson, 1986.

Horowitz, M., N. Adler, and S. Kegeles. "A Scale for Measuring the Occurrence of Positive State of Mind: A Preliminary Report." *Psychosomatic Medcine* 50 (1988): 477–83.

Ibañez, T. "Some Critical Comments about the Theory of Social Representations." *Ongoing Production on Social Representations* 1 (1992): 21–26.

Ignatieff, M. *The Warrior's Honour: Ethnic War and the Modern Conscience.* London: Chatto & Windus, 1998.

Instituto Latinoamericano de Salud Mental (ILAS). *Reparación de los derechos humanos y salud mental.* Santiago: ILAS, 1996.

International Federation of Red Cross and Red Crescent Societies (IFRC). *World Disasters Report 1993.* Dordrecht: Martinus Nijhoff, 1993.

IWGIA. *Poblaciones indígenas. 3.* Geneva: IWGIA, 1992.

James, W. "Managing Food Aid: Returnees' Strategies for Allocating Relief." *Refugee Participation Network* 13 (1992): 3–6.

Janoff-Bulman, R. *Shattered Assumptions: Towards a New Psychology of Trauma.* New York: Free Press, 1992.

Jean, E. "Crisis e Intervencion." In Doctors without Borders, *Escenarios de Crisis.* Madrid: Acento, 1993.

Jodelet, D. "Memoire de Masse: Le côté moral ed affectif de l'histoire." *Bulletin de Psychologie* 45 (1992): 239–56.

———. "El lado moral y afectivo de la historia: Un ejemplo de memoria de masas: el proceso a K. Barbie, 'el carnicero de Lyon.'" In D. Páez et al., eds., *Memoria colectiva de procesos culturales y políticos.* Lejona: Editorial de la Universidad del País Vasco, 1997.

Jones, L. *Adolescent Groups for Encamped Bosnian Refugees: Some Problems and Solutions.* Paper delivered at Third International Conference on Health and Human Rights, Manila, 1995.

Kane, S. *Asistencia a las personas de diferentes culturas, víctimas de la violencia organizada: Manual de la Cruz Roja y la Media Luna Roja.* Geneva: FICR, 1995.

Kluckhon, C. *Por los senderos de la psicología intercultural.* Mexico: Fondo de Cultura Económica, 1952.

Knoppers, M. In M. Hart and S. Van Praet, "Sudán: Morir de muerte lenta." In Doctors without Borders, *El mundo en crisis.* Madrid: Acento, 1996.

Kordon, D., Edelman, L., et al. *Efectos psicológicos de la represión política.* Buenos Aires: Editorial Sudamericana-Planeta, 1986

Lavelle, J., et al. *Harvard Guide to Khmer Mental Health.* Cambridge, Mass.: Harvard University Program in Refugee Trauma, 1996.

Levav, I., et al. "An Epidemiological Study of Mortality among Bereaved Parents." *New England Journal of Medicine* 319 (1988): 457–61.

Lieberman, M. A. "Bereavement Self-help Groups: A Review of Conceptual and Methodological Issues." In M. S. Strobe, W. Stroebe, and R. O. Hansson, eds., *Handbook of Bereavement: Theory, Research and Intervention.* New York: Cambridge University Press, 1993.

Lippman, W. *Public Opinion.* New York: Macmillan, 1922.

Loncaveric, M. "Socio-Cultural Integration Project for Bosnian Refugees." In G. Perren, ed., *Trauma: From Individual Helplessness to Group Resources.* Vienna: Paul Haupt Publishers Berne, 1996.

López-Ibor, J. J., et al. "Psychopathological Aspects of the Toxic Oil Syndrome Catastrophe." *British Journal of Psychiatry* 147 (1985): 352–65.

Mandela, N. "La reconciliación en Sudáfrica." *El País Semana* 1158 (1998):26

Marc, P. *De la bouche à l'oreille: Psychologie sociale de la rumeur.* Cousset: Eds. Del Val, 1987.

Markus, H. R., S. D. Kitayama, and R. J. Heiman. "Culture and Basic Psychological Principles." In E. T. Higgins and A. W. Kruglanski, eds., *Social Psychology: Handbook of Basic Principles.* New York: Guilford Press, 1996.

Marqués, J., D. Páez, and A. F. Serra. "Procesos de memoria colectiva asociados a experiencias traumáticas de guerra: Reparto social, clima emocional y la transmisión de la información transgeneracional en el caso de la guerra colonial portuguesa." In D. Páez et al., eds., *Memoria colectiva de procesos culturales y políticos*. Lejona: Editorial de la Universidad del País Vasco, 1997.

Marsella, A. J., et al. *Ethnocultural Aspects of Posttraumatic Stress Disorder*. Washington, D.C.: American Psychological Association, 1997.

Marsella, J. "Thoughts on Cross-Cultural Studies on the Epidemiology of Depression." *Culture, Medicine and Psychiatry* 2 (1978): 343–58.

Martín-Baro, I. *Sistema, grupo y poder*. San Salvador: UCA, 1989.

———. *Psicología social de la guerra*, San Salvador: UCA, 1990.

Martín Beristain, C. *Viaje a la memoria*. Barcelona: Virus, 1997.

———. "Procesos de duelo en comunidades mayas afectadas por la violencia política." Ph.D. diss., Universidad del País Vasco, 2005.

Martín Beristain, C., and G. Donà. *Psychosocial Approach to Humanitarian Aid*. Luxemburg: Network on Humanitarian Assistance, 1997.

Martín Beristain, C., and F. Riera. *Afirmación y resistencia: La comunidad como apoyo*. Barcelona: Virus, 1993.

Martín Beristain, C., M. Valdoseda, and D. Páez. "Coping with Fear and Loss at an Individual and Collective Level: Political Repression in Guatemalan Indigenous Communities." In G. Perren-Klinger, ed., *Trauma: From Individual Helplessness to Group Resources*. Berne: Paul Haupt Publishers, 1996.

Maslow, A. H. *Motivation and Personality*. New York: Harper & Row, 1970.

McIvor, R. J., and S. W. Turner. "Assessment and Treatment Approaches for Survivors of Torture." *British Journal of Psychiatry* 166 (1995): 705–11.

Mental Health Handbook. *Promoción de salud mental: Un manual para comunidades bajo represión*. San Francisco: No Means Press, 1993.

Mesquita, B., and N. H. Frijda. "Cultural Variations in Emotions: A Review." *Psychological Bulletin* 112 (1992): 179–204.

Meza, V. "Hurricane Mitch." *Infopress Centroamericana* 1296 (1998): 3.

Middleton W., et al. "The Bereavement Response: A Cluster Analysis." *British Journal of Psychiatry* 169 (1996): 167–71.

Moghaddan, F. M., D. M. Taylor, and S. C. Wright. *Social Psychology in a Cross-Cultural Perspective*. New York: W. H. Freeman, 1993.

Mollica, R. F. "The Trauma Story: The Psychiatric Care of Refugee Survivors of Violence and Torture." In E. Ochberg, ed., *Post-Traumatic Therapy and Victims of Violence*. New York: Brunner/Mazel, 1987.

———. "Efectos psicosociales y sobre la salud mental de las situaciones de violencia colectiva." In P. Pérez, ed., *Actuaciones psicosociales en guerra y violencia política*. Madrid: ExLibris, 1999.

Mollica, R. F., et al. "Repatriation and Disability: A Community Study of Health, Mental Health, and Social Functioning of the Khmer Residents of Site Two." Working document. Harvard University Program in Refugee Trauma, Cambridge, Mass.: 1993.

Moore, F., and J. Collins. *World Hunger: 12 Myths*. London: Earthscan Publications Ltd., 1988.

Morales, J. F., et al. *Psicología Social*. Madrid: McGraw-Hill, 1994.

Needham, R. "Refugee Participation." *Refugee Participation Network* 17 (1994): 17–19.

Nilchaitovit, T., J. M. Hill, and J. C. Holland. "The Effects of Culture on Illness Behavior and Medical Care: Asian and American Differences." *General Hospital Psychiatry* 15 (1993): 41–50.

Nolen-Hoeksema, S., A. McBride, and J. Larson. "Rumination and Psychological Distress among Bereaved Partners." *Journal of Personality and Social Psychology* 72 (1997): 855–62.

Oberg, J. "Coping with Unfamiliar Cultures." In N. Worren, ed., *Studies in Cross-Cultural Psychology*, vol. 1. London: Academic Press, 1961.

ODHAG (Oficina de Derechos Humanos del Arzobispado de Guatemala). "Informe Project Interdiocesano de recuperación de la Memoria Histórica." In *Guatemala: Nunca Más*, vols. 1–4, *Impactos de la Violencia*. Tibás, Costa Rica: LIL/Arzobispado de Guatemala.

Oliver-Smith, A. "Anthropological Research on Hazards and Disasters." *Annual Review of Anthropology* 25 (1996): 303–28.

Páez, D. "Análisis sentimental de nuestra cultura: Cultura, emoción y conocimiento de sí en España e Iberoamérica." In C. Nieto, ed., *Saber, sentir, pensar*. Madrid: Debate, 1997.

Páez, D., E. Arroyo, and I. Fernández. "Catástrofes, situaciones de riesgo y factores psicosociales." *Mapfre Seguridad* 57 (1995): 43–55.

Páez, D., and N. Basabe. "Trauma político y memoria colectiva: Freud, Halbwachs y la psicología política contemporanea." *Psicología Política* 6 (1993): 7–34.

Páez, D., and A. Blanco. "Psicología social latinoamericana." *Revista Antropos* 44 (1994).

Páez, D., J. L. González, and N. Aguilera. *Identidad cultural, aculturación y adaptación de los inmigrantes latinoamericanos en el país vasco*. Bilbao: Centro Cultural Chileno Pablo Neruda, 1997.

Páez, D., and J. Marqués. "Rumores y conductas colectivas." In J. F. Morales et al., eds., *Psicología social*. Madrid: McGraw Hill, 1999.

Páez, D., et al. "Cultura y emoción en Europa y América Latina." In D. Páez and A. Blanco, eds., *Psicología social latinoamericana anthropos suplementos* 44 (1994): 44–53.

———, eds. *Memoria colectiva de procesos culturales y políticos*. Lejona: Editorial de la Universidad del País Vasco, 1997.

Pedersen, D., quoted in J. W. Berry et al., *Cross-cultural Psychology: Research and Applications*. Cambridge: Cambridge University Press, 1988.

Peltzer, K., *Counselling and Psychotherapy of Victims of Organized Violence in Sociocultural Context*. Frankfurt: IKO, 1996.

Pennebaker, J. W. *Opening Up*. New York: Morrow, 1990.

Pérez, P. "Contradicciones respecto al papel de las organizaciones no gubernamentales en el trabajo psicosocial en situaciones de guerra y violencia organizada." In P. Pérez ed., *Actuaciones psicosociales en guerra y violencia política*. Madrid: ExLibris, 1999.

Pérez, P., C. Santiago, and R. Álvarez. *Ahora le apuestan al cansancio*. San Cristóbal de las Casas: GAC y Centro de DDHH "Miguel Agustín Pro Juárez" AC, 1999.

Pérez Sales, P. *Psycho-Social Care in War and Political Violence*. Madrid: ExLibris, 1999.

Pérez Sales, P., R. Bacic, and T. Durán. *Muerte y desparición forzada en la Araucanía: una aproximación étnica*. Santiago de Chile: Lom, 1998.

Perren-Klinger, G. "Human Reactions to Traumatic Experience: From Pathogenic to Salutogenic Thinking." *Trauma: From Individual Helplessness to Group Resources*. Vienna: Paul Haupt Publishers Berne, 1996.

Pichinao, J. "Sueños y premoniciones." In P. Pérez Sales, R. Basic, and T. Durán, *Muerte y desaparición forzada en la Araucanía: Una aproximación étnica*. Santiago de Chile: Lom, 1998.

Pradelles, C. "Les morts et leurs rites en Afrique," *L'Homme* 138 (1996): 137–42.

PRAIS. http://www.inp.cl/inicio/exo-prais.php. Accessed January 20, 2006.

Price-Williams, D. R. "Cultural Psychology." In G. Lindzey and E. Aronson, eds., *Handbook of Social Psychology*. New York: Random House, 1985.

"Programme in the Net of Psycho-Social Help in Croatia." In L. T. Arcel, ed., *War Victims, Trauma and Psychosocial Care*. Zagreb: Nakladnistov Lumin, 1985.

Prunier, G. "Humanitaire: Un Droit Hypocrite." *Le Monde des debates* 1 (1993): 15–18.

Punamaki, R. L. "Political Violence and Mental Health." *International Journal of Mental Health* 17 (1989): 3–15.

Raphael, B. *When Disaster Strikes*. London: Hutchinson, 1986.

Rawnsley, M. M. "Minimizing Professional Burnout: Caring for the Care Givers." In D. T. Wessels, Jr., A. H. Kutscher, and I. B. Seeland, eds., *Professional Burnout in Medicine and the Helping Professions*. New York: Haworth Press, 1989.

Report of the National Commission for Truth and Reconciliation, Chile (*Informe de la Comisión Nacional de Verdad y Reconciliación*). Santiago: Corporación Nacional de Reparación y Reconciliación, 1991.

Rieff, D. *Slaughterhouse: Bosnia and the Failure of the West*. New York: Simon and Schuster, 1995.

Rimé, B., et al. "Social Sharing of Emotion: New Evidence and New Questions." In W. Stroebe and M. Hewstone, eds., *European Review of Social Psychology* 8 (1998).

Rockeach, M. (1968). "Beliefs, Attitudes and Values." In J. F. Morales et al., *Psicología social*. Madrid: McGraw Hill, 1988.

Ross, L. E., and R. E. Nisbetter. *The Person and the Situation: Perspectives in Social Psychology*. New York: McGraw Hill, 1991.

Rubonis, A. V., and L. Bickman. "Psychological Impairment in the Wake of Disaster: The Disaster—Psychopathology Relationship." *Psychological Bulletin* 109 (1991): 384–99.

Rushing. W. A. *The AIDS Epidemic: Social Dimensions of an Infectious Disease*. Boulder, Colo.: Westview Press, 1995.

Saavedra, M. del R. *Desastre y riesgo: actores sociales en la reconstrucción de Armero y Chinchind*. Bogatá: Centro de Investigación y Educación Popular, 1996.

Sarea, T. *El dolor invisible de la tortura*. Hernani: Sarea, 1994.

Sepúlveda, L. "Las fracturas de Chile." *El País* December 24, 1998, p. 10.

Sichrowsky, P. "Nacer culpable, nacer víctima." *Memoria* 3 (1987): 56–57.

Silver, R. C., and C. Wortman. "Effective Mastery of Bereavement and Widowhood." In P. B. Baltes and M. M. Baltes, eds., *Successful Aging*. London: Cambridge, 1990.

Smith, P. B., and M. H. Bond. *Social Psychology across Cultures*. New York: Harvester, 1993.

Solares, A. *Estado y nación: Las demandas de los grupos étnicos de guatemala*. Guatemala: Flacso, 1993.

Solomon, Z. D. "Does the War End when the Shooting Stops?" *Journal of Applied Social Psychology* 20 (1990): 1733–45.

Sondorp, E. "Croyances et pratiques lieés à la diarrhée infantile chez les refugies afghans." *Medical News* 1 (1992): 12–15.

Stearns, S. D. "Psychological Distress and Relief Work: Who Helps the Helpers?" *Refugee Participation Network* 15 (1993): 9–11.

Steinglass, P., and E. Gerrity. "Natural Disasters and Post-Traumatic Stress Disorder: Short-term versus Long-Term Recovery in Two Disaster-Affected Communities." *Journal of Applied Social Psychology* 20 (1990): 1746–65.

Stroebe, M. S., W. Stroebe, and R. O. Hansson, *Handbook of Bereavement: Theory, Research and Intervention.* New York: Cambridge University Press, 1993.

Summerfield, D. "The Impact of War and Atrocity on Civilian Populations: An Overview of Major Themes." In D. Black et al., eds., *Psychological Trauma: A Development Approach.* London: Royal College of Psychiatry, 1996.

Summerfield, D., and F. Hume. "War and Post-Traumatic Stress Disorder: The Question of Social Context." *Journal of Nervous and Mental Disease* 181 (1993): 522.

Sveass, N. "The Psychological Effects of Impunity." In *An Encounter at the Crossroads of Human Rights Violations and Mental Health.* Oslo: Centre for Refugees, University of Oslo, 1995.

Sydor, G., and P. Philippot. "Prevalence du stress post-traumatique et intervention de prevention secondaire auprés des cooperants belges exposés à une catastrophe humanitaire." Paper delivered at Louvain, Université de Louvain, 1995.

Taft, R. "Coping with Unfamiliar Cultures." In N. Warren, ed., *Studies in Cross-Cultural Psychology.* London: Academic Press, 1977.

Teter, H. "Mass Violence and Community Treatment." In G. Perren-Klinger, ed., *Trauma: From Individual Helplessness to Group Resources.* Berne: Paul Haupt Publishers, 1996.

Thompson, P. *La voz del pasado.* Valencia: Alfons el Magnànim, 1988.

UNDP. *Report of Human Development.* New York: United Nations, 1994.

UNHCR. *Guidelines on the Evaluation and Care of Victims of Trauma and Violence.* Utrech Consultation. Geneva: WHO, 1994.

———. *La situación de los refugiados en el mundo.* Madrid: Alianza, 1994.

UNHCR and World Health Organization (WHO). *Refugee Mental Health: Draft Manual for Field Testing.* Geneva: WHO, 1992.

Van der Pligt, J. "Risk." In A. S. R. Manstead and M. Hewstone, eds., *The Blackwell Encyclopedia of Social Psychology.* Oxford: Blackwell, 1995.

Vázquez, Á., and A. M. Araujo. *La maldición de Ulises: Repercusiones psicológicas del exilio.* Santiago de Chile: Sudamericana, 1990.

Vesti, P., and S. Bojlom. "Antithesis of Therapy: Extreme Man-made Stress. Torture: Sequels and Rehabiliation." *Psychiatria Danubina* 2 (1990): 297–312.

Weiss, R. S., and T. A. Richards. "A Scale for Predicting Quality of Recovery Following the Death of a Partner." *Journal of Personality and Social Psychology* 72 (1997): 885–91.

Wilches, G. "Particularidades de un desastre." In *Características del terremoto y la avalancha de 6 de junio de 1994 y sus efectos sobre las comunidades afectadas.* Popayán: Corporación Nasa Kiwo, 1995.

Wilson, J. P., and J. Lindy. *Countertransference in the Treatment of Post-Traumatic Stress Disorder.* New York: Guilford Press, 1994.

Zonabend, F. "Au pays de la peur déniée." In J. Delumeau, *La peur en Occident.* Paris: Fayard, 1993.

Zubieta, E., et al. "Cultura y emoción América." *Boletín de Psicología* (1999).

Zur, J. "Making Sense of Violent Experiences: The Reconstruction of Meaning of la Violencia." *Refugee Participation Network* 16 (1994): 10–12.

Zwi, A., and A. Ugalde. "Towards an Epidemiology of Political Violence." *Social Science and Medicine* 28 (1989): 633–42.

Acknowledgments

The author wishes to extend profound gratitude to collaborators who assisted the development of the book's content and its English-language edition by sharing their experiences and insights. The following individuals made this work possible: Darío Paez, Itziar Fernández, Giorgia Donna, Pau Pérez, Jena Laske, and Arancha García del Soto.